WRITERS ON THE SOUTH-WEST COAST

Cover: 'A Cornish Haven' by Joseph Edward Southall
© Royal Society of Water Colours

Portland Bill Lighthouse

Writers on the South-West Coast

*A Literary Journey from Dorset
via Land's End to the Bristol Channel*

Compiled and presented by
Eric Bird & Lilian Modlock

EX LIBRIS PRESS

First published 1994 by
Ex Libris Press
1 The Shambles
Bradford on Avon
Wiltshire

Typeset in 10 point Palatino

Design and typesetting by Ex Libris Press

Cover printed by Shires Press, Trowbridge
Printed and bound in Britain by
Cromwell Press Ltd., Broughton Gifford, Wiltshire

ISBN 0 948578 67 X

CONTENTS

Mullion Cove

Introduction

In *Writers on the Coast* we journeyed from Kent round the south-east coast of England to the Hampshire-Dorset border. In this sequel we shall explore the Literary Coast of south-west England, travelling westward along the coastlines of Dorset, South Devon and Cornwall to Land's End, voyaging out to the Isles of Scilly, then following the Atlantic coast of Cornwall to North Devon, and the southern shores of the Bristol Channel through Somerset and Avon. This south-western coast of England is highly varied, with scenery that can be awe-inspiring, and inlets that take the sea far inland to branching valleys. It has had a long and eventful history and, as we shall see, many writers have referred to it.

We have taken as 'literary' those pieces that seemed to us to have been written memorably, and with style; something more than mere factual reporting, or casual comment. This is subjective, of course: our selection inevitably reflects our own interests, opinions, and prejudices. We have tried to avoid 'flowery' writing, especially if it is inaccurate; and we have put aside the flat prose of purely technical description.

It is remarkable how much literary activity has gone on along these south-western shores. We have tried to avoid simple descriptive pieces, items that merely extol the scenic beauty and tourist attractions of a part of the coast. There are "guide book" accounts of almost all these seaside places, but we have quoted only those that we felt had gone beyond a straightforward description, including some that described places as they used to be, not as they are now.

Several books have dealt with places along the south-west coast where writers were born, or lived, or died, and some mention the works they generated there, but few quote what was actually written about the landscape, and this deficiency we now seek to remedy. Many writers have portrayed the coastal features, or used them as a setting for their narratives: most notably Thomas Hardy. Others completely ignored the local landscape: there is nothing in *Dr Jekyll and Mr Hyde*, for example, to indicate that Stevenson wrote it in Bournemouth, or in Sir Walter Scott's *Marmion* to show that he was writing in Mudeford, near Christchurch, in what was then Hampshire. Our concern is with descriptions, evocations and dramatisations of the south-west coast.

Literary figures, such as Hardy, Betjeman, A.L. Rowse and Daphne Du Maurier, have written so prolifically about this coast that we have had to make a selection of pieces which seemed particularly appropriate.

We also had to decide how far to travel up the marine inlets. We have included some towns which are not actually coastal but have considerable maritime connections, places such as Exeter, Bideford and Barnstaple.

Some writers invented names for coastal locations. Prominent here was Thomas Hardy, whose names for places around the Wessex coast included, in the sequence we have followed: 'Sandbourne' (Bournemouth), 'Havenpool' (Poole), 'Anglebury' or 'Southerton' (Wareham), 'Corvsgate' (Corfe), 'Bollard Head' (Ballard Down), 'Knollsea' (Swanage), 'Lulstead' or 'Lulwind Cove' (Lulworth Cove), 'Ringworth' (Ringstead), 'Budmouth' or 'Melport' (Weymouth), 'Isle of Slingers' (Isle of Portland), 'The Beal' (Portland Bill), 'Deadman's Bay' (West Bay), 'Chesil Bank' or 'The Pebble Bank' (Chesil Beach), 'Abbot's Beach' or 'Abbotsea' (Abbotsbury), 'Port Bredy' (Bridport), 'Idmouth' (Sidmouth), 'Exonbury' (Exeter), 'Pen-Zephyr' (Penzance), 'Barwith Strand' (Trebarwith Strand), 'Castle Boterel' (Boscastle), 'Dundagel' (Tintagel), and 'Stratleigh' (Bude). Other disguised south-west coastal places include Thackeray's 'Baymouth' (Sidmouth), Quiller-Couch's 'Troy Town' (Fowey) and Beatrix Potter's 'Stymouth' (Falmouth, or possibly Dartmouth or Newlyn). 'Buddlecombe', as we shall see, has been used twice: by Henry Handel Richardson for Lyme Regis and by James Payn for Newquay.

Where we have given several quotations for a particular place (as for Bournemouth and Plymouth) we have arranged them in chronological sequence, but in some cases it seemed useful to group several on one theme. Generally we have retained the grammar, spelling and punctuation of the original works.

Most of the literary descriptions we have quoted are still recognisable in the present landscape. Much of the scenery of the south-west coast has been maintained, despite strong pressure for development, thanks especially to the National Trust; to planners who have curbed development which would otherwise have occurred; to the Countryside Commission's Heritage Coasts; and to English Nature and local conservation organisations which have established Nature Reserves. There are, unfortunately, areas of sprawling suburbia, particularly around Torbay, but there are also areas of quite outstanding coastal scenery, especially along the Dorset coast, and parts of Devon and Cornwall.

Our book is thus a journey of about 400 miles. It is covered by a set of 13 of the Ordnance Survey Landranger maps, scale 1 to 50,000 (about an inch and a quarter to the mile), which show coastal pathways and access points, as well as place-names. The journey can be made on foot, walking along coastal pathways and seaside promenades, in two or three weeks. With careful study of time-tables it can be achieved largely on local buses and trains, but these give only tantalising glimpses of the coast. Most people will want to travel by car, turning off down side roads to park for a while at the seaside, and perhaps take a short walk. In this way the journey will take them about ten days.

We have numbered the quotations and given a brief reference to the sources of each literary extract, in the hope that some of these pieces will persuade readers to go back to the original books.

The quotations show great variety in the way people have seen places, interpreted them, and written about them. Some items tell us as much about the personality, pre-conceptions and moods of the writer as about the areas mentioned. When we found places described in ways that seemed curious or inappropriate, we realised that our own response to these coastal landscapes was influenced by memories and associations, as well as the mood of the moment. In localities we knew well, our reaction was rather like that of Sir Arthur Quiller-Couch, in his story of the journalist's visit to Cornwall (quoted on page 120): "Q" valued his own impressions of his beloved Fowey, built up over many years of residence, above the opinions of a day visitor. Both are interesting, and a transient writer may notice things that the long-term resident has overlooked.

As in *Writers on the Coast*, our primary aim is to enhance the enjoyment of those who travel along this coast (and those who will make an imaginary, arm-chair journey from Dorset to Land's End and round to the Severn estuary) by providing this added dimension of local literature.

Our thanks goes to Dorchester Library, the West Country Studies Library in Exeter, the Cornwall Local Studies Library in Redruth, and Sevenoaks Library; also to Sheila Bird and Gareth James for their assistance.

Eric Bird & Lilian Modlock
August 1994

About the Editors:

Dr. Eric Bird, lives in a seaside suburb of Melbourne, Australia, but spends part of each year in Britain. He has published books and monographs, as well as numerous scientific articles, on coastal topics.

Lilian Modlock, a Londoner, is a keen coastal traveller who lives and writes in Kent.

DORSET

Chewton Bunny and Highcliffe

Our literary journey around south-west England begins on the road between Lymington and Christchurch, where the Hampshire-Dorset boundary runs down the little wooded valley known as Chewton Bunny to the shores of Christchurch Bay. The name Bunny is used hereabouts to describe a chine or ravine opening between cliffs, and if you climb down to the beach you can look eastward to the Needles and the Isle of Wight and westward to the bold promontory of Hengistbury Head.

Highcliffe Castle, on the western side, is a nineteenth century edifice on the site of an earlier house built for John Stuart, the third Earl of Bute, and Prime Minister in the reign of George III. The Earl was a keen botanist, who had financed the setting up of Kew Gardens and endowed the Pagoda. Sheila Herringshaw has told how:

'While he was searching for botanical specimens in the New Forest he came to the high cliffs surrounding Christchurch Bay. He was so thrilled with the view that he camped on the cliffs, and subsequently engaged the architect, Robert Adams, to build him a house there'.[1]

From the gardens, steps lead down the cliff through a grove of holm oaks to Avon Beach.

Sir Walter Scott at Mudeford

A lane that turns left from the main road at Shelley Hill, descends to the fishing village of Mudeford, beside the narrow entrance to Christchurch Harbour. The little River Mude, which rhymes with Bude, flows through Mudeford, pronounced Muddy-ford, to reach the sea beside Haven House Inn, once a haunt of smugglers. William Stuart Rose, a parliamentarian and poet, built a house which he called Gundimore, on the dunes. It can be found near the western end of Avon Beach, facing out across the sea to The Needles. In 1807 Sir Walter Scott stayed with him while he was writing *Marmion*, but this poetic work, set in Scotland, makes no reference to Dorset. Samuel Taylor Coleridge and Robert Southey were other visitors. Their host produced this rhyme:

Here Walter Scott has wooed the northern muse;
Here has with me rejoiced to walk or cruize;
        ....And these "ribbed sands" was Coleridge pleased to pace,
While ebbing seas have hummed a rolling bass
To his rapt talk.... [2]

Mudeford

Christchurch

A little to the west is Christchurch, an old walled town, once the stronghold of Alfred the Great against Danish marauders. It is notable for its priory, the longest parish church in Britain, and has a lengthy list of Rectors including the seventeenth century satirist and dramatist John Marston, here from 1616 to 1631.

Christchurch Harbour

South of the town is the wide expanse of Christchurch Harbour, described by the naturalist C.J. Cornish in 1895: 'The waters of the Avon and Stour which meet at Christchurch and hurry in great swirling pools past the grey towers and arches of the ancient priory, and under the many bridges of the town, are cut off from their natural impetuous entry to the sea by the long ironstone ridge of Hengistbury Head. Between the town and the sea this great dyke thrusts itself across the skyline, and at flood tide ponds back the whole of the tidal and river water into a broad lake, the exit from which into the sea might, for all that can be seen from this inland harbour, be by some subterranean passage beneath the cliff itself. The actual gate by which the outflow from the hundreds of acres of swollen waters escapes at the ebb into the sea is a short and narrow channel called the Run, which cuts its way between two overlapping claws of sandspit. It is in the narrow waters of the Run that the salmon are caught, as they begin to ascend the river at the turn of the tide'.[3]

At low tide the reed swamps, salt marshes and mudflats are threaded by winding tidal creeks. There is a Nature Reserve, rich in bird and insect life.

Hengistbury Head

South of the harbour entrance a spit of sand and shingle, carrying a line of beach huts, runs out from Hengistbury Head, a peninsula covered by heath and scrub, with a commanding position between Christchurch Bay and Bournemouth Bay. John Grimson wrote that: 'Hengistbury Head has been a particularly fruitful site for archaeologists. Its crowning hill has yielded evidence of human settlement through the Stone, Bronze and Iron Ages, and the work of Iron Age man is still there to be seen, in the form of the stout earthwork of the Double Dyke, which strikes across the base of the headland from cliff top to harbour side, some two thousand years after its raising. The Celts of the Iron Age were great ones for defence. They liked to know when their enemies were coming and be adequately fortified when they came, and Hengistbury Head is typical of their coastal fortifications. They favoured prominent headlands, like this one, with water on three sides, and sought to cut themselves off from the rest of Britain by building a great double embankment and ditch on the fourth'.[4]

In 1929 Gordon Selfridge, founder of the Oxford Street department store, bought Hengistbury Head with the idea of building himself a palace on it, but fortunately nothing came of this, and in 1930 he sold it to Bournemouth Corporation. It is now a public open space with a nature trail and visitor centre and in summer you can ride out to the headland on a rubber-tyred train.

Bournemouth

The Hengistbury cliffs decline towards Southbourne, which is an eastern suburb of Bournemouth. The undercliff walk begins at Point House café, and follows the gentle curve of Bournemouth Bay round to Sandbanks in the distance. It is backed by steep bluffs, cut by a succession of deep wooded ravines: Boscombe Chine, Alum Chine, Branksome Chine, and Canford Chine. There are two piers, and several miles of sandy beach. On top of the cliffs the plateau was empty heathland until the nineteenth century, when houses began to appear. After the coming of the railway in 1870 Bournemouth grew into a sprawling resort and residential town, with conifers and rhododendrons in its gardens and parks.

The Casa Magni Shelley Museum is devoted to the poet, whose son Percy Florence Shelley lived in the house from 1849 to 1889.

In 1884 Robert Louis Stevenson and his wife Fanny returned from France to live for three years in Bournemouth, first in lodgings on West Cliff with a view of The Needles and the Isle of Wight, and then in a house close to Alum Chine, bought for him by his father and re-named Skerryvore after the most beautiful and difficult of all the lighthouses built by the Stevenson family:

> *For love of lovely words, and for the sake*
> *Of those, my kinsmen and my countrymen,*
> *Who early and late in the windy ocean toiled*
> *To plant a star for seamen, where was then*
> *The surfy haunt of seals and cormorants:*
> *I, on the lintel of this cot, inscribe*
> *The name of a strong tower.*[5]

His biographer, James Pope Hennessy, says that the pine woods reminded Stevenson of Scotland, and the sunny summertime Channel recalled the Mediterranean, but the truth seems to be that local landscapes made little impression on him. While living in Bournemouth he wrote *Kidnapped*, with his mind on Mull and the Scottish Highlands, and *Dr Jekyll and Mr Hyde*, but he was already a sick man and any local travelling went unrecorded, although some scenes from his story *The Wrong Box* were set nearby in the New Forest. In 1887 he abandoned Bournemouth for America and Samoa. The house called Skerryvore was destroyed in an air raid in 1940, and the site is now a Memorial Garden.

The French poet Paul Verlaine came here to teach at St. Aloysius' School in 1876, and set a Bournemouth scene to start off one of his poems:

> *Le long bois de sapins se tord jusqu'au rivage*
> *L'étroit bois de sapins, de lauriers et de pins,*
> *Avec la ville autour déguisée en village:*
> *Chalets éparpillés rouges dans le feuillage*
> *Et les blanches villas des stations de bains.*

Le bois sombre descend d'un plateau de bruyère,
Va, vient, creuse un vallon, puis monte vert et noir
Et redescend en fins bosquets où la lumière
Filtre et dore l'obscur sommeil du cimitière
Qui s'étage bercé d'un vague nonchaloir.[6]

John Wells offered a translation:

The long wood of Scotch firs twists down towards the shore
A narrow wood of firs, laurel and spruce. All round,
The town has, masquerading as a village more,
Strewn in among the trees, red bungalows galore,
The whitewashed seaside villas on the lower ground.

A gloomy wood that starts high up against the sky
And zigzags down, digs dells, then climbs up inky-green
To fall again in spinneys. single trees awry
Where daylight gilds the graves, a sleepy cemetery
Of dappled terraces, cool, vague and dimly seen.[7]

John Betjeman disliked the petty bureaucrats who wanted uniform counties for the sake of streamlined administration, and parodied them in 'The Town Clerk's Views':

Bournemouth is looking up. I'm glad to say
That modernistic there has come to stay.
I walk the asphalt paths of Branksome Chine
In resin-scented air like strong Greek wine
And dream of cliffs of flats along those heights,
Floodlit at night, with green electric lights.
But as for Dorset's flint and Purbeck stone,
Its old thatched farms in dips of down alone -
It should be merged with Hants and made to be
A self-contained and plann'd community
Like Flint and Rutland, it is much too small
And has no reason to exist at all.[8]

Thomas Hardy's name for Bournemouth was 'Sandbourne'. It was at first 'a sprinkling of houses at the edge of heathland': but when Christopher Julian returned there, towards the end of *The Hand of Ethelberta*, he was 'directed to the outskirts, and into a fir plantation where drives and intersecting roads had been laid out, and where new villas had sprung up like mushrooms'.[9]

Fifteen years later, in *Tess of the D'Urbervilles*, ' Sandbourne' had become a large, 'Mediterranean lounging-place on the English Channel'.

'This fashionable watering-place, with its eastern and its western stations, its piers, its groves of pines, its promenades, and its covered gardens, was, to Angel Clare, like a fairy place suddenly created by the stroke of a wand, and allowed to get a little dusty. An outlying eastern tract of the enormous Egdon Waste was close at hand, yet on the very verge of that tawny piece of antiquity such a glittering novelty as this pleasure city had chosen to spring up. Within the space of a mile from its outskirts every irregularity of the soil was prehistoric, every channel an undisturbed British trackway; not a sod having been turned there since the days of the Caesars. Yet the exotic had grown here, suddenly as the prophet's gourd. The sea was near at hand, but not intrusive; it murmured, and he thought it was the pines; the pines murmured in precisely the same tones, and he thought they were the sea'.[10]

It was in this 'city of detached mansions' that Tess was to murder Alec D'Urberville.

Malcolm Muggeridge came to Bournemouth in 1934: 'On a warm sunny afternoon you see the place perhaps, in its most characteristic mood. A crowd gently washes up and down the lower promenade; deck-chairs are spread out under a colonnade, and in these sedentary persons sun themselves, and watch the passers-by; open and closed motor-cars, their speed limited to eight miles per hour, amble back and forth; further along the Front, and towards Poole, are little cabins arranged like boxes at the theatre, in which family parties make tea and chatter, half domestic and half public; the chines, connecting the shore and the town, are black with moving people, rivulets of people following their winding course; on the upper promenade the same scene, only more sparse; occasional stragglers climbing or dropping from one promenade to the other; the cliff-lifts methodically running.

'No one crowd is quite like another. Each has its own rhythm and character. The Bournemouth crowd is sedate and unribald. If its respectability is a trifle oppressive, its assurance and air of economic well-being are restful. There is the very word. Bournemouth is restful. Its merry-making has no flavour of hysteria'.[11]

Sandbanks

Westward, past Canford Cliffs, is Sandbanks, built on a narrow promontory. A car ferry, guided by chains, grinds to and fro across this tidal entrance to the South Haven Peninsula. John Grimson found that 'After ploughing through all the miles of bricks and mortar of Barton-on-Sea, Highcliffe, Christchurch, Bournemouth and Poole, to step off the ferry at South Haven Point is like being released from enforced detention. All around, there is an emptiness of marsh, heath and forest spreading back from the southern shore of Poole Harbour, whose waters seem to be the only tangible barrier preventing that great flood tide of development from sweeping across from the north'.[4]

Poole Harbour

Poole Harbour is an estuary, with extensive salt marshes and several high islands. Some say it is the second biggest harbour in the world after Sydney Harbour, over ninety miles in circumference although the harbour entrance is only a quarter of a mile wide. C.J. Cornish sailed in on a summer's day in the eighteen-nineties: 'As we came slowly in over the blue water, and passed over the bar, our surprise and admiration increased. On the right was a spit of sand-hills, covered with masses of purple heather and a few wind-blown pines. To the left lay Brownsea Island, with its castle and trees; to the left a wide inland sea, lying between Brownsea Island and the long sweep of Purbeck, with the keep of Corfe Castle standing up far off, black against the evening sun. In front lay the way up to Poole town, with quaint ports and sea-marks, and one or two pretty wooden sailing vessels dipping down with the tide. On either side of Poole the sea seemed to run inland till lost in heather and pines. The chart showed the enormous expanse of 'slob-lands' in proportion to navigable water in these inland lagoons.

'At the end of the great frost of the beginning of the year 1895 I paid another visit to the harbour. The sand-hills were quite beautiful even in the frost. The heather and moss which contrive to exist even on the sand were of the richest dark plum and green respectively. The frost had nipped all the dead heather blossom off, and this lay in little piles and patches, like dark seed-pearls, daintily scattered on the sand. In other places the wind-blown sand had been quite freshly piled, and was covered with the tracks of mice, and strange to say, of rats, which had been out foraging for food the night before. On the other side of the sand-hills the wind was blowing down the harbour, bitterly cold. Nearly all the harbour was ice-bound, and the swans, to avoid being nipped by the ice, had collected together in a flock in one of the bays, where by constantly swimming and keeping together, they kept a little circle of still unfrozen water. All other fowl seemed to have forsaken the harbour for some less frozen sea'.[3]

This landscape has changed. The spit of sand-hills is now Sandbanks, covered with hotels and houses, and the muddy 'slob-lands' have become wide swards of tidal grassland following the introduction of Spartina, brought from Southampton Water in 1899.

Frederick Treves, Dorset Writer and Royal Physician, described the area in 1906: 'The Poole estuary extends inland for some seven miles, a tortuous sea inlet encompassed on all the sides by the famished heath.

'It is a maze of waterways, of capes and creeks, of islands and shoals, of gleaming water that here scoops a bay out of the heather-tinted sands and there flickers like a light between the trunks of a clump of pines. The shores of this sea labyrinth belong to the moorland, so that by the water's edge will be found a ruddy sand cliff, a garden of gorse, a biscuit-coloured beach, a waving flat of drowned grass, a strand of stones and fir trees. Go back ten centuries and this Wessex estuary is still the same, the same as when up the fairway came, with thud of rowlocks, the long boats of the Danes, lined with glistening shields, while on the shore were burning huts and folk fleeing across the heath.

'On the brightest day, when the tide is rising, the sea pours into Poole and floods the harsh moor with blue. The water shines like metal. When the sky is overcast and the tide on the ebb, the lagoon is a flat of snaky channels and slimy pools; its islands are black as if their trees were charred, its grey waters stagnate over jade-green shoals, its mud banks seem to be puffed up by a baneful air. It is then that the place appears to belong to the primeval world, so that it would not be unfitting if monstrous saurians with spiny backs, were to be seen wading in the dismal ooze'.[12]

Tidal creeks thread the marshlands of Poole Harbour, converging into larger channels. At the eastern end is a Nature Reserve with brackish lagoons, lakes, salt and fresh marshes, thronged with waterfowl, herons, gulls and terns. The double high tide experienced in the Solent occurs here also, so that Poole Harbour is a broad lagoon for up to 14 hours each day. Kenneth Allsop found the saltings 'lush with cord grass and sea-lavender, harriers drift through in the autumn; far across on the mud flats were vivid pepperings of oystercatchers, and a cormorant sat on a spar-buoy, its wings arched to dry, like a heraldic emblem'.[13]

On the north shore, Poole is a busy port and industrial area. The Old Town, with its quays and fine Georgian buildings, has a long history: it was sacked by the Danes in 787, and several times thereafter; it received its charter in 1248, and in the 18th and 19th centuries gained prosperity from the Newfoundland trade. 'This place is famous for the best, and biggest oysters in all this part of England,' wrote Daniel Defoe, 'more pearls are found in the Poole oysters and larger than in any other oyster about England'.[14]

J.M.W. Turner wrote some verse to accompany his engraving 'Poole and Distant View of Corfe Castle, Dorsetshire':

> *Westward the sand by storm and drift have gained*
> *A barrier, and that barrier maintained,*
> *Backed by a sandy heath, whose deep-worn road*
> *Deny'd the groaning wagon's ponderous load.*
> *This branches southwards at the point of Thule,*
> *From the harbour to the town of Poole.*
> *A little headland on a marshy lake*
> *Which probably contemptuously was given*
> *That deeps and shallows might for once be even.*[15]

Perhaps Turner was more a painter than a poet?

Brownsea Island

The largest island in Poole Harbour is Brownsea, some 560 acres, the site of Lord Baden-Powell's famous camp in 1907 which led to the founding of the Boy Scout Movement. The Block House built in the reign of Henry VIII, became the foundations of Brownsea Castle, which overlooks the entrance to Poole Harbour. It can be reached by passenger ferry from Sandbanks or Poole Quay, and is owned by the National Trust.

Celia Fiennes, diarist and traveller, toured England on horseback and came to Poole late in the 17th century: 'From thence by boate we went to a little Isle called Brownsea 3 or 4 leagues off, where there is much Copperice [iron ore from which liquids used in dyeing, tanning and ink making were derived] made, the stones being found about the Isle in the shore in great quantetyes, there is only one house there which is the Governours, besides little fishermens houses, they being all taken up about the Copperice workes; they gather the stones and place them on the ground raised like the beds in gardens, rows one above the other, and all are shelving so that the raine discolves the stones and [it] draines down into the trenches and pipes made to receive and convey it to the house; that is fitted with iron panns foursquare and of a pretty depth at least 12 yards over, they place iron spikes in the panns full of branches and so as the liquor boyles to a candy it hangs on these branches: I saw some taken up it look't like a vast bunch of grapes, the coullour of the Copperace not being much differing. This is a noted place for lobsters and crabs and shrimps, there I eate some very good'.[16]

Jack Battrick, who was born and lived on Brownsea Island has written an account of the Island's history. 'Brownsea is of low elevation, almost entirely covered with heath and fir plantations, fringed and embroidered with broad embankments of flowering rhododendron. North and west the coast rises to a height of ninety feet where a hard stratum of sandstone runs through the steep banks. These cliffs are, in turn, adorned with a thick growth of golden gorse, bell heather and masses of bracken with the lofty Scotch and pine firs towering behind them. Here the rich warm colours of the rock, mixed with every shade of green and brown on the crags and ledges, present a refreshing spectacle of colour.' In the nineteen-twenties, said Battrick: ' We in Brownsea experienced part of the extraordinary birth of wireless. During these years Marconi worked at Sandbanks and his large, highly varnished yacht with its white superstructure came and anchored in Brownsea Roads just off our pier. Marconi worked from a transmitting station on Sandbanks. He had worked there for nearly thirty years and he was often seen there, walking up and down the beach, with an extraordinary helmet on his head. This head-gear was in fact headphones and his curious antics of walking about on the beach there was apparently his attempts to find a spot at which he could pick up a wireless message'.[17]

Wareham

The A351 leads west from Poole, round to Wareham, between the Frome and the Piddle Rivers. Donald Maxwell, touring in the 1920s described Wareham as: 'One of those places that does not make a very vivid impression upon the traveller when he first sees it. Unlike Rye, which is another stranded seaport, it lies somewhat unobtrusively between its two rivers and is not visible as a town from very far away. Yet I know few historic sites that appeal more to the imagination on closer acquaintance.

'There is a haunting quality about its lanes and streets, its green ramparts standing abruptly above a green land – a land which proclaims on all sides that it was once part of the sea. The plan of the town is almost exactly square.

'The principal quay of later days was the one by the Frome, by the church, but it must be remembered that the two rivers were once part of the sea, a tidal estuary, in which Wareham appeared at high water more or less as an island'.[18]

The quays beside the Frome were a port until the silting of the river diminished it to a yacht harbour. T.E. Lawrence lived at Clouds Hill Cottage, six miles to the north-west, and met his death in a motorcycle accident nearby in 1935. In the church of St. Martin, Wareham, is an effigy of Lawrence carved in Purbeck Stone by Eric Kennington.

The Isle of Purbeck

South of Wareham a chalk ridge marks the boundary of the so-called Isle of Purbeck, a region of clay vales and limestone plateaux evoked in Paul Hyland's poem:

> *Salt mists creep on the sunlit hills*
> *as if the sea beyond reclaimed*
> *its own pure chalk whose calcined bone*
> *under cropped grass is Purbeck's spine,*
> *ocean's upswelling laid-down dead.*
>
> *Below are clay-scapes, gravel troughs,*
> *relicts of repetitious seas'*
> *transgressions and retreats; the waste*
> *acidic heath whose flagrant furze*
> *like yeast, works in the sun's oven.*
>
> *Furrows, like ripples in the rough,*
> *struggle from farmsteads, and revert.*
> *Seawards, ramparts raised on the chalk,*
> *strip-lynchets, stones chart human tides*
> *while mounds like sea-marks compass them.*

Those barrows of trussed bones disperse
in mist up on the chilling ridge.
The humming heath lies undisturbed;
men settled on the sun-baked earth
that soon must break over their heads.[19]

Studland

On the southern shores of Poole Harbour are heathy promontories with pine plantations and intervening muddy inlets. South Haven Peninsula is an area of heathy dunes, and small lakes, a National Nature Reserve; the Dorset Coast Path begins here. Studland Bay, sheltered from the prevailing westerly winds, and much used by small boats, is backed by a long sandy beach and grassy dunes. During his journey around the British coast in 1982, Paul Theroux came across the ferry from Sandbanks and 'stepped on to an empty mile of sand dunes and scrub, called Studland Heath. It was an old wind-blown place. There were lovers on this beach, plainly copulating in the sandy craters. I walked on, past men standing up in waist-high heather. Some were naked and watchful. I took them to be perverts. Some stood on hillocks and just stared into the middle distance. It was littered with blowing paper – magazine pages, which I examined and found to be pornographic. In the remotest parts of this wild place there were girlie magazines and book pages, some of them torn into small pieces. I supposed that lonely men had taken them here, crept into the dunes by the sea and examined them, feeling safe and hidden'.[20]

This may be a jaundiced view. When we walked through this part of the Dorset Coast Path on a warm summer afternoon there were about fifty nudists – men, women and children – on the beach behind a very English notice warning that 'Beyond this point nudists may be seen'. They seemed quiet, happy and relaxed. By contrast, the conventional beach at Studland had a large crowd of noisy, restless people attired in bathing trunks and bikinis.

Old Harry Rocks

On the southern shore of Studland Bay chalk cliffs appear, running out to chalk stacks. Early this century there were two of these – known as Old Harry and his Wife – but in 1925 Hilaire Belloc wrote: 'Old Harry is an isolated chimney of chalk rock which still stands, expecting doom. He had a wife standing beside him for centuries – a lesser (but no doubt nobler) pillar. She crashed some years ago and now he is alone'.[21]

The present group of outlying stacks is known as Old Harry Rocks, and there are more pinnacles off the shore to the south. Paul Hyland found that: 'The gap between the Foreland and the biggest stack, finally breached in 1921, is called St. Lucas Leap; only a saint could jump it now and, if he did, a flurry of screaming gulls would not thank him for so peremptory an invasion of their colony. Spare grass caps its hard chalk, but resistant as it is, the sea ineluctably gnaws at its foundations; slowly the needles' eyes that pierce it widen, and will eventually split it into smaller stacks like that of slim, upstanding Old Harry, finally reducing them to seaweed-festooned footings, like those of Old Harry's Wife, fallen in 1896, that squat in the sea between them. Old Harry is a synonym for the devil, and the cliff-top is named Old Nick's Ground; but on sunny days when leisurely gulls wheel below and cormorants skim and plunge into smooth, clear water, it is hard to appreciate such black designations. Swap holiday weather for wintry storms, when heavy seas hack at the rocks, when birds rise tattered into the wind or cling to exposed perches, when you must fight to keep your footing on the cliff, and all your sympathy will be with St. Lucas, poised somewhere between the devil, his ground, and the deep, angry sea'.[19]

Old Harry Rocks

Ballard Down

The cliffs ascend to Ballard Down, a ridge from which the chalk of The Needles, on the Isle of Wight, can usually be seen in the distance. In *The Hand of Ethelberta* Hardy described the view: 'Silver sunbeams lighted up a many-armed inland sea [Poole Harbour] which stretched round an island with fir-trees and gorse [Brownsea Island], and amid brilliant crimson heaths wherein white paths and roads occasionally met the eye in dashes and zigzags like flashes of lightning. Outside, where the broad Channel appeared, a berylline and opalized variegation of ripples, currents, deeps, and shallows [Studland Bay] lay as fair under the sun as a New Jerusalem, the shores being of gleaming sand'.[9]

This ridge crest was also a viewpoint in E.M. Forster's *Howard's End*: 'If one wanted to show a foreigner England, perhaps the wisest course would be to take him to the final section of the Purbeck Hills, and stand him on their summit, a few miles to the east of Corfe. Then system after system of our island would roll together under his feet. Beneath him is the valley of the Frome, and all the wild lands that come tossing down from Dorchester, black and gold, to mirror their gorse in the expanses of Poole. Bournemouth's ignoble coast cowers to the right, heralding the pine-trees that mean, for all their beauty, red houses, and the Stock Exchange. Seen from the west, the Wight is beautiful beyond all laws of beauty. It is as if a fragment of England floated forward to greet the foreigner – chalk of our chalk, turf of our turf, epitome of what will follow. And behind the fragment lies Southampton, hostess to the nations, and Portsmouth, a latent fire, and all around it, with double and treble collision of tides, swirls the sea. How many villages appear in this view! How many castles! How many churches, vanished or triumphant! How many ships, railways and roads! What incredible variety of men working beneath that lucent sky to what final end! The reason fails, like a wave on Swanage beach; the imagination swells, spreads and deepens, until it becomes geographic and encircles England'.[22]

Swanage

Swanage, in its bay to the south of the chalky cliff of Ballard Down, was described in 19th century guide books as 'a pleasant little watering-place with a good beach'. Its pier was added in 1896. It was from Swanage that Hardy's Ethelberta rode her donkey to Corfe (Corvsgate) Castle, starting along the shore, then climbing to 'the lofty ridge which ran inland' along Ballard Down, 'rounding off at the top in vegetation, like a forehead with low-grown hair'.[9] Hardy's name for Swanage was 'Knollsea'.

Swanage is still a fairly small and secluded seaside resort, which retains its old-fashioned air. Hardy wrote a poem, 'Once at Swanage':

> *The spray sprang up across the cusps of the moon,*
> *And all its light loomed green*
> *As a witch-flame's weirdsome sheen*
> *At the minute of an incantation scene;*
> *And it greened our gaze – that night at demilune.*
>
> *Roaring high and roaring low was the sea*
> *Behind the headland shores:*
> *It symboled the slamming of doors,*
> *Or a regiment hurrying over hollow floors...*
> *And there we two stood, hands clasped; I and she![23]*

In *The Hand of Ethelberta* 'Knollsea was a seaside village lying snug within two headlands as between a finger and thumb. Everybody in the parish who was no boatman was a quarrier, unless he were the gentleman who owned half the property and had been a quarryman, or the other gentleman who owned the other half, and had been to sea.

'The knowledge of the inhabitants was of the same special sort as their pursuits. The quarrymen in white fustian understood practical geology, the laws and accidents of dips, faults and cleavage, far better than the ways of the world and mammon; the seafaring men in Guernsey frocks had a clearer notion of Alexandria, Constantinople, the Cape, and the Indies than of any inland town in their own country'.[9]

In the final stages of *The Hand of Ethelberta* the steamer *Spruce*, unable to berth at 'Knollsea' because of a stormy sea, turns back towards 'Sandbourne' (Bournemouth): 'The direction and increase of the wind had made it necessary to keep the vessel still further to sea on their return than in going, that they might clear without risk the windy, sousing, thwacking, basting, scourging Jack Ketch of a corner called Old-Harry Point, which lay about halfway along their track, and stood, with its detached posts and stumps of white rock, like a skeleton's lower jaw, grinning at British navigation. Here strong currents and cross currents were beginning to interweave their scrolls and meshes, the water rising behind them in tumultous heaps, and slamming against the fronts and angles of cliff, whence it flew into the air like clouds of flour. Who could now believe that this roaring abode of chaos smiled in the sun as gently as an infant during the summer days not long gone by, every pinnacle, crag, and cave returning a doubled image across the glassy sea?'[9]

Christopher Somerville, depicted an earlier Swanage in *Britain Beside the Sea*: 'As recently as the eighteenth century there was no effective communication by road between Swanage and the outside world. Everything came and went by sea. Purbeck marble had gone into just about every medieval cathedral in the land, and the workable, durable Purbeck freestone into houses, walls, harbours, streets and roads; but roadless, isolated Swanage missed out on the profits until new quarries by the town were opened at about the same time as old London was burning in the Great Fire. Swanage acquired quays and jetties, great mounds of stone along its sea frontage, crowds of sweating quarrymen and stone-shifters, stone-dust in the summer, mud in the winter. None of this added to the scenic attractions of the area. Quarrying doesn't do the landscape any favours at the best of times, and the dusty little stone port shipping out tens of thousands of tons a year was more concerned with business than appearance. Rebuilding London gobbled up whatever the Purbeck quarries could supply. So did the turnpikes and sea defences of Georgian England and, in their turn, the Victorian new towns and new roads. It wasn't until the enormous quarries above Swanage at last began to give out towards the end of the nineteenth century that the town relinquished its long grip on stone, cleaned up, broadened out and put on a well-scrubbed smile for the holidaymaker'.[24]

W.J. Arkell also wrote about the area: 'Swanage Stone and Purbeck Marble have been quarried for building and interior decoration from time immemorial. The building stones are quarried mainly south-west of Swanage, at Herston and Acton, but nearly the whole outcrop is riddled with old shafts and much land spoilt with tip-heaps. Formerly the stone was also tunnelled in the cliffs of Durlston Bay, but all traces of these workings have now disappeared. Swanage originated essentially as a quarrying town, and it was not until the present century that any other building material was seen in its house walls or roofs. Until after the turn of the century masons' yards and piles of stone occupied the sea frontage adjoining the quay and as far north as the mouth of Swan Brook'.[25]

Peveril Point and Tilly Whim Caves

To the south, at Peveril Point, the 'sinister ledge of limestones, like a crocodile's teeth'[9] was a threat to navigation. Cliffs of limestone continue to Durlston Head, where the Country Park includes a Great Globe (diameter 10 feet, weight forty tons) of Portland limestone, bordered by walls on which literary quotations and geographical information have been engraved. Nearby are the Tilly Whim caves, former limestone quarries: Tilly was a quarryman and whim the dialect word for winch. Freestone and Purbeck marble, veined red, grey and other colours, have long been cut from this southern ridge, and used in the building of Westminster Abbey and several cathedrals. Anvil Point lighthouse stands on a grassy slope, the turf nibbled by numerous rather tame rabbits.

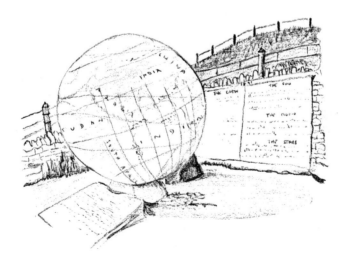

Limestone Globe, Swanage

Moonfleet

J. Meade Falkner set part of his story *Moonfleet* here. After a narrow escape from soldiers on White Nothe the smuggler, Elzevir Block, had carried the injured fifteen-year old John Trenchard along the coast, to find sanctuary 'in the land of the old marble quarries at the back of Anvil Point', at Tilly Whim Caves. John Trenchard was the narrator: 'These quarries were made by men centuries ago, some say by the Romans themselves; and though some are still worked in other parts of Purbeck, those at the back of Anvil Point have been disused beyond the memory of man.

'It was by the side of one of these old shafts that Elzevir laid me down at last. "There", he said, "this is Joseph's Pit, and here we must lie hid until thy foot is sound again".' The shaft led down into a cave: 'On one side was that passage through which we had come in, and on the other opened a sort of door which gave on to a stone ledge eight fathoms above high-water mark. For the cave was cut out just inside the iron cliff-face which lies between St Alban's [St. Aldhelm's] Head and Swanage'.[26]

Here they remained through the summer until John could walk freely again. 'I could walk across the cave without the help of a stout blackthorn that Elzevir had cut me: and so I went out on to the ledge to watch the growing sea. There I sat down, with my back against a protecting rock, in such a place that I could see up-Channel and yet shelter from the rushing wind. The sky was overcast, and the long wall of rock showed grey with orange-brown patches and a darker line of sea-weed at the base like the under strake of a boat's belly, for the tide was but beginning to make. There was a mist, half-fog, half-spray, scudding before the wind, and through it I could see the white-backed rollers lifting over Peveril Point;* while all along the cliff-face the sea-birds thronged the ledges, and sat huddled in snowy lines, knowing the mischief that was brewing in the elements'.

In due course Elzevir and John moved out of the caves, and after further adventures, they were tricked, trapped, and imprisoned in the Netherlands, then sentenced to deportation to work on the sugar farms of Java, and put on board the brig *Aurungzebe*. We shall meet them again on page 34.

Strip Lynchets

Paul Theroux, having trudged west from Durlston Head:'walked on, a little inland, so I would not have to go up and down the bluffs. The gorse bushes had bright yellow flowers and the land was open – it was like traipsing around the edge of a great country, on top of its sliced-off side. I went across Dancing Ledge and through Seacombe and up Winspit, and various notches in the coast with steep terraces, and valleys of sheep browsing under ivy-strangled haw-

---

* We think he was looking at Durlston Head, not Peveril Point, which is round the corner, and out of sight from Tilly Whim Caves.

thorns. These terraces, the ridges of the edge of the valley, were caused by ploughing six hundred years ago. At the village of Worth Matravers, I read that these furrows were called 'strip-lynchets' and the tourist sign said, "The need to plough such steep terraces was probably learned after the dramatic population decline caused by the Black Death of 1348-9." Most of these Dorset villages were a great deal smaller than they had once been'.[20]

Dancing Ledge

Paul Hyland came along this coast on: 'a day to make for Dancing Ledge along the cliff-path, watching yachts and fishing-boats ploughing gulf-strewn furrows in the pacific Channel, while you tread turf-cushioned rock which only sailors can see is undermined by the gaping mouths of cliff quarries like Blacker's Hole. Natives, impatient with tourists' demands for entertainment, have been known to direct those in search of a glittering night-spot to Dancing Ledge. But the broad platform of rock there is rutted with the wheels of man-drawn horn-carts with shafts like out-curving antennae, though it is an ideal place from which to dive into the sea for a final swim as the sun goes down behind St. Aldhelm's Head. Songs cried out to be sung and you could dance if you liked, so long as you conserved enough wind for the steep smugglers' path up to Spyway and Langton Matravers'.[19]

Kimmeridge

A coastal ridge culminates in St Aldhelm's Head, with its square and sturdy 12th century Norman chapel, 354 feet above sea level. Beneath the cliffs the sea has cut out a cove called Chapman's Pool, and to the west layers of limestone run across the shore as Kimmeridge Ledges.

Frederick Treves wrote of this scene: 'The traveller who follows the coast now passes the fine hill of Swyre Head, and so comes to Kimmeridge. The downs here are in long rolling lines, like terrific sea combers about to break upon a shoal. On the slope of one of these is the hamlet - a cosy place of thatched cottages in a clump of trees. A rough road leads to a bay surrounded by low, earth-coloured cliffs. But for a ridiculous tower, a lifeboat shed, and a coastguard station, made up of unpleasantly formal houses, the place is as desolate as it is dingy'.[12]

Paul Theroux was in a better mood: 'The sun and the wind made the long grass flicker like fire. There were pastures on the cliffs, and just to the left of the overgrown path two hundred vertical feet of gull-clawed air to the sliding surf, and the whole ocean beyond. This was the most beautiful stretch of coast I had seen so far, and I was alone on it.

'There was a tower at the edge of the cliff ahead. It stood on its own, it was attached to nothing, it looked like a ruined lighthouse. This was at Kimmeridge Bay. A man with a pamphlet told me that it was called the Clavell Tower and that it was almost two hundred years old. Clavell was a clergyman and also stargazer. He used the tower for his astronomy. It was a delicate structure, and the steeps and headlands of the coast made it seem more delicate, because there was no other building near it'.[20]

Clavell Tower, Kimmeridge

The tower on the cliff top at Kimmeridge was in fact built in 1820 by the Reverend John Clavell of Smedmore as a summer-house. It was *The Black Tower* in P.D. James's thriller set hereabouts and featured in the television series. Attempts have been made to use the oil shale layers in the cliffs near Kimmeridge Bay as a fuel, but it burns smelly and smoky. In 1958 drillers found much better quality oil at a depth of 1800 feet, and large quantities have been extracted by the 'nodding donkey' pumps on the cliffs to the west. The coastal footpath then ascends to where John Trenchard, the hero of *Moonfleet*, 'had once been over Gad Cliff in a basket, to get two peregrines' eggs'.[26]

Tyneham

Just inland is the ruined village of Tyneham, in an area closed to the public for much of the year because of the Army firing ranges. John Grimson told the story: 'The military occupation of the Purbeck ranges is a long story of enforced evacuation, broken promises and – more recently – of nationwide controversy and clashes of interests. The Army has been here since 1916, when almost a thousand acres of land near Lulworth Cove were taken over as a tank gunnery school, but the big expansion came in 1943, when more than five thousand additional acres were taken. In the middle of it lay the village of Tyneham, whose three hundred inhabitants were evacuated just before Christmas, taking with them what they regarded as a solemn pledge that they could return to their homes when the war was over. On the door of their church they pinned a notice which read: "We have given up our homes to help to win the war to keep men free. We shall return one day and thank you for treating the village kindly". Now, more than a third of a century later, although some Tynehamians still live in hope of being allowed to return, it is clear to most that the pledge will never be fulfilled.

'Since the war we have seen the rise of the environmental movement. There have been calls for the Army to leave and for the whole of Purbeck to be designated a National Park. Indeed, many people believe that the area would have become a National Park long ago, had it not been for the military presence. It has for long been part of a designated Area of Outstanding Natural Beauty, and has more recently been included in the defined twenty-four-mile frontage of the Purbeck Heritage Coast.

'However, thirty years have passed since the betrayal of those villagers, and Tyneham as a community is gone beyond recall. And if the story of their betrayal presents the unacceptable side of the Army's occupation of this vast tract of land, it must be said in fairness that there is today another, more acceptable side, which finds widespread local support. The Army is a considerable employer of local labour, a payer of local rates, and much of the servicemen's pay is spent locally. Also the military presence has certainly prevented other, more unsightly forms of development in an area of spectacular and unspoilt coast, and has effectively conserved its wildlife.

'When one compares the untamed, unspoilt wilderness of the Purbeck ranges with poor little strangulated Lulworth Cove, striving to survive beneath an ever-increasing welter of summer tourists, its lovely little cliff-girt bay overfaced by the stark glitter of reflected sunlight from a thousand cars parked on its western hill, the question must be faced: is the Army any more of a despoiler than the rest of us?'[4]

Lilian Bond had memories of a happier Tyneham in the late nineteenth century, long before the arrival of the army. She remembered picnics when 'we came in triumph to the top of the cliffs, where we left the cart and scrambled down the stairway, cut in the shale, to the shelf of rock below. Broadbench's level platform stretched away round the foot of the cliff to the west into Hobarrow Bay. At its seaward edge it formed a small cliff of its own where the upper shelf ended a few feet above a boulder strewn floor. This miniature cliff was indented and had little headlands and inlets where rock pools held bright sea anemones. The shelf made an excellent table for picnics and legs could be comfortably swung as the picknicker sat on the edge overlooking the four feet abyss. At low tide the games to be played round the rocks and ankle-deep basins of clear, lukewarm water were legion. I can still feel the warmth of the smooth sleek rock face on the soles of my feet'.[27]

Arish Mell

The high chalk Purbeck Hills which back the undulating Kimmeridge area have been cut by the sea behind broad Worbarrow Bay, and almost penetrated at Arish Mell gap. F.J. Harvey Darton, admired the view in the 1920s: 'The tiny village of Arish Mell (an old Celtic name) is a place of warm peace, where kine drift down from the meadows to the seashore itself. Their friendly brown coats are not the brightest colour here. The face of the coast, from Worbarrow Point to Mupe's Rocks, is like a many-hued puzzle, a geological jigsaw. The shingle is yellow and blue-grey; the down turf wears its eternal green; Bindon, its flank dark with pines, has a face of gleaming silver: but Ring's Hill contains every shade from scarlet to purple, while the little headland of Worbarrow is striped with contorted formations, of grey and drab and black. Mupe's dark rocks are of a threatening brown, with the white snow of waves at their base. I do not know whom this desolate and lovely place may most fully satisfy; the geologist, the artist, the historian, the mere walker may all take delight in it'.[28]

Lulworth Cove

At Lulworth Cove the Portland and Purbeck limestones form a steeply dipping rampart, cut through by the sea. which then invaded a valley of softer clays and washed out a beautifully rounded bay, backed by an arcuate beach of flint shingle. This is a coastline of remarkable diversity and beauty. Frederick Treves, who lived at Lulworth, wrote of it: 'In this sea line are cliffs of jagged rocks, sheer as a bastion wall, as well as green lawns which creep lazily to the water's edge. There are wide, open bays, and fissured sea-echoing chines. There are round coves, inlets reached through arched rocks, level sands and moaning caves. There are beaches of shingle, of pebbles, of colossal boulders, and of the clay of crumbling banks; precipices of every colour, from the white of chalk to the black of the shale; and walls of stone streaked with tints of yellow, buff, or red',[12] He described the 'fearful fall' of an 11 year old girl down the chalk cliff in 1892: she survived, battered and scratched, but the notice commemorating this misadventure seems to have disappeared.

It was at Lulworth Cove, in September 1820, that John Keats, sailing to Italy, was delayed because his ship lay becalmed, and spent a day ashore, clambering over the rocks. Then he went back on board to complete his final sonnet:

> *Bright Star, would I were steadfast as thou art –*
> *Not in lone splendour hung aloft the night*
> *And watching, with eternal lids apart,*
> *Like nature's patient, sleepless Eremite,*
> *The moving waters at their priestlike task.*[29]

The story of Keats' brief landing at Lulworth Cove, his last glimpse of England, inspired Hardy to write 'At Lulworth Cove a Century Back':

> *Had I but lived a hundred years ago*
> *I might have gone, as I have gone this year,*
> *By Warmwell Cross on to a Cove I know,*
> *And Time have placed his finger on me there:*
>
> *'You see that man?' – I might have looked, and said,*
> *'O yes: I see him. One that boat has brought*
> *Which dropped down Channel round Saint Albans Head.*
> *So commonplace a youth calls not my thought'.*
>
> *'You see that man?' – 'Why yes; I told you; yes:*
> *Of an idling town-sort; thin; hair brown in hue;*
> *And as the evening light scants less and less*
> *He looks up at a star, as many do'.*
>
> *'You see that man?' – 'Nay, leave me!' then I plead,*
> *'I have fifteen miles to vamp across the lea,*
> *And it grows dark, and I am weary-kneed:*
> *I have said the third time; yes, that man I see!'*
>
> *'Good. That man goes to Rome – to death, despair;*
> *And no one notes him now but you and I:*
> *A hundred years, and the world will follow him there,*
> *And bend with reverence where his ashes lie'.*[23]

In the summer of 1907, Rupert Brooke, then a Cambridge undergraduate, was in Lulworth with a 'reading party', and wrote two versions of an incident there, the first to his mother:

'One day we were reading on the rocks, and I had a Keats in my pocket, and it slipped out, and falling into a swift current, was borne out to sea. So we leapt into a boat and rowed up and down the coast until we espied it off some rocks. But the sea was rather rough and we could not land on that rocky part, or get near Keats. So we landed half a mile off on a beach, and came over the rocks to the Keats; and we found it, I stripped and went in after it and got it'.[30]

The second was to fellow-student Maynard Keynes:

'On Tuesday we sat on seagirt rocks and read J. Keats. When I leapt from rock to rock J.K. fell from pocket into swirling flood beneath; and, ere aught could be done, was borne from reach on swift current. We rushed to the harbour, chartered a boat, and rowed frantically along the rocky coast in search of it. At length we spied it close in, by treacherous rocks, in a boat we could not get to it alive. We beached our barque (at vast risk) half a mile down the coast and leapt lightly over vast boulders to the spot.

'With a hurried misquotation from Diodorus Siculus I cast off my garb, and plunged wholly naked, into that "fury of black waters and white foam" - Enough. J.K. was rescued, in a damaged condition. All (except my Stomach) is well'.[30]

Thomas Hardy described Lulworth Cove as 'Lulstead Cove' in *Desperate Remedies*, in which Cytherea Graye and her brother Owen came in on the paddle steamer from Weymouth, and climbed the hill behind the cove. Owen decided to walk inland in search of a friend, leaving Cytherea behind:

'She remained on the summit where he had left her till the time of his expected return, scanning the details of the prospect around. Placidly spread out before her was the open Channel, reflecting a blue intenser by many shades than that of the sky overhead and dotted in the foreground by half-a-dozen small craft of contrasting rig, their sails graduating in hue from extreme whiteness to reddish brown, the varying actual colours varied again in a double degree by the rays of the declining sun.

'Presently the distant bell from the boat was heard, warning the passengers to embark. This was followed by a lively air from the harps and violins on board, their tones, as they arose, becoming intermingled with, though not marred by, the brush of the waves when their crests rolled over – at the point where the check of the shallows was first felt – and then thinned away up the slope of pebbles and sand'.[31]

Hardy gave it another name, 'Lulwind Cove', in *Far From the Madding Crowd*, in which Sergeant Troy walked up to the crest of the ridge: 'A wide and novel prospect burst upon him with an effect almost like that of the Pacific upon Balboa's gaze. The broad steely sea, marked only by faint lines, which had a semblance of being etched thereon to a degree not deep enough to disturb its general evenness, stretched the whole width of his front and round to the right, where, near the town and port of Budmouth [Weymouth], the sun bristled down upon it, and banished all colour, to substitute in its place a clear oily polish. Nothing moved in sky, land, or sea, except a frill of milkwhite foam along the nearer angles of the shore, shreds of which licked the contiguous stones like tongues.

'He descended and came to a small basin of sea enclosed by the cliffs. Troy's nature freshened within him; he thought he would rest and bathe here before going further. He undressed and plunged in. Inside the cove the water was uninteresting to a swimmer, being smooth as a pond, and to get a little of the ocean swell, Troy presently swam between the two projecting spurs of rock which formed the pillars of Hercules to this miniature Mediterranean. Unfortunately for Troy a current unknown to him existed outside, which, unimportant to craft of any burden, was awkward for a swimmer who might be taken in it unawares. Troy found himself carried to the left and then round in a swoop out to sea.

'He now recollected the place and its sinister character. Not a boat of any kind was at present within sight, but far in the distance Budmouth lay upon the sea, as it were quietly regarding his efforts, and beside the town the harbour showed its position by a dim meshwork of ropes and spars. After well-nigh exhausting himself in attempts to get back to the mouth of the cove, he perceptibly approached the extremity of a spit of land yet further to the right, now well defined against the sunny portion of the horizon. While the swimmer's eyes were fixed upon the spit as his only means of salvation on this side of the Unknown, a moving object broke the outline of the extremity, and immediately a ship's boat appeared, manned with several sailor lads, her bows towards the sea.

'All Troy's vigour, spasmodically revived to prolong the struggle yet a little further. Swimming with his right arm, he held up his left to hail them, splashing upon the waves and shouting with all his might. From the position of the setting sun his white form was distinctly visible upon the now deep-hued bosom of the sea to the east of the boat, and the men saw him at once.'

Thus rescued, he decided to vanish, and soon Bathsheba, his wife, was told that "Her husband was drowned this week while bathing in Lulwind Cove. A coastguardsman found his clothes, and brought them into Budmouth yesterday".[32]

Durdle Door

There are the remains of a fossil forest in the steep rocks near the entrance, and the limestone rampart becomes more broken to the west, where Durdle Door is all that remains of it in front of high chalk cliffs. 'How individual a feature of Dorset coast', wrote Llewelyn Powys, 'is the great oolite archway situated westward of Lulworth Cove known as Durdle Door. The Durdle Door is sometimes called the Barn Door, and the homeliness of this title accords well with its shape for, viewed either from sea or land, this broken cliff has the simple look that often belongs to the entrances of old out-buildings of agrarian husbandry, entrances wide enough to admit a broad-beamed country waggon burdened high with corn sheafs. The appearance of this rugged, firmly standing portal of the open sea suggests an ancient human building, the weathering it has received differing little from the weathering that has fallen upon the square belfry tower of Sherborne Abbey.

'On a summer's morning the Durdle Door can present a very harmless and tranquil appearance. At intervals curling waves break upon its shingle, waves not high enough to overset a child's toy boat. Samphire, flower of St. Peter, that has managed to root itself in the rough interstices of the huge sea gate, seems as naturally placed as are patches of mistletoe upon an apple tree bowed down with age'.[33]

White Nothe

West from Durdle Door the cliffs undulate in front of wide grassy chalk combes. In one of these, in the 1967 film of *Far From the Madding Crowd*, Gabriel Oak's dog drove his sheep over the cliff edge, although in Hardy's story this 'pastoral tragedy' occurred at an inland chalk quarry.[32]

The chalk cliffs then sweep up to White Nothe, where underlying sandstone and clay forms a tumbled landslip, in which an outcrop of oil shale, on fire for a few years from 1826, gave the name Burning Cliff. In *Moonfleet*, J. Meade Falkner set a smuggling scene here, with White Nothe disguised as 'Hoar Head': 'the highest of that line of cliffs, which stretches twenty miles from Weymouth to St Alban's Head, it stands up eighty fathoms or more above the water. The seaward side is a great sheer of chalk, but falls not straight into the sea, for three parts down there is a lower ledge or terrace, called the under-cliff'.

The smuggler Elzevir Block and the boy John Trenchard had walked across from Moonfleet (Fleet) by way of the hills behind Weymouth, and John Trenchard took up the story: 'Twas to this ledge that we were bound; and though we were now straight above, I knew we had a mile or more to go before we could get down to it. So on we went again, and found the bridle-path that slopes down through a deep dip in the cliff-line; and when we reached this under-ledge, I looked up at the sky, the night being clear, and guessed by the stars that 'twas past midnight. I knew the place from having once been there for blackberries; for the brambles on the under-cliff being sheltered every way but south, and open to the sun, grow the finest in all those parts'.

Here the *Bonaventure* came ashore at three in the morning to unload kegs of liquor, and all went well until the smugglers were ambushed by a posse of soldiers, and a stray shot broke John Trenchard's leg. Elzevir and John could not return by way of the bridle path, but Elzevir knew of an alternative: 'Just at the end of this flat ledge, farthest from where the bridle-path leads down, but not a hundred yards from where we stand, there is a sheep-track leading up the cliff. It starts where the under-cliff dies back again into the chalk face, and climbs by slants and elbow-turns up to the top. The shepherds call it the Zigzag, and even sheep lose their footing on it'.

Elzevir carried the wounded John up the Zigzag to make an escape. As they reached the top: 'The day was still young, and far below us was stretched the moving floor of the Channel, with a silver-grey film of night-mists not yet lifted in the offing. A hummocky up-and-down line of cliffs, all projections, dents, bays, and hollows, trended southward till it ended in the great bluff of St Alban's Head, ten miles away. The cliff face was gleaming white, the sea tawny inshore, but purest blue outside, with the straight sunpath across it, spangled and gleaming like a mackerel's back'. [26] They made their way, Elzevir carrying John, eastward along this coast to a hiding place, in Purbeck, where we found them on page 26.

Chaldon Herring

A little way inland the village of Chaldon Herring (also known as East Chaldon) was the home of two of the Powys brothers. Theodore lived in a house called Beth Car (from 1904 to 1940) and Llewelyn lived with his wife and sisters at Chydyok Farm (from 1931 to 1936), while John Cowper Powys, who wrote several novels, including *Weymouth Sands*, was a travelling lecturer in the United States (from 1909 to 1936).

Llewelyn Powys told in *Skin for Skin* how Theodore left Studland in 1904 'to find some unpretentious village, where he would be altogether free from molestation. He walked on and on, over the downs. He went into Corfe, into Kimmeridge, into Arishmell Bay, until eventually he arrived at Winfrith and from there debouched to East Chaldon, which very possibly is the most hidden village in Dorset. And here, for twenty years, he has lived, occupied with his own queer mystical illuminations, with his books, his writing, and his wife and two boys. His house is surrounded by bare downs, over the huge, supine shoulders of which sea-gulls and black rooks alternately cast their shadows'. [34]

Llewelyn Powys

Llewelyn Powys had lived for six years in one of the coastguard cottages on top of White Nothe, which he preferred to call White Nose; in this he was supported by Thomas Hardy, who said that the cliff had the shape of the Duke of Wellington's nose. Although this cliff 'approaches an altitude of six hundred feet, it is not as high as Golden Cap, but both its position and its "countenance" render it the noblest of all the Dorset headlands. This proud sea headland, conspicuous from the Esplanade at Weymouth, is a promontory of many mysteries. It would take a boy longer than a summer's holiday to explore all the secret Robin-Hood-retreats of the under-cliff, the giddy ledges and castle rocks to be found in that strip of broken ground. In the winter this under-cliff is entirely deserted, a forest abandoned to the partridge, to the raven, and to the red fox. In the early summer, when there are forget-me-nots in the turf by the cliff's edge, minute as the bright chips of enamel in a brooch, a pair of shiftless magpies translated into dutiful fowls of troth, give themselves to the exacting task of rearing young in a clumsy "nitch" of prick-thorns. This happens during that fugitive period when the voice of the cuckoo is audible far out over the waves of Weymouth Bay, and larks are singing all day long high up above open strategic foot-square platforms where zigzag figured adders lie curled for hour after hour in a voluptuous torpor warming their close dry scales'.[33]

Llewelyn spent many hours walking, in this, his favourite area: 'One morning, as I walked I noticed a rabbit disappear over the cliff's edge. On coming to the place, I made out a kind of ledge, down which a man might possibly clamber to a rocky projection, some forty feet below. Immediately I was seized with a great desire to reach this point.

'Smugglers in the old days had frequented this bay, and it seemed to me that I had probably found the top of the path used by them when scaling the cliff. Very slowly, scarcely venturing to look at the wrinkled sea below me, I clambered down, foot by foot. Once on the other side of the rock, I came upon a rusty iron bar, deeply imbedded in the face of the bluff. I reached it, and held to it with both hands, as the only stable thing on the side of that tilted precipice. My knees trembled. The idea of climbing back terrified me, the idea of climbing down terrified me. And yet, how exciting, if only I could manage to reach that purged and chastened beach, at which I had so often gazed! Again I descended. There was a kind of track. Once I dislodged a small stone and shivered to see how it fell with scarcely a break to the pebbles so far below.

'I was a full hour in the solitary cove. I trudged from one end to the other of its virginal beach, shaped like a horned moon. Under Bat's Head I found a cave, and crawled into its further recesses where I lay for a time listening to the boom-boom of the waves, as they rolled in upon the hollow tunnels, honeycombing that solitary headland. The cave was full of seaweed, and I picked up a long brown riband and bound it round my forehead. Its surface was smooth and slippery, and no mermaid could have smelt more intimately of the sea.

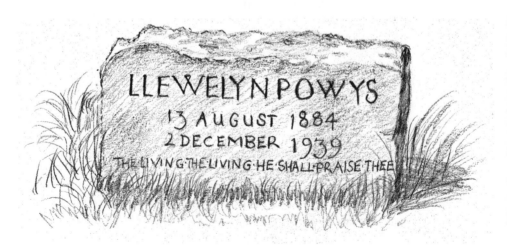

LLEWELYN POWYS
13 AUGUST 1884
2 DECEMBER 1939
THE LIVING THE LIVING HE SHALL PRAISE THEE

'Walking back to the place where I would have to begin the ascent, I looked up. All was blue and white - white cliffs and blue sky, white surf and blue sea, white birds and blue, curling waves! I felt giddy, I could see the smuggler's stake sticking out of the precipice like a nail in a white-washed wall. When I had scaled some fifty feet, I looked round. There below me were the tracks I had made on the wet, red shingle. Above, the cliff flanked itself against the sky like a snow-covered alp. I began climbing again, and in a few minutes was once more clinging to the corroded iron stake. Only faintly now there came to my ears the montonous ebb and flow of the sea'.[33]

Up on the hill, to the east of White Nothe, a memorial stone to Llewellyn Powys stands high above the sea.

The Sailor's Return

Chaldon Herring was also the scene of David Garnett's novel, *The Sailor's Return*, in which it was called 'Maiden Newbarrow'. The Sailor's Return is the local Inn to which William Targett came to live with his wife Tulip, a Princess of Dahomey, and their little son, Sambo. One night they went down to the beach near White Nothe for a swim: 'Over the hill was the sea. There they went cautiously down a winding path that led them to a gap in the cliffs. Soon they dismounted, tied their horses to a tree, and ran down onto the beach. It was high tide, and the sea was so calm that it might have been a great saucer of milk, gently moving but without a wave it brimmed up to the very lip of the shingle beach. William threw off his coat, his shirt and his trousers.

"Are there no sharks?", asked Tulip.

"No, not in England".

'Tulip had slipped on her seaman's trousers and an old coat of William's when she came riding. Now she flung them off and raced after him into the water. It was warmer to their bodies than the air of the August night. They swam out in silence, Tulip's curly black head bobbing in the wake of William's fair one'.[35]

Osmington White Horse

The chalk scarp curves behind Ringstead Bay, which occupies an amphitheatre of low undulating hills. Osmington Mills, with its 13th century Smugglers Inn, is where John Constable, honeymooning in 1816, produced the painting of Weymouth Bay, now in the National Gallery, and several views of Osmington Bay. On the chalk scarp inland has been cut a white horse with King George III riding away from Weymouth, the most coastal of all the chalk horses, and the only one visible from out at sea. It also is the only white horse hill-figure in Britain to carry a rider and was, probably cut to commemorate the first visit of George III to Weymouth. Thomas Hardy mentioned it under construction early in the nineteenth century, when the Trumpet Major and Anne Garland came there: 'When they reached the hill they found forty navvies at work removing the dark sod so as to lay bare the chalk beneath. The equestrian figure that their shovels were forming was scarcely intelligible to John and Anne now they were close, and after pacing from the horse's head down his breast to his hoof, back by way of the king's bridle-arm, past the bridge of his nose and into his cocked hat, Anne said that she had had enough of it, and stepped out of the chalk clearing upon the grass'.[36]

Sutton Poyntz

Sutton Poyntz, to the west, was Hardy's 'Overcombe' in *The Trumpet Major*. At the time of the Napoleonic threat, the village people climbed to the top of the Chalk downs to watch a parade of red- coated soldiery: 'It was a clear day with little wind stirring, and the view from the downs, one of the most extensive in the county, was unclouded. The eye of any observer who cared for such things swept over the wave-washed town, and the bay beyond, and the Isle [of Portland], with its pebble bank, lying on the sea to the left of these, like a great crouching animal tethered to the mainland. On the extreme east of the marine horizon, St. Aldhelm's Head closed the scene, the sea to the southward of that point glaring like a mirror under the sun to the west, Dogbury Hill and Black'on near to the foreground, the beacon thereon being built of furze faggots thatched with straw, and standing on the spot where the monument [to Admiral Hardy] now raises its head'.[36]

George III at Weymouth

When he visited Weymouth in 1789, George III became the first king to use a bathing machine on the sandy beach. Fanny Burney, in royal service here, recorded this event in her diary: 'Think of the surprise of his Majesty when, the first time of his bathing, he had no sooner popped his royal head under water, than a band of music, concealed in a neighbouring machine, struck up "God Save Great George Our King"'.[37]

Thomas Hardy worked the same incident into *The Trumpet Major*: 'It was the 3rd of September, but the King's watering-place still retained its summer aspect. The royal bathing-machine had been drawn out just as Bob reached Gloucester Buildings, and he waited a minute, in the lack of other distraction, to look on.

'Immediately that the King's machine had entered the water a group of florid men with fiddles, violoncellos, a trombone, and a drum, came forward, packed themselves into another machine that was in waiting, and were drawn out into the waves in the King's rear. All that was to be heard for a few minutes were the slow pulsations of the sea; and then a deafening noise burst from the interior of the second machine with power enough to split the boards asunder; it was the condensed mass of musicians inside, striking up the strains of 'God save the King', as his Majesty's head rose from the waters. Bob took off his hat and waited till the end of the performance, which, intended as a pleasant surprise to George III by the loyal burghers, was possibly in the watery circumstances tolerated rather than desired by that dripping monarch'.[36]

Thus popularised, the little town became a coastal resort. In 1798 the Dorset poet William Holloway, composed an invitation:

> Wouldst thou enjoy health, contemplation, ease.
> Salubrious waters and a purer breeze:
> Can friendship charm thee, or can ease excite,
> Philander haste, fair Weymouth's scenes invite.
> Come let us stray, yon winding cliffs along,
> To hear the cheerful lark's shrill matin song;
> Thro' blooming fields of clover, pea and bean,
> Rich, various, blooming midst their native green,
> High o'er the misty margin of the main
> Now mounts the sun and gilds the wat'ry plain;
> There white with flowing saile behold afar,
> Or barks of trade, or bulky ships of war.[38]

A Georgian Resort

Weymouth flourished, and became a seaside town with fine Georgian houses and a clock tower (built to celebrate Queen Victoria's jubilee in 1887) on its esplanade. The Queen's statue frowns westward from St. John's church along the seafront to the more cheerful and colourful monument to George III.

As 'Budmouth', the town was prominent in Hardy's *The Trumpet Major*, and in his preface to *The Return of the Native*, Hardy remarked that 'between 1840 and 1850 the old watering-place herein called "Budmouth" still retained sufficient afterglow from its Georgian gaiety and prestige to lend it an absorbing attractiveness to the romantic and imaginative soul of a lonely dweller inland'. Later in the book the reddleman, Diggory Venn, said 'Now Budmouth is a wonderful place – wonderful – a great salt sheening sea bending into the land like a bow – thousands of gentle people walking up and down – bands of music playing – officers by sea and officers by land walking among the rest – out of every ten folk you meet nine of 'em in love'.[39]

In Hardy's *The Dynasts*, the Hussar recalled Budmouth:

> *When we lay where Budmouth beach is,*
> *O, the girls were fresh as peaches,*
> *With their tall and tossing figures and their eyes of blue and brown!*
> *And our hearts would ache with longing*
> *As we paced from our sing-songing,*
> *With a smart Clink! Clink! up the Esplanade and down.*[40]

Weymouth's sandy beach is ideal for the building of sand castles: there are summer competitions when the most elaborate structures are shaped, to be judged before the rising tide consumes them. One worker in sand was the young John Cowper Powys: 'The grand delight of those months of lodging in Weymouth was digging with a wooden spade in the wet sand near the sea's edge. Oh, how deep a pleasure, oh how quivering and trembling a pleasure·it was to watch the salt-water flow into an estuary that you yourself had prepared for it! What a commentary it is upon the ways of mortal life that such a proverbially vain thing, such an ultimate example of useless activity, as digging in sea-sand should be attended with such ravishing transports of happiness. But that incredible sensation when the sea at last really rushes in and our sand-banks grow paler and whiter, as the long ripples reach them; till they begin to yield and to sink and to flatten out, and their edges are overpoweringly smoothed away and rounded off and silted into indistinction; and the sand we have piled up comes sliding down, sinking, sinking, sinking; till finally there is nothing left but the smooth sea-floor, just as it has been for a thousand years'.[41]

In *Weymouth Sands* Powys wrote of Lodmoor, the swampy area east of Weymouth: 'All visitors to Weymouth remembered Lodmoor as a curious and interesting phenomenon amid their other impressions. The Preston Road is bounded on its southward flank by a picturesque, grey sea-wall and by the pebbly shore. Across its level expanse, if they debouched amid its peat-smelling cattle paths, could be seen seaward, beyond the low roof of the Coast-Guard Station, the towering facade of the great cliff called the White Nose [Nothe], and land-ward, above the grassy undulations of the Downs, the far-seen image of the White Horse'[42]

Weymouth Harbour
John Cowper Powys described the harbour at the mouth of the Wey, with 'a picturesque row of old-fashioned houses on the western side of the little harbour.

Some of these time-mellowed habitations had lights in their rooms; and the rays from their windows fell upon stone steps leading down into the rushing tide, and upon quite a fleet of small rowing-boats that rocked up and down in the darkness. Above the roofs of these houses rose the grassy promontory known locally as the Nothe',[42] where the harbour has been protected since 1539 by Sandsfoot Castle, which Hardy, in *The Well-Beloved* correctly called Henry VIII's Castle.

Thomas Hardy began a poem on the quay beside Weymouth harbour:

> *From here, the quay, one looks above to mark*
> *The bridge across the harbour, hanging dark*
> *Against the day's-end sky, fair-green in glow*
> *Over and under the middle archway's bow:*
> *It draws its skeleton where the sun has set,*
> *Yea, clear from cutwater to parapet;*
> *On which mild glow, too, lines of rope and spar*
> *Trace themselves black as char.*
>
> *Down here in shade we hear the painters shift*
> *Against the bollards with a drowsy lift,*
> *As moved by the incoming stealthy tide.*
> *High up across the bridge the burghers glide*
> *As cut-black paper portraits hastening on*
> *In conversation none knows what upon:*
> *Their sharp-edged lips move quickly word by word*
> *To speech that is not heard.*[23]

The Changing Coastline

The coastline we have just traversed, from Swanage to Weymouth, is geologically famous because of the variety and interest of the rock formations and structures it displays. The geologist W.J. Arkell, who wrote about it in 1939 in a Geological Memoir, asked: 'What will be the future of this 30 miles of coastline, so richly endowed as a training ground and museum of geology? Few tracts of equal size could raise so many claims, scientific, aesthetic and literary, for preservation as a national park. At present, however, it seems that little can be done to save it falling piecemeal before the builder. Weymouth and Swanage are expanding apace and must continue to do so. In the past five years the rural road to Portland Ferry has become a street. Wyke Regis has been engulfed. The villas are marching out to Chickerell and round the back of Lodmoor. They have captured Jordan Hill. The next to fall will be Redcliff. A new building estate with unlimited possibilities has appeared at Ringstead: a red-roofed villa has sprung up on the skyline of the White Nothe itself. If the English of this present generation allow this heritage of the community to be irreparably spoilt for private gain they will be held by posterity to have been unworthy to possess it. To all geologists who have enjoyed and profited by this coast, an appeal is made to do their utmost to preserve it.' [25]

Fortunately there were others who shared Arkell's view, and the emergence of post-war town and country planning, together with the declaration of Heritage Coasts and sites of scientific interest has curbed exploitative development and urban sprawl, so that half a century later the coast between Swanage and Weymouth is still scenically and scientifically of very high quality. But we will need to maintain vigilance if these values are to be perpetuated along the South Coast of England.

Portland Harbour

Weymouth is a ferry port with links to the Channel Islands. It was the building of a French naval base at Cherbourg that prompted the similar enclosing of the bay south of Weymouth as Portland Harbour. The huge stone breakwaters, designed by Sir John Coode, a harbour engineer, were built between 1849 and 1872. Charlotte Mason described how 'great heaps of waste stone have been used for several years to make a breakwater on the plan of that at Plymouth. Some fifteen hundred men were employed about this breakwater, who marched to and from their work in dull-looking gangs – men who never spoke to, rarely looked at one another, and who never dared to stop their work; men with hard-looking, heavy faces for the most part, wearing the same sort of clothes, with the same badge. These men were the convicts from the large and dreary prison upon the island'. [43] Many of them were about to be transported to Australia.

Stone for the breakwaters, and also for Buckingham Palace and St. Paul's Cathedral, came from the vast quarries on the Isle of Portland. This great limestone peninsula slopes southwards from 496 feet above sea level to less than 20 feet at the Bill of Portland, where the lighthouse built in 1844 overlooks the turbulent waters of Portland Race and the Shambles Shoal. Portland Castle was another Henry VIII fortress, occupied in 1592 by Sir Walter Raleigh, as Governor of Portland.

In his novel *The Laughing Man*, set in the seventeenth century, Victor Hugo wrote that: 'The peninsula of Portland, viewed geometrically, presents the appearance of a bird's head, of which the bill is turned towards the ocean, the back of the head towards Weymouth; the isthmus is its neck. Portland exists now only for commerce. The value of the Portland stone was discovered by quarrymen and plasterers about the middle of the seventeenth century. Ever since that period [use] has been made of the Portland Stone – a valuable industry, enriching the district but disfiguring the bay. Two hundred years ago these coasts were being eaten away as a cliff; to-day, as a quarry. The pick bites meanly, the wave grandly;

hence a diminution of beauty. To the magnificent ravages of the ocean have succeeded the measured strokes of men.'[44]

The Gibraltar of Wessex

The opening scenes of Victor Hugo's novel are set in a wintery, bleak Portland: 'The sea, like the land, was white - the one with snow, the other with foam. There is nothing so melancholy as the light produced by this double whiteness. Certain lights of night are very clearly cut in their hardness; the sea was like steel, the cliff like ebony; the bay of Portland appeared almost like a geographical map, pale, in a semicircle of hills. There was something dreamlike in that nocturnal landscape. From cape to cape, along the whole coast, not a single spark indicating a hearth with a fire, not a lighted-window, not an inhabited house, was to be seen. Here and there came sudden risings in the great expanse of waters in the gulf, as the wind disarranged and wrinkled the vast sheet.'[44]

The Isle of Portland is a grey, stony, treeless, windswept landscape, described as the 'Isle of Slingers' and 'The Gibraltar of Wessex' by Thomas Hardy: 'The peninsula carved by Time out of a single stone has been for centuries immemorial the home of a curious and well nigh distinctive people, cherishing strange beliefs and singular customs now for the most part obsolescent.'[45]

A gravelly causeway links this Isle of Portland to the mainland, with a gap at Small Mouth, the entrance to the tidal lagoon known as the Fleet which runs behind Chesil Beach to the north-west. Hardy described Anne Garland passing this way in *The Trumpet Major*, on the way to Portland Bill where she hoped to catch a glimpse of Admiral Lord Nelson's flagship, *Victory*, on which Bob Loveday was sailing from Portsmouth to Plymouth, and on towards Spain: 'She soon finished her shopping [in Weymouth], and then, crossing over into the old town, pursued her way along the coast-road to Portland. At the end of an hour she had been rowed across the Fleet (which then lacked the convenience of a bridge) and reached the base of Portland Hill. The steep incline before her was dotted with houses, showing the pleasant peculiarity of one man's doorstep being behind his neighbour's chimney, and slabs of stone as the common material for walls, roof, floor, pig-sty, stable-manger, door-scraper, and garden-stile. Anne gained the summit, and followed along the central track over the huge lump of freestone which forms the peninsula, the wide sea prospect extending as she went on. Weary with her journey, she approached the extreme southerly peak of rock, and gazed from the cliff at Portland Bill.

'The wild, herbless, weather-worn promontory was quite a solitude, and, saving the one old lighthouse about fifty yards up the slope, scarce a mark was visible to show that humanity had ever been near the spot. Anne found herself a seat on a stone, and swept with her eyes the tremulous expanse of water around her that seemed to utter a ceaseless unintelligible incantation. Out of the three hundred and sixty degrees of her complete horizon two hundred and fifty were covered by waves, the *coup d'oeil* including the area of troubled waters known as the Race, where two seas met to effect the destruction of such vessels as could not be mastered by one. She counted the craft within her view: there were five; no, there were only four; no, there were seven, some of the specks having resolved themselves into two. They were all small coasters, and kept well within sight of land.'[35]

Marie Stopes, pioneer of birth control in Britain, lived in the Old Higher Lighthouse on Portland Bill and started the Portland Museum by buying a cottage and land in Easton and giving them to the islanders for this purpose. A lane leads down beneath a stone archway beside a limestone crag on which stands Rufus Castle, originally a Norman structure. Frederick Treves found the island agreeable :'There lies on the east side [of the Portland peninsula] a tiny, green-wooded dell, which for charm and picturesqueness can hardly be surpassed. This is the Cove of Church Hope. The glen is narrow and full of shade, a most gentle hollow in the cliffs opening to the sea. On the summit Pennsylvania Castle, a modern castellated house, built in 1800 for John Penn, governor of the island, and grandson of the founder of Pennsylvania. It is surrounded by a luxuriant garden, in vivid contrast with the rest of the barren and dusty rock. The trees in this genial nook were planted by the said John Penn. At the bottom of the dell is a small cove of shingle, where a wet beach glistens among a waste of rocks and brambles. There are some tarred fisher huts on the shore, together with a few boats, lobster-pots, and nets. Close to the margin of the cove are the ruins of the old parish church of Portland. It came to an end through a landslip, and of it little remains but ivy-covered walls, an arched doorway or two, and certain venerable tombs buried among the grass of the churchyard. The eternal quiet of the place is broken only by the sound of the sea.'[12]

Novelist and travel writer, Ethel Mannin visited Portland quarries in the 1970s in search of stones marked by Christopher Wren but discarded when he was building St. Paul's Cathedral: 'My daughter found the Wren rejects by chance and was puzzled by the curious markings. but looking for them is another matter, for apart from the sheer quantity of these huge blocks and boulders they almost all bear strange markings in the form of the imprint of fossilised shells. The cliffs are high here, and gulls and guillemots nest on the rock ledges. All is so uniformly grey here that any other colour stands out with a quite startling brilliance – I do not mean the obvious brightness of a red cardigan but quiet greens and blues which in another setting would be dull and unremarked.'[46]

Portland Bill

The sea off Portland Bill was also described by Thomas Hardy in *A Pair of Blue Eyes*, from a steamer: '....due south of Portland Bill. Those are the lights abeam us: look. A terrible spot that, on a stormy night And do you see a very small light that dips and rises to the right? That's a light-ship on the dangerous shoal called The Shambles, where many a good vessel has gone to pieces. Between it and ourselves is the Race – a place where antagonistic currents meet and form whirlpools – a spot which is rough in the smoothest weather, and terrific in a wind.'[47] The lightship was removed in 1971.

Pulpit Rock, Portland Bill

The waters off Portland Bill are certainly dangerous for sailors. In 1948 Ann Davison and her husband Frank set out from Fleetwood in Lancashire in an old seventy-foot fishing trawler, the *Reliance,* to sail round the world, but they ran into gales which drove them up the English Channel. She described what then happened: 'Inevitably the wind eased off: we bucketed slowly away from the shore, out of green into grey water, up towards Portland Bill. If only we could get clear of the horns of this damned Bay and get into mid-Channel again. If only this infernal wind would blow from another direction. It was in melancholy mood that I waited in the saloon for a weather report from the radio. The sky had been full of wind at dawn, and I hoped to hear that the sky was a liar. We listened to a gale warning, and Frank said "We'd better fix the engine in that case". He seemed quite brisk and cheerful.

'By night we were coming up to the Bill, having pinched and scraped all the sea-room possible. The sou'westerly wind had hardened considerably. *Reliance* under jib and mizzen was tugging away to clear the Bill, upon which the light flashed brightly'. But things went wrong, and as they drifted round Portland Bill the engines failed, and *Reliance* was driven ashore. 'Then the tall cliff face was upon us with a tremendous splintering crash. The bowsprit snapped like kindling. Before our horrified eyes the bows of the vessel buried into the very face of the cliff. And above the roaring sea came the terrible noise of a dying ship'.

They took to their float, 'a lozenge-shaped ring of cork, or some other unsubmersible substance, canvas-bound and painted red and yellow' but the Portland lifeboat failed to find them and they drifted out past the end of Portland Bill. 'Wilder and wilder came the seas. Wilder and whiter. Instead of the float riding over the crests, the crests rode over the float. We paddled one-handed, holding on to the life-lines. The current took us into the very centre of Portland Race. The sea was white with insensate rage. Towering pinnacles of water rushed hither and yon, dashing into one another to burst with a shrapnel of foam – or to merge and grow enormous.'

They were flung repeatedly into the sea, and fought their way back on to the float; but soon Frank was dead: 'Nothing mattered now. No point in trying any more. The fight was over. I laid my head on my arms and closed my eyes, engulfed in a blessed darkness.'[48] Ann Davison was washed up on some rocks, and managed to scramble ashore. Remarkably, this experience did not cure her of the sea: she went on to make further voyages, including a solo crossing of the Atlantic.

Chesil Beach

As the rocky cliffs of Portland end, Chesil Beach begins. It is a sixteen mile long bank of shingle, with a gradation westward from large cobbles at Chiswell to pea-sized pebbles at Bridport. 'I cannot conceive of any portion of the English coast more calculated to arouse a boy's imagination', wrote Llewelyn Powys of Chesil Beach at Chiswell. 'It is possible even when the weather is rough to stand in comparative safety and look down into the dragon throat of the terrible bay. A prodigious Atlantic roller, visible for a long time to a rain-drenched onlooker above the turbulence of all lesser waves far out at sea, dashes itself at last against this huge natural breakwater, and a second later, its pride broken, withdraws with an irresistible suction down, down, down, foam and tumbling pebbles together, until with a snarl, the very ocean floor is, for the duration of a moment, exposed under the curved suspended arch of a tottering wall of water, high towering as a church steeple, broad and awe-inspiring as the Niagara in flood.'[32]

Frederick Treves, described the Chesil Bank as 'a magnificent beach of pebbles which swings in a stately curve from the foot of Portland to Burton Bradstock, a distance of from seventeen to eighteen miles. For about half the way it is separated from the mainland by the reedy waters of the Fleet, the home of many hundreds of swans. Between the Fleet and the sea the beach stands up as a bank, steep and smooth, with a deadly slope towards the Western Bay. No sea rampart can surpass it in bluster, in massiveness, in truculence. It stands alone defying the tide. The Fleet is a mere moat or ditch behind it. In a westerly gale it is a place terrible to behold. The ice-smooth combers crash down upon the glacis with the force of battering rams; the beach is torn at by the receding waves as if the straitened foam were a myriad of claws.'[12]

H.M. Tomlinson lived much of his life beside Chesil Beach: 'There is no harbour on the curved sweep of this bank of shingle for many miles in either direction. The line of the beach in the north curves so imperceptibly that to the eye it looks straight; towards the southern end it sweeps round like the blade of a sickle, and is as sharp in the run. The five-fathom mark is close inshore, so the first line of breakers is direct upon the shingle. The usual weather, of course, is westerly; nearly always south of west. And in that direction I suppose the next land would be the Bahamas, but I have only local maps, and can lay no exact course to what landfall is in the eye of the wind. Anyhow, there is so much ocean between us and the next land that the waves come in, with any seaward breeze, in regular and massed attacks. They growl as they charge. In summer weather like this it is a cheerful noise, for they are only playing roughly. Then they break and make the shingle fly, with a roar; and a myriad little stones, as a wave draws back, follow it with thin cries.'[49]

It is alleged that fishermen coming ashore on Chesil Beach at night, or during a foggy day, can judge how far they are along the shore by the size of the pebbles. The crest ranges up to 40 feet above sea level, forming an inhospitable shore on which many ships have been wrecked. From time to time it has been overwashed by storm surges, as in 1824 when the sloop *Ebenezer* was swept over it into the Fleet lagoon, and part of Chesilton was swept away. The beach has been overwashed several times in more recent gales.

In Hardy's *The Well-Beloved* Jocelyn Pierston and Marcia Bencomb were walking along Chesil Beach. 'While overtaking and conversing with her he had not observed that the rising wind, which had proceeded from puffing to growling, and from growling to screeching, with the accustomed suddenness of its changes here, had at length brought what it promised by these vagaries – rain. The drops, which had at first hit their left cheeks like the pellets of a popgun, soon assumed the character of a raking fusillade from the bank adjoining, one shot of which was sufficiently smart to go through Jocelyn's sleeve.

'To windward was the long, montonous bank, too obtusely piled to afford a screen, over which they could hear the canine crunching of pebbles by the sea without; on their right stretched the inner bay or roadstead, the distant riding-lights of the ships now dim and glimmering; behind them a faint spark here and there in the lower sky showed where the island rose; before there was nothing definite, and could be nothing, till they reached a precarious wood bridge, a mile further on, Henry the Eighth's Castle being a little further still.'[45]

In Jonathan Raban's novel *Foreign Land* his hero, George, saw from his boat that 'the unearthly level straightness of its piled shingle looked as bleak as a line in a ledger. Nothing seemed to grow on it. He could see no people. Even the sea, sucking along its edge, seemed repelled by it. It had the comfortlessness of a cold outpost of Sahara; though the Sahara, George thought, at least had some curves to its name. There were no curves on Chesil Beach. For more than a mile in front, and many miles behind, it stretched away, ruled and rigid, as unfriendly a coast as George had ever seen.'[50]

Fleet Village

Fleet village, on the inner shore behind Chesil Beach, was mentioned in *Moonfleet*, Meade Falkner's stirring tale, from which we have already quoted. The story began with an account of his village by John Trenchard: 'Moonfleet lies half a mile from the sea on the right or west bank of the Fleet stream. This rivulet, which is so narrow as it passes the houses that I have known a good jumper clear it without a pole, broadens out into salt marshes below the village, and loses itself at last in a lake of brackish water. The lake is good for nothing except sea-fowl, herons, and oysters, and forms such a place as they call in the Indies a lagoon; being shut off from the open Channel by a monstrous great beach or dike of pebbles.'[26]

John Trenchard became involved in smuggling with Elzevir Block, keeper of the Why Not? Inn at the bottom of the village. We have already quoted their adventure at White Nothe and their escape to a hiding place on the Purbeck cliffs. After their imprisonment in Holland they were sentenced to deportation aboard the brig *Aurungzebe* and were only a few days out from Scheveningen when they ran into a wild storm. The prisoners were released, and came up on deck: 'In the mist to which we were making a sternboard I saw a white line like a fringe or valance to the sea; and then I looked to starboard, and there was the same white fringe, and then to larboard, and the white fringe was there too. "We are on a lee shore", Elzevir shouted, and then the murk and the driving rain lifted ever so little, and we saw a misty bluff slope down into the sea, like the long head of a basking alligator poised upon the water'. It was Portland Bill. By coincidence, the storm had caught them just off Moonfleet, and was washing the ship towards Chesil Beach, where the villagers had gathered.

The Dutch crew and most of the prisoners clambered into the lifeboats, against the advice of Elzevir: ' "Friends, any man that takes to boat is lost. I know this bay and know this beach, and was indeed born hereabouts, but never knew a boat come to land in such a sea, save bottom uppermost. So if you want my counsel, there you have it, namely, to stick by the ship. In half an hour we shall be in the breakers; and I will put the helm up and try to head the brig bows on to the beach; so every man will have a chance to fight for his own life, and God have mercy on those that drown".'

The *Aurungzebe* grounded on the beach. 'Then we stood waiting side by side till a great wave came in, turning the space 'twixt ship and shore into a boiling cauldron: a minute later 'twas all sucked back again with a roar, and we jumped. I fell on hands and feet where the water was a yard deep under the ship, but got my footing and floundered through the slop, in a desperate struggle to climb as high as might be on the beach before the next wave came in. There was a roar of water in my ears, with a great shouting of the men upon the beach, and then I caught the rope'. John Trenchard was the only survivor, for that next wave took Elzevir away with it.[26]

The Fleet

The lagoon behind Chesil Beach, known as The Fleet, is backed by undulating hills. Fleet House, built on the inner shore in 1603 has become the Moonfleet Hotel. An attempt was made to drain The Fleet in the 17th century, when Sir George Horsey built a wall between the mainland and the inner shore of Chesil Beach. The site of this wall remains a mystery, but the project failed because the shingle bank, Chesil Beach, is permeable, and sea water simply leaked through to prevent the enclosed area being reclaimed.[51]

C.J. Cornish came here in the eighteen-nineties: 'Whether judged by the strangeness and beauty of its surroundings, or the number and variety of the wild birds that make it their home, there is no more attractive spot for the naturalist than the Fleet, the straight lagoon which runs for nine miles from the Isle of Portland to Abbotsbury, behind the barrier of Chesil Beach. There is not an acre of water on the narrow shining lagoon, or a rood of shingle on the Chesil Beach which banks it in, that is not the chosen home of the wild-fowl of the river or the shore. During the winter, wild-ducks and coots in thousands crowd the sheltered waters of the Fleet; in summer, the hot and hazy surface of the shingle swarms with the young of the terns and dotterels; and at the head of the water, in an almost tropical growth of pampas grass and fuchsias, and the rankest luxuriance of the herbage of the marsh, is the swan paradise of Abbotsbury.

'Whether viewed from the land seawards, or from Chesil Beach across the Fleet, the scene was alike rich in life and colour. The strangeness of the view from Chesil Bank inwards makes it perhaps the more striking. To the right stretches an apparently endless line of dark-blue sea, separated from the lighter waters of the Fleet by the golden shingle of "the Bank" which vanishes in yellow haze towards Portland. On the Fleet opposite floated hundreds of white swans, among which the black coots and cormorants swam and dived like imps among the angels. The further shore was again fringed with the dead-gold of the reed-stumps, backed by the rich green of the hills beyond. As the evening drew on, the birds and animals of the shore and the lake seemed to enjoy an exclusive do-minion over their respective haunts. No human being was in sight, and the nine miles of Chesil Beach were probably untrodden by any creature larger than the hares which came hopping down from the hills to feed upon the wild vetch which grows among the shingle on the shore.'[3]

The Swannery

Abbotsbury Swannery, at the western end of The Fleet, has had a protected colony of mute swans among the reeds, at least since the 11th century. The Abbot Orc, who founded the Benedictine Abbey in about 1040, was granted rights to this part of The Fleet by King Canute in 1023. According to Ward Lock's Guide: 'There are about 900 swans, and several score of cygnets hatched yaerly. Some are fattened for the table. Those that escape that fate and continue to thrive take eighteen months before becoming fully decked in their white plumage. Then perhaps they are sold, or given to add charm to some public or private piece of ornamental water. The Swannery is seen at its best in April or May, when the birds are nesting. It is well to be cautious when going near a sitting bird; the keeper can tell of encounters he himself has experienced when approaching the nest of an angry swan. All day long swans can be seen in the Fleet Estuary (which is salt water), coming up to the Swannery to drink, and then sailing away after refreshment.'[52]

Abbotsbury

A short distance inland is the yellow-brown stone village of Abbotsbury, with 14th century St Catherine's Chapel on a nearby hill-top, and a large 15th century stone tithe barn. Along the shore, Abbotsbury Gardens shelter 20 acres of subtropical vegetation on part of the estate given to the Earl of Strangways by Henry VIII in 1543.

J.B. Priestley walked down to the coast from Abbotsbury: 'A turn of the road brought us into Roman Italy. That is really the most delightful thing about

England. You never know – you could never guess – what is waiting for you round the corner. Eccentric aristocrats have worked their wills on this island for centuries, with the result that anything may happen in it.

'Some time during the eighteenth century, the local lord of the manor here paid a visit to Italy, returning with a head humming with eclogues and Virgilian tags and plans for improving the estate. We found a carved stone seat at the side of the road, antique Italy in every line and crevice of it, and sat there in the vague trembling sunlight. After that, for the next half mile or so, England disappeared. We moved in a tiny world of sharp light and shadow, of grave dark beauty, of fine lines and harsh surfaces. Virgil himself could have passed that ilex-bordered avenue at ease, waiting for the magic of his thunder and tears. Here and there, between the dark trees, were great clumps of some gigantic alien grass, pale yellow and as dry as new matches. If a leopard had suddenly poked its head out of that blanched rustling stuff, I should not have been surprised.'[53]

St. Catherine's Chapel, Abbotsbury

At the bottom of the hill Chesil Beach is readily accessible. Priestley climbed to the shingle crest to examine it: 'When you lie down at full length and see them close, these pebbles are enchanting. They have every colour and every combination of colours, and you can spend hours and hours collecting black ones with red stripes or cream ones banded with brown, and all you have to do, to bring up a fresh assortment, is to sweep your hand across the top and then begin collecting again. Ali Baba in his cave had no richer profusion of stones. The sun scattered the last shreds of mist and smote the south ridge of the bank so strongly that you could see the shimmer of heat above the pebbles. The whole land disappeared, but sent a singing lark to remind us it was still there somewhere. Ours was a world of sun, air, water, pebbles, and this mad trilling in the blue. Nobody came. Nothing happened. For a few hours we were out of it, living richly on a current account in Chesil Bank.'[53]

Hardy's Monument
High on the hills behind The Fleet, on Black Down, stands the octagonal sandstone tower which is a monument to Admiral Sir Thomas Masterman Hardy, commander of Nelson's flagship H.M.S. Victory at the Battle of Trafalgar in 1805, and later a resident of nearby Portesham. The chalk scarp runs westward to Abbotsbury Hill, then swings inland to Eggardon. The ramparts of an Iron Age fort crown Abbotsbury Hill, beneath which Chesil Beach curves on until it abuts the cliffs of yellow sandstone between Burton Bradstock and West Bay, and ends against the breakwaters of Bridport Harbour.

Bridport
Bridport began a rope-making industry early in the 13th century, using locally grown flax processed in mills along the River Brit. The need for space to stretch ropes and make nets resulted in unusually wide streets and rope walks. It retains a reputation for the making of ropes and fishing nets, and tennis nets for Wimbledon. In Hardy's time it was a compact town: 'The shepherd on the east hill could shout out lambing intelligence to the shepherd on the west hill, over the intervening town chimneys, without great inconvenience to his voice, so nearly did the steep pastures encroach upon the burghers' backyards. And at night it was possible to stand in the very midst of the town and hear from their native paddocks on the lower levels of greensward the mild lowing of the farmer's heifers, and the profound, warm blowings of breath in which those creatures indulge. But the community which had jammed itself in the valley thus formed a veritable town, with a real mayor and corporation, and a staple manufacture.'[54]

West Bay
South from Bridport, the road runs down the Brit valley to the little harbour of West Bay. Hardy described the scene in *Fellow-Townsmen*:'The harbour-road soon began to justify its name. A gap appeared in the rampart of hills which shut out the sea, and on the left of the opening rose a vertical cliff, coloured a burning orange by the sunlight, the companion cliff on the right being livid in shade. Between these cliffs, like the Libyan bay which sheltered the shipwrecked Trojans, was a little haven, seemingly a beginning made by Nature herself of a perfect harbour, which appealed to the passer-by as only requiring a little human industry to finish it and make it famous, the ground on each side as far back as

the daisied slopes that bounded the interior valley being a mere layer of blown sand. But the Port-Bredy burgesses a mile inland had, in the course of ten centuries, responded many times to that appeal, with the result that the tides had invariably choked up their works with sand and shingle as soon as completed. There were but few houses here: a rough pier, a few boats, some stores, an inn, a residence or two, a ketch unloading in the harbour, were the chief features of the settlement.'[54] Hardy mentioned the Harbour Inn, which is now the Bridport Arms.

Treves called West Bay 'probably the queerest seaport in any part of the British Isles'. In 1747 piers and wharves were constructed, and in 1823 sluices were built to hold back the river, then release it suddenly to sweep away the shingle and revive a navigable entrance. This became history after the protruding stone piers were completed in 1866.

The prominent block of flats was built in 1885, and (to the regret of some) survived a fire in 1925. At about that time, Hilaire Belloc sailed his yacht into West Bay, which he called Bridport Haven: 'Never was I more fascinated by any little haven, for it has the delightful qualities of a model. I had been running for Portland Bill in a fairly fresh wind, which rose more than I liked [so] turned round and ran to Bridport. We sailed in through the long narrow bottle-neck of an entrance, more like a canal than a harbour, to find ourselves in a basin about the size of a large drawing-room, but with everything complete - a Lloyds office, a harbour master, and a signal station, a hotel, and all on the scale of the place.'[21]

Bennet Copplestone began his story *The Treasure of Golden Cap* beside this harbour: 'The windows of the inn looked out over the harbour basin towards the great West Bay, which in splendid and almost unbroken curve runs from Start Point in Devon to Portland Bill in Dorset. Modern shipping does not know the West Bay – for it steams hurriedly along the sea chord, leaving the curve of coast unvisited – but for all that the Bay is now neglected, a kind of maritime backwater, it is a Bay of deep memories.'[55]

Eype Mouth

From the A35, west of Bridport, a narrow lane winds down to Eype Mouth. Rachel Lloyd described smugglers landing here: 'No worse place to land a boat could be found, for the shingle beach formed a wall and below it the sea tugged and twisted, rushing up the precipice, then falling back, the pebbles rolling with the rattle of artillery. A small stream wound through the creek, and disappeared into the head of the shingle, threaded its way through it and trickled out into the sea. A boat trying to land must be wound up by a winch and the dinghy that plies to and fro between the *Grace of Eype* and the shore must have had a hard task. She landed Spanish iron on that beach at night in large quantities, the men's feet scrunching on the bank of rolling pebbles, the sea rushing up and lassooing their legs.'[56]

Seatown

Seatown is at the end of another lane, off the A35 at Chideock, but John Grimson walked here by way of the cliff path: 'Beyond Eype Mouth the cliff of Thorncombe Beacon takes us up to more than five hundred feet before letting us down into the next dip where Seatown (a cluster of houses and the 'Anchor Inn') basks in the glitter of caravans which sprawl up the vale towards Chideock. Here a plateful of Dorset knobs (the crusty bread rolls which are baked at nearby Morecombelake) and a lump of blue vinney (the local Stilton-type cheese) go down well, especially when assisted by a tankard of the local brew. After that, we are in good enough fettle to tackle the climb to Golden Cap, which, at 625 feet, is the highest cliff on the south coast, and has a crowning stratum of orange sandstone which gleams to seaward in the sunlight and gives the cliff its name.'[4]

Golden Cap

It was here, in Bennet Copplestone's story, that Dickie and Betty Grenville came while sailing on Lyme Bay in 1920: 'Betty, who was at the helm, had so little to do that she could permit her eyes to rove over the splendid line of coast. Standing out, solitary, conspicuous, dwarfing the gentler cliffs on either hand, towered a flat-topped summit. Its seaward face, yellow as the lichen on old Dorsetshire cottages, seemed to fall sheer to the water's edge. Midway between Lyme and Bridport this bare, flat summit, with its fringe of heather and its scarped yellow seaward face, stood forth as an unmistakable and unforgettable landmark.'

This was Golden Cap, to which they were drawn in search of treasure hidden by Elizabethan sailors. Later, on closer inspection: 'They could see that the seaward front was less sheer than it looked from the Bay. As the sea had eaten into the base of it the soft rock had peeled off in huge flakes which, sliding down, build up a barrier at the foot. Golden Cap was receding, foot by foot, century after century, yet the process of destruction was slow. Though the yellow edge of the cliff touched the flat top and the area of the summit had aforetime been much more extensive, a great many acres still remained to fight dauntlessly an ultimately losing battle.'[55]

Charmouth
The cliffs then decline towards Charmouth, which Jane Austen admired for its 'high grounds and extensive sweeps of country, and still more its sweet retired bay, beached by dark cliffs, where fragments of low rock among the sands make it the happiest spot for watching the flow of the tide; for sitting in unwearied contemplation.'[57]

Catherine of Aragon stayed at the Queen's Armes Hotel in 1501, and after the Battle of Worcester in 1651, Charles II fled, disguised as a groom, and spent a night in the Queen's Armes in Charmouth, hoping to escape to France. The plan failed because the wife of Stephen Limbry, the boatman who was to help the King, became suspicious, and decided to protect him by locking him in a room without his trousers. Narrowly escaping capture the King left on horseback towards Bridport.

Aaron Elkins set his murder yarn in this area. 'The little Queen's Armes was reputed to be over five hundred years old, and although the outside had been stuccoed and modernized many times through the years, the Tudor stonework and age-blackened woods inside gave credence to the reputation. Gideon and Julie had the afternoon to themselves, and they spent it walking east over the deserted, rocky beach from Charmouth toward Golden Cap, along the base of the blue lias cliffs. It was the kind of time they had dreamed of when they planned the trip: mesmerized into a tranquil stupor by the sound of the surf, they wandered aimlessly along the shore in the thin November sunlight, talking now of one subject, now of another – all of it desultory and haphazard, and lost as soon as the next thundering wave washed their minds clean. Now and then they kissed gently or simply embraced without a word. They held hands most of the time and paused frequently to look at the sea, or so that one of them could show the other some small, perfect spiral of a petrified sea creature embedded in the rocks at their feet.'[58] An archaeology student had been murdered on Stonebarrow Fell.

Black Ven
Between Charmouth and Lyme Regis the cliffs of Black Ven have been slumping, with landslides down to the shore. Paul Theroux walked along the shore from

Charmouth on a May day in 1982: 'I set off, jumping from rock to rock. The fossils were visible on the rock surfaces, petrified snails on one slab and fossilized fish on another.... Lyme was shining gently above its stone pier. Behind me I could see where I had walked all the way from the Chesil Bank and Weymouth. The Isle of Portland was indistinct and blubberlike; it could have been a whale that had blundered against the Dorset coast to die. Because of the tide, I was the only person on this stretch of beach. It was deserted and full of cracks and corners, another of the places where I expected to find a corpse, a murder victim, a suicide, or more likely someone who had accidentally drowned and been washed ashore.'[20]

Francis Bickley had similar feelings, walking from Lyme to Charmouth seventy years previously: 'They look so forlorn, these tumbledown cliffs, like neglected houses or the brick-heaps of Titan builders. You are barely out of Lyme before you feel the loneliness. Charmouth smiled invitation: in the distance the golden brow of Golden Cap was radiant. Nevertheless I felt myself in one of the waste places of the earth.'[59]

Landslides in the winter of 1986-87 took a bite out of the Lyme Regis golf course on top of the Black Ven cliff, and so interrupted the coastal footpath.

Fossils

It was under the cliffs of Black Ven, in 1811, that 12 year old Mary Anning discovered her colossal fossil, the reptile *Ichthyosaurus platyodon*. She went on to make many other palaeontological discoveries, notably *Pleisiosaurus* and the winged reptile *Pterodactylus*, in the slumping cliffs along the Lyme Bay shore, and founded the Old Fossil Shop in Lyme. There is a stained glass window, endowed by the Geological Society as a memorial to her in the local church, but, as John Fowles remarked: 'One of the meanest disgraces of British palaeontology is that although many scientists of the day gratefully used her finds to establish their own reputation, not one native type bears the specific *anningii*.'[60] The Philpot Museum in Lyme has assembled an exhibition dedicated to Mary Anning and her fossils.

Fossil hunting continues to attract many visitors to these cliffs: a hazardous activity, for rock falls occur frequently, and hammering by fossickers can bring about sudden slumping. Brian Jackman wrote that 'sometimes these fossil remains occur in such numbers that whole strata are stuffed with shells as thick as currants in a Christmas pudding. Witness the Green Ammonite beds under Golden Cap' or the 'Fuller's Earth clay at Watton Cliff peppered with belemnites, ammonites, rare brachiopods and brittle-starfish.'[61] These fossils continue to stimulate the literary: it was the discovery of an ichthyosaurian at Lyme Regis in 1844 that disrupted the life and faith of the clergyman Matthew Pearce in Graham Swift's recent novel, *Ever After.*

Church Cliffs

Towards Lyme, the Blue Lias Church Cliffs were once quarried. Back in 1922, E.M.Ward grumbled that: 'The erosion at Lyme has been accelerated by human agency, for while the townsfolk were engaged in ceaseless warfare against the sea their best defence against it was being removed. In spite of the fact that as early as the reign of James I an edict forbade the taking of stones from the sea or seashore near the borough of Lyme, thousands of tons of limestone were being quarried from the ledges of rock before the town in the early nineteenth century. The quarrying of lime of both reefs and cliffs continued here until recently, thus accelerating the recession of the coast both directly and indirectly through the resultant deepening of the water in front of the town.'[62]

A sea wall and groynes have been built beneath Church Cliffs in the hope of retaining a shingle beach but the shore is still submerged as the tide rises. A gloomy Theroux arrived to find the tide 'high near Lyme, washing against the cement fringe of the sea wall. There was room to walk, but the wall was covered in green sea-slime, and so it was very slippery. I crossed it on all fours and at Lyme I felt as if I had won a close race.'[20]

Lyme Regis and The Cobb

John Fowles has written about the long history of Lyme Regis and the ancient harbour, the Cobb, which juts seaward from its western end. He tells us that in 774 Lyme received permission from Sherborne Abbey to manufacture salt, and its royal charter (and so the appendage Regis) was granted in the thirteenth century by Edward I, when it was a port to face the French: 'Despite its royal blessing in 1284, Lyme soon suffered from the perennial nightmare of its history - its very peculiar geological situation. The town is built on, and surrounded by, some of the most unstable land in Britain; and perhaps even worse, it is exposed to the full fury of the sea. The first thing any stranger to Lyme must realize is that the Cobb is not only a harbour; it is just as importantly a gigantic breakwater protecting the town from the great storms out of the south-west. This was fully realized by Sir Francis Walsingham, when he came to Lyme in 1586 to report on it (the previous winter the Cobb had suffered severe damage) for Elizabeth. He says the Cobb and "an exceeding number of great piles" protect "from the violence and fretting of the sea, which otherwise would in short time eat out both the town and the land thereunto adjoining".'[63]

The Cobb is certainly very old. It was first mentioned (as "Le Cobbe") in a document dated 1295. It was damaged in a 1378 storm, then rebuilt to serve a fishing village. The Cobb sent ships to meet the Spanish Armada in 1588, and in 1685 the Duke of Monmouth landed on the cobble beach hoping to seize the throne of England. He failed, but the beach was named after him.

Daniel Defoe described The Cobb in the 1720s: 'It is a massy pile of building, consisting of high and thick walls of stone. The towns' people have the benefit of this wonderful harbour, and it is carefully kept in repair, as indeed it behoves them to do; but they could give me nothing of the history of it; nor do they, as I could perceive, know anything of the origin of it, or who built it; it was lately almost beaten down by a storm, but is repair'd again. The custom-house officers have a lodge and warehouse upon it, and there were several ships of very good force, and rich in value, in the basin of it when I was there.'[14]

Celia Fiennes passed this way early in the 18th century: 'We went to Colway near Lime in Somersetshire [Celia wasn't good on counties] to a relations house Mr Hendlys, from thence to Lime a seaport place open to the main ocean, and so high a bleake sea that to secure the Harbour for shipps they have been at great charge to build a Mold from the town with stone, like a halfe moon, which they call the Cobb, its raised with a high wall and this runns into the sea a good compass, that the Shipps rides safely within it; when the tide is out we may see the foundations of some part of it; that is the tyme they looke over it to see any breach and repaire it immediately, else the tide comes with so much violence would soone beate it down; there is some part of it low and only is to joyne the rest to the land, and at high water is all cover'd of such a depth of water that shipps may pass over it to enter the Cobb. From Lime the wayes are also difficult by reason of the very steep hills up and down.'[16]

Christopher Morris quoted another early 19th century description of the Cobb, by Roger North: 'The Cobb is a mole built in the sea – there is not any one like it in the world, for although it is an immense mass of stone no one stone that lies there was ever touched with a tool, or is bedded in any sort of cement; but all, being pebbles of the sea, are piled up, and hold by their bearings only, and the surge plays in and out through the interstices of the stone, in a wonderful manner.'[16]

In 1906 Frederick Treves said that 'The Cobb is the chief glory and delight of Lyme. It is a sturdy work, laid down on mysterious lines and bearing a resemblance to no marine structure of like intent. It combines in one series of stone banks the functions of a breakwater, a quay and a pier. It has somewhat the curve of a shepherd's crook, with an adventitious tentacle of masonry projecting from the summit of its bend. It wanders into the water in a hesitating manner which is quite in keeping with the uncertainty of the town.'[12]

Three decades later, Llewelyn Powys wrote that 'Perhaps it is the Cobb, the extraordinary Breakwater of the royal city of Lyme Regis, that helps give to the place its idiosyncratic character. If you look down upon this old structure from the hills above, it takes on the appearance of a vole's flat tail left dangling on the water outside its slippery retreat. The old monosyllabic word Cobb in mediaeval times had many uses. A male herring was called a Cobb, a black-backed gull, a miller's thumb; and with no great stretch of the imagination the Breakwater to-day may in truth be thought to resemble the king digit of the miller's "cluster o' vive". It is probable, however, that this odd barricade against the Channel waves earned its name from actually being "a rounded heap of stones".[33]

Eighteenth Century Lyme

During the 18th century Lyme Regis became a fashionable resort, visited by Bath society. Jane Austen visited in 1804, when she described sea bathing in a letter to her sister: 'The bathing was so delightful this morning, and Molly so pressing with me to enjoy myself that I believe I stayed in rather too long, as since the middle of the day I have felt unreasonably tired.'[64]

Later, in *Persuasion*, she told of the winter visit of the Musgrove family, with Captain Wentworth, to Lyme: 'After securing accommodations, and ordering a dinner at one of the inns, the next thing to be done was unquestionably to walk directly down to the sea. They were come too late in the year for any amuse-ment or variety which Lyme, as a public place, might offer; the rooms were shut up, the lodgers almost all gone, scarcely any family but of the residents left. The principal street almost hurrying into the water, the walk to the Cobb, skirting round the pleasant little bay, which in the season is animated with bathing machines and company, the Cobb itself, its old wonders and new improvements, with the very beautiful line of cliffs stretching out to the east of the town, are what the stranger's eye will seek; and a very strange stranger it must be, who does not see charms in the immediate environs of Lyme, to make him wish to know it better'.

They had come to meet Captain Wentworth's friend, Captain Harville, wintering in Lyme with his family in a small house near the Cobb. The next day, when they were about to leave, they walked again 'to make the proper adieus to the Cobb. There was too much wind to make the high part of the new Cobb pleasant for the ladies, and they agreed to get down the steps to the lower, and all were contented to pass quietly and carefully down the steep flight, excepting Louisa; she must be jumped down them by Captain Wentworth. In all their walks, he had had to jump her from the stiles; the sensation was delightful to her. The hardness of the pavement for her feet, made him less willing upon the present occasion; he did it, however; she was safely down, and instantly, to shew her enjoyment, ran up the steps to be jumped down again. He advised her against it, thought the jar was too great; but no, he reasoned and talked in vain; she smiled and said "I am determined I will": he put out his hands; she was too precipitate by half a second, she fell on the pavement on the Lower Cobb, and was taken up lifeless!'[57]

Much consternation, and the inert Louisa was carried back to the inn where the surgeon determined that the bang on the head had knocked her out, and that she would soon recover, but would have to stay a few more days in Lyme.

Tennyson in Lyme

Llewelyn Powys is one of several writers who have recounted how 'when Tennyson visited Lyme Regis in 1867 people were eager to show him the place where the Duke of Monmouth landed. "Don't talk to me of the Duke of Monmouth," he said impatiently, "Show me the exact spot where Louisa Musgrove fell." [32] Tennyson's son's version of the story is that his father 'was led on to Lyme by the description of the place in Miss Austen's 'Persuasion', walking thither the nine miles over the hills from Bridport. On his arrival he called on Palgrave, and, refusing all refreshment, he said at once: "Now take me to the Cobb, and show me the steps from which Louisa Musgrove fell". '[65] These steps are known locally as 'Granny's Teeth'.

John Fowles was sceptical about this story: 'Since Tennyson had just walked the whole way from Bridport to Lyme, the "at once" must be taken with a pinch of salt'. F.T. Palgrave, who Tennyson came to visit, was the compiler in 1865 of an anthology, *The Golden Treasury of the best songs and lyrical poems in the English Language,* and author of some local poems, *A Lyme Garland,* one of which, 'The Sea Gods', depicts the eighteenth century atmosphere:

> *A red fog hangs on the horns of the moon*
> *In a haven of breeze and rain;*
> *And voices come from the silvery sea,*
> *On the cliff the station is white and high,*
> *But sees not, snug and low*
> *Where their mate lies dim on the silvery sea,*
> *With a light just shown in a flash of glee*
> *As they near the weather bow.*[66]

Australian Buddlecombe

Fowles also recalled that 'Lyme appears in the Australian novel *The Fortunes of Richard Mahony,* by Henry Handel Richardson, where the Victorian seaside resort, 'Buddlecombe', is in fact Lyme Regis, Buddle being an alternative name for the River Lim. Henry Handel Richardson was really a woman, and her secretary was Maria Raymond, a daughter of the manager of Lyme's first cinema, at the Assemby Rooms. It was she who seemingly gave Ethel Richardson the details for her picture of Lyme.'[63]

In the second book of her trilogy, *The Way Home,* Richardson described how Richard Mahony, a medical graduate from Edinburgh University, having spent time on the Ballarat goldfields in Australia, returned to England in the eighteensixties to work as a general practitioner. After a short period in Leicester he came to the south coast resort, where: 'The ancient little town of Buddlecombe, originally pressed down the mouth of a narrow valley to the sea, from which it is protected by rampart and breakwater, has, in the course of the centuries, scaled the nearer of the two hills that confine it. Nowadays its streets go every-where up and down. A precipitous lane is climbed by the ridge-like steps of an Italian donkey-path; the old town gardens, massively walled, are built in tiers, so that the apple-trees on the higher levels scatter their blossoms on the gardens beneath. Coming from the upland, three driving-roads drop into the town at a bold gradient; and vehicles, whether they mount or descend, creep like snails. Half-way down the sheerest of the three, the quaint little old houses, that set in oddly enough just where the road is steepest, appear to cling shoulder to shoul-der, each a storey or a half-storey lower than the last, their lines all out of drawing with age and the insecurity of their footholds; while those at the bottom of the hill, seen from this point but as a dimpling cluster of gables, dormers, chimneys, look, till you are virtually upon them, as if they were standing in the sea. The roofs of one and all are silvered with the mortar of innumerable repairs, some of their ancient tiles flying off afresh in every rowdy equinox'.

Lyme Regis: The Cobb

The sea-front he described was then: 'crescent-shaped; and a high, wooded cliff, which leaves room for no more than a footpath between it and the surf-rolled shingle, cuts the town in two. The smaller half, grouped about the harbour, includes the old custom-house, a couple of ramshackle magazines and their yards, an ancient inn or two, all bustling places once on a time, when elephants' teeth and gold dust were unshipped here, and the stuffs and linens of England arrived on pack-horses for transit to France; when, too, much lucrative wine and spirit-running went on with the French coast.

'To get the best view of the town you must row out beyond harbour and mole, or, better still, swim out, on one of those dead-calm days that every summer brings – days when the yellow cliffs across the bay send down perfect golden shadows in the blue mirror of the sea. Then, lying pillowed on this saltest, most buoyant water, glance back to where, grouped in that perfect symmetry that seems the lost secret of old town-builders, the little place on its gun-cliffs lies curved to the bay. Viewed thus, it looks like a handful of grey shells clustered on a silver shingle – pearl, not stone grey – for there is no dourness about Buddlecombe.'[67]

In the great storm of 1824 the breakwater was badly damaged, but by 1826 it had been rebuilt more strongly, using blocks of limestone shipped across from Portland.

Literary Lyme

Up the hill in Silver Street is The Mariners, a pink hotel which was used in one of the illustrations for Beatrix Potter's story *The Tale of Little Pig Robinson*.[68] In 1804 Lyme was the birthplace of John Gould, who worked with his father as a gardener at Windsor Castle, and became first a taxidermist, then a writer of large, lavishly illustrated books on birds. His visit to Australia in 1838-40 resulted in seven volumes on the Birds of Australia and four more on the Mammals of Australia. In 1895 Whistler came to Lyme, staying at The Lion and painting local scenery.

It is strange that Thomas Hardy, who had code-names for most of the towns and many of the villages of Dorset, did not invent one for Lyme Regis or The Cobb: he seems never to have mentioned either in his novels. Cecil Day-Lewis, eventually Poet Laureate, began to take holidays in Lyme in 1936, and subsequently lived in Musbury, over the hills towards Axminster. He wrote detective stories under the pen-name Nicholas Blake and one of these, *The Beast Must Die*, began and ended at Lyme, where the narrator, Felix Lane, looked 'out of the window at Golden Cap glowing in the evening sun, and the crisped leaf-metal waves of the bay, and the curved arm of the Cobb enfolding the baby boats a hundred feet below me', planning a murderous revenge.[69]

John Fowles began his story *The French Lieutenant's Woman* on The Cobb: 'The Cobb has invited what familiarity breeds for at least seven hundred years, and the real Lymers will never see much more to it than a long claw of old grey wall that flexes itself against the sea. In fact, since it lies well apart from the main town, a tiny Piraeus to a microscopic Athens, they seem almost to turn their backs on it. Certainly it has cost them enough in repairs through the centuries to justify a certain resentment. But to a less tax-paying, or more discriminating, eye it is quite simply the most beautiful sea-rampart on the south coast of England. And not only because it is, as the guide-books say, redolent of seven hundred years of English history, because ships sailed to meet the Armada from it, because Monmouth landed beside it – but finally because it is a superb fragment of folk-art.

'Primitive yet complex, elephantine but delicate; as full of subtle curves and volumes as a Henry Moore or a Michelangelo; and pure, clean, salt, a paragon of mass.'[60]

It was on the Cobb, on a blustery March day in 1867, that the hero, Charles Smithson, first encountered Sarah Woodruff, known locally as the French Lieutenant's Woman. In 1980 the book became a successful film, and the image of cloaked actress Meryl Streep standing on the stormy breakwater, went around the world on publicity posters for the film and video.

'Lyme', wrote Fowles, 'is situated in the centre of one of the rare outcrops of a stone known as the blue lias. To the mere landscape enthusiast this stone is not attractive. An exceedingly gloomy grey in colour, a petrified mud in texture, it is a good deal more forbidding than it is picturesque. It is also treacherous, since its strata are brittle and have a tendency to slide, with the consequence that this little stretch of twelve miles or so of blue lias coast has lost more land to the sea in the course of history than almost any other in England. But its highly fossiliferous nature and its mobility make it a Mecca for the British palaeontologist. These last hundred years or so the commonest animal on its shores has been man – wielding a geologist's hammer.'[60]

Devonshire Head

Devonshire Head, to the west, is a headland no longer. Fowles, in a local history, suggested that it once protruded further seaward to give better shelter to the harbour that grew up in the lee of the Blue Lias reefs: 'The old name for where the county boundary with Devon meets the shore some 600 yards west of the Cobb is Devonshire Head, and though there is no headland to be seen today, it is quite possible that the earliest Cobb (first mentioned in 1294, but a date before 1250 is likely) was built in the at least partial lee of a cape long lost to the sea.'[63]

There is an 1814 print, 'Lyme Regis, Dorsetshire: a squall', by J.M.W. Turner, in the Glasgow Art Gallery, which shows a more protrusive headland west of the Cobb. Today the shingle of Monmouth Beach fades into limestone ledges beneath the cliffs which run out to Seven Rock Point, and into Devonshire.

SOUTH DEVON

The Landslip

If you walk out on The Cobb at Lyme Regis, and climb the steps to the top of the high wall, you can look westward past Devonshire Head to the beginning of the curious region known as The Landslip, which extends along the coast as far as Axmouth. A footpath leads up to it from behind the tennis courts and bowling greens, through the undulating meadows of Ware Common, with its farm and cottages, backed by a high chalk cliff. In *The French Lieutenant's Woman* John Fowles gave this description:

'There runs, between Lyme Regis and Axmouth six miles to the west, one of the strangest coastal landscapes in Southern England. From the air it is not very striking: one notes merely that whereas elsewhere on the coast the fields run to the cliff-edge, here they stop a mile or so short of it. The cultivated chequer of green and red-brown breaks, with a kind of joyous indiscipline, into a dark cascade of trees and undergrowth. There are no roofs. If one flies low enough one can see that the terrain is very abrupt, cut by deep chasms and accented by strange bluffs and towers of chalk and flint, which loom over the lush foliage around them like the walls of ruined castles. From the air – but on foot this seemingly unimportant wilderness gains a strange extension. People have been lost in it for hours, and cannot believe, when they see on the map where they were lost, that their sense of isolation – and if the weather be bad, desolation – could have seemed so great.

'The Undercliff – for this land is really the mile-long slope caused by the erosion of the ancient vertical cliff-face – is very steep. Flat places are as rare as visitors in it. But this steepness in effect tilts it, and its vegetation, towards the sun; and it is this fact, together with the water from the countless springs that have caused the erosion, that lends the area its botanical strangeness – its wild arbutus and ilex and other trees rarely seen growing in England; its enormous ashes and beeches; its green Brazilian chasms choked with ivy and the liana of wild clematis; its bracken that grows seven, eight feet tall; its flowers that bloom a month earlier than anywhere else in the district. In summer it is the nearest this country can offer to a tropical jungle. It has also, like all land that has never been worked or lived on by man, its mysteries, its shadows, its dangers – only too literal ones geologically, since there are crevices and sudden falls that can bring disaster, and in places where a man with a broken leg could shout all week and not be heard.'[1]

Tennyson came here in 1867 with his friend Palgrave from Lyme. His son, Hallam Tennyson, described their finding 'a noble natural terrace, edging the sea and tossed into endless small mounds and valleys', and quoted Palgrave's account of Tennyson's reaction: 'This exactly represents some of the romantic landscape before my minds's eye in the 'Idylls': little winding glades, closed all round with grassy mounds and wild shrubs, where one might fancy the sudden appearance of a knight riding, or a spell-bound damsel.'[2]

In front of the vertical upper chalk cliff is a tumbled mass of broken rock and slumping clay, mostly covered by dense forest. In *The French Lieutenant's Woman*, John Fowles' hero, Charles Smithson, came here in search of fossils. Above the crumbling slopes of Pinhay Bay, where the cliffs are still very active, with heaps of flint, clay and boulders, and uprooted trees sliding down on to the beach, he again encountered the beautiful and wayward Sarah Woodruff, notorious in the Lyme of 1867 for her liaison with Varguennes, a French naval officer. It was an encounter that was to lead to an affair, much anguish, some distress, and (this being a 'modern' novel) a great deal of confusion.[1]

Pinhay Bay

Pinhay was mentioned by Jane Austen as 'Pinny, with its green chasms between romantic rocks, where the scattered forest trees and orchards of luxuriant growth declare that many a generation must have passed away since the first partial falling of the cliff prepared the ground for such a state, where a scene so wonderful and so lovely is exhibited, as may more than equal any of the resembling scenes of the far-famed Isle of Wight'.[3]

There had been intermittent landslips before the nineteenth century, but the big one was during Christmas1839; Sheila Bird told the story: 'Just before the dramatic landslide of 1839 the undercliff was a hummocky area, rather as Ware Common is now, and there were farmworkers' cottages on it. 1839 had been a year of continuous heavy rainfall with perpetual gales which had washed ashore large numbers of the giant sub-tropical jellyfish known as "Portuguese man-of-war". A few weeks before Christmas, cracks had begun to appear in the cliff-top fields by Dowlands Farm, and William Critchard, a farm labourer, had noticed signs of subsidence in his undercliff cottage.

'On Christmas Eve, Critchard, his wife, and their neighbours made their way to Dowlands Farm to join the Yuletide celebrations and the traditional burning of the faggot, to which all the farm labourers were annually invited by the farmer, Mr Chappell. Returning home at one in the morning, Critchard knew it was not just the effects of a good night out which made the homeward path seem as if it had dropped about a foot. The cottage had suffered further subsidence. It turned out to be a night to remember, for around four o' clock there came "a wonderful crack" as the plaster split and the beams settled. They had the greatest difficulty in getting their door open, and when, with the aid of a crowbar, they eventually succeeded, it was to behold a network of deep fissures in their garden. Critchard alerted the other cottagers to the danger of the situation, and they hurriedly retrieved possessions from their cottages as he stumbled his way across yawning fissures to tell Mr Chappell of these happenings. The earth was on the move, for the wagon sent down to fetch their belongings had great difficulty in getting back as the road had vanished by that time. Critchard's cottage and his neighbour's had been contorted, and an isolated cottage was wrecked'.[4]

On Christmas Day a large section of land subsided noisily into the sea, including slabs of cultivated land, complete with hedgerows, which dropped into an immense cavern. It was known for a time as Goat Island. A reef of rock was thrown up offshore. Several months later, in August 1840, the crop was harvested from the subsided fields with, according to Sheila Bird, 'the assistance of young ladies dressed as Nymphs of Ceres, and an audience of thousands. The place had already become quite a tourist attraction, and even Queen Victoria came to view the landslip, wrongly described by some as an "earthquake", from a yacht anchored offshore'.[4]

The geologist William Buckland made his report: 'The recent sinking of the land and elevation of the bottom of the sea at Axmouth, Devon, which occurred during the two days, 25 and 26 December [1839], have no analogy to the motions of an earthquake, but come from an entirely different cause. The cliffs on that part of the coast consist of strata of chalk and cherty sandstone, resting on a thick bed of loose sand or foxmould, beneath which is a series of beds of fine clay impervious to water. Owing to the long continuance of wet weather in the last autumn, the lower region of the foxmould had become so highly saturated with water as to be reduced to semifluid quicksand. The coast from Axmouth to Lyme Regis presents vertical cliffs of chalk about 50 feet above sea level, between which cliffs and the beach a space varying from a quarter to half a mile in extent, is occupied by ruinous fallen masses of chalk and sandstone, forming an undercliff similar to that in the south coast of the Isle of Wight.

'The landslip at Axmouth began on the night of 24 December 1839 and during the following day slight movements of the undercliff were noticed; a few cracks also appeared in the fields above. About midnight of 25 December two coastguards observed a huge reef of rocks gradually rising out of the sea at a short distance from the shore; they moved slowly upward during 26 December, until a reef or breakwater was formed half a mile long and ranging from ten to forty feet in height, between which and the shore was a basin of salt water about five acres in extent and in some parts twenty five feet deep. The men who saw the reef rising fled to the top of the cliffs, where they soon found the field on which they trod intersected by chasms, from which they made their escape with difficulty.

'Fifty acres were gradually severed from the mainland during 26 December. Of these a portion subsided about fifty feet below its former level, and the rest sank into a tremendous chasm extending three-quarters of a mile from east to west and varying in breadth from 200 to 400 feet. Towards the face of the new cliff, a portion of the mass presents a most picturesque appearance of ruin and confusion, arising from the fact of its having broken up into fragments, which having sunk to unequal depths and being divided by deep chasms give the appearance of castles, towers and pinnacles. The upward movement of the reef was simultaneous with the downward movement of the land'.[5]

The Undercliff Walk

After a century and a half of abandonment the Landslip is covered by a fine ash forest, part of the Axmouth to Lyme Regis National Nature Reserve, best seen by walking the coastal footpath. It can be walked briskly in a couple of hours, or sauntered through enjoyably in half a day. The A35 climbs the hill out of Lyme and runs along the plateau behind the Landslip, through Rousdon and down into the Axe valley, where a left turning leads to Axmouth and Seaton.

John Grimson entered the Undercliff from the western end: 'The South Devon coast path begins by striking straight through the middle of this thickly wooded tumble of undercliff. One walks, sometimes bent double in the long, twisting tunnel which passing bodies such as ours have forced through the rampart jungle, through a twilight world which echoes to the cooings and flappings of invisible wood pigeons and a lot of unidentified forest noises. From somewhere deep in the wood, the screech of an owl pierces eerily through the trees, and in the constantly changing light from forest to clearing and back to forest again, it is difficult to keep one's eyes focussed on the narrow path ahead. Long ropes of ivy drape from the trees like trailing lianas in an Amazonian rain forest, and one would not be surprised to come upon a bunch of ill-intentioned Indians in the next thicket, or alligators in the next swamp. In reality, the predominantly ash forest abounds with grey squirrels and rabbits, stoats and weasels, badgers and foxes, buzzards and hawks. There are red deer also, and the nightingale nests here. In this wild and overgrown lost world of landslips, there are few glimpses of the sea, even fewer of the cliff above. And along a narrow path which frequently passes close along the edge of a crumbling undercliff, with the danger invisible beneath a fringe of overgrowth, it is all too easy to find one's seaward foot descending into space. So it is probably fortunate that we do not have the distractions of extensive coastal scenery'.[6]

This is a little exaggerated: the walking track through the Landslip is clear and well-maintained, although one should take care not to sprain an ankle in the occasional cracks and crevices.

The River Axe

There is said to have been a Roman port at the mouth of the River Axe, which is now encumbered by drifting shingle. Sea-birds haunt the salt marshes and tidal mudflats and the village of Axmouth stands a mile inland. In his account of the valley, *The Book of the Axe*, in 1875, G.P.R. Pulman wrote: 'Prior to the construction of the pier, about 1803, the river did not regularly flow into the sea, but remained kept back like a three-quarter tide and overflowed a portion of the Marsh. Even at high tide the stream had a flow at its mouth of not more than four or five feet, and at other times the water percolated through the shingle, as the Char does at Charmouth. The erection of the pier had the effect of enabling vessels of a hundred tons to enter at high water.

'A few years ago two trading vessels sailed regularly to and from London, and other vessels used the harbour. But the introduction of the railway transferred the considerable carrying trade of the neighbourhood from the water to the land. The operation of the tides and shingle pressing the mouth to the eastward, along with the diminution of the volume of the river, and the discontinuance of harbour repairs, accounts for the present dilapidated condition of the place'.[7]

It is now a cheerful little estuarine harbour beside the Axe Yacht Club, founded in 1935.

River Axe

Seaton

At the mouth of the Axe is the old Seaton Bridge, built in 1877, the oldest surviving concrete bridge in England. It has been preserved beside a modern curving bridge which sweeps over the estuary and into the seaside town. Seaton is a Victorian and Edwardian resort that grew up at the mouth of the Axe valley, and part of the old branch line railway that ran to Seaton survives in the form of a tramway which offers rides inland to Colyford and Colyton.

Seaton Tram

In 1835 the Reverend J.B. Smith wrote a very long poem about Seaton, 'descriptive of the various phenomena of the ocean and a summer spent by the sea-side' and dedicated to Sir William Templer Pole, Baronet, of Shute House, some miles inland. We shall quote only the first few lines:

> *Ye Visitors! who seek our sea-girt shore,*
> *Where ocean's billows musically roar,*
> *In search of health, or objects that amuse,*
> *Charm'd with our crescent strand, and varied views.*
> *O! deign to listen to a minstrel's lay –*
> *His theme the beach – the time a summer's day –*
> *Thro' that, your roving steps he fains would guide*
> *Along the margin of the flowing tide,*
> *And to the whisp'ring winds and waves proceed*
> *To tune with artless hand his simple reed...* [8]

The rhyming couplets (and occasional triplets) go on, in similar vein, for more than 1500 lines, and offer a good deal of comment on local natural history.

Seaton Beach

On Monday 7th August 1871 the Reverend Francis Kilvert, diarist and traveller, visited the beach at Seaton on a burning hot day: 'The beach was thronged,
swarming, a gay merry scene, light dresses, parasols, straw hats and pugenees,
lovers sitting under the shade of boats, unloved girls looking jealously on at
undisguised blandishments, and girls with shoes, stockings and drawers off
wading in the tide, holding up their clothes nearly to their waists and naked from
the waist downwards. A collier, heavy laden and sitting low in the water, had
come into the bay and coal barges were unloading her and plying between the
collier and the beach. One barge was lying close to the beach and was surrounded
by carts into which a gang of men were discharging the coal with marvellous
rapidity. The other barge was alongside the collier.

'It was a bright busy scene, the thronged beach, the pretty dresses, the galloping
horses and carts, the black collier, the deep blue sea, the dazzling white cliffs
towering perpendicularly from blue sea to the sky, and the brilliant sunshine
poured over all. I never saw the sea more intensely wonderfully blue'.[9]

Beer

To the west, chalk reappears in the cliffs around Beer, a village behind a cove
where fishing boats are hauled up to a cobble beach. A stream runs down the
side of the main street and once there was a pier at the harbour mouth, used for
the shipment of Beer Stone.

Smuggling was rife here, and Beer was the birthplace in 1778 of Jack Rattenbury, prominent in this activity until the onset of gout led to his early retirement to Seaton. His exploits earned him the title 'Rob Roy of the West'. He
recalled his childhood in Beer in *Memoirs of a Smuggler*, allegedly compiled from
his Journals: 'Beer, where we resided, lying open to the sea, I was continually
by the waterside; and as almost all I heard or saw was connected with that element,
I early acquired a partiality for it, and determined, almost from my infancy, when
I grew up, to be a sailor'. His career took him on numerous journeys over to
the Channel Islands and Cherbourg, and back to Dartmouth, Topsham and
Weymouth, in the course of which he indulged in 'smuggling and privateering'.
He was arrested and escaped from custody several times, and spent some terms
in jail, but was finally pardoned, and came under the patronage of Lord Rolle.[10]
These reminiscences were written in an elegant style that seems unlikely for a
rough old sailor, and their authorship remains a mystery.

Beer Head

The chalk cliffs run out from Beer Cove to Beer Head, which J.L.W. Page described
in his book of the Devonshire coast in 1895: 'Beer Head rises 426 feet almost straight
from the water, and is the most defined promontory between Berry Head and
Portland. It is the most southerly outcrop of the chalk in England; in fact, the

most westerly too, as the traces in the cliffs towards Branscombe are really part of the same mass. With its white pinnacles and ivy-hung crags it is a beautiful object. Below it is eaten out into caverns, where the water is a ghastly green with the reflections of the overhanging crags of chalk. The lower rocks are dotted with black objects. If you approach you will find that they become instinct with life, and move their heads uneasily from side to side. They are cormorants, or 'Beer Head fishermen' as the Sidmouth folk facetiously term them'.[11]

Beer Stone

There was a landslip at Hooken in 1790 which left hummocks and pinnacles, now scrub-covered, below the chalk cliffs. Just inland are the Beer Caves, a network of tunnels cut to excavate the fine chalk known as Beer Stone. In the words of J.L.W. Page: 'Beer Stone is excellent for building purposes. Lying at the junction of the chalk and greensand, it is principally composed of carbonate of lime, soft and easily cut, but hardening with exposure, owing to evaporation of the moisture with which it is charged. After a few years the creamy white weathers to a soft grey, which imparts an air of substantial comfort to the neighbouring cottages'.[11]

Brian Le Messurier added: 'Beer Stone was known to the Romans, but came into its own in the Middle Ages, during the time of great church and cathedral building. It is said that when first split from bed rock it can be sawn with a carpenter's saw'.[12] It can easily be carved into quite intricate forms, such as statues and gargoyles, and has been used in the decoration of such buildings as Westminster Abbey and St. Paul's, Norwich and Exeter cathedrals, as well as in nearby Branscombe Church.

Branscombe

Branscombe

The coast hereabouts is a high plateau trenched by deep valleys that open to the shore at Branscombe and Weston Mouth. W.H. Hudson 'spent hours of rare happiness' near Branscombe 'watching the birds. I could not have seen and heard them to such advantage if their breeding-place had been spread with other species. Here the herring-gulls had the rocks to themselves, and looked their best in their foam-white and pearl-grey plumage and yellow legs and beaks. While I watched them they watched me. Standing motionless, beautiful in form and colour, they looked like sculptured figures of gulls, set up on the projections against the rough dark wall of rock, just as sculptured figures of angels and saintly men and women are placed in niches on a cathedral front'.[13]

A Cliff Walk

John Seymour gave some advice: 'You can walk along the cliff top to Sidmouth, but better perhaps to plod laboriously along the shingle beach, because from here you get a view of the fine and weird *arêtes* of the cliffs. The cliff here is crowned with Upper Greensand (we have left the white cliffs of Old England behind us for good now: no more chalk from here on westwards. There was chalk once but it has all been eroded away). This soft Greensand has been cut into strange peaks and pinnacles. It is inadvisable to sit close to the bottom of these cliffs - lumps fall off. Below the Greensand there is [pink] Keuper Marl, and below that, just before you get to the Sid, you will see [red] Triassic sandstone appearing at the foot of the cliffs'.[14]

Sidmouth

Sidmouth, once described as 'a little fisher town', stands at the mouth of the wider Sid valley. Like several south coast resorts, it developed during the Napoleonic War, when European travel was curtailed, and the gentry sought sunny but English places for their holidays. Jane Austen was in Sidmouth on holiday from Bath, in 1801. An incidental remark by her older sister, Cassandra, many years later, suggested that during that summer, Jane Austen met a young man, probably a clergyman, and fell in love; but very soon afterwards received a letter annoucing that he had died. The identity of the gentleman in question remains a mystery.

Edmund Butcher, in his book *An Excursion from Sidmouth to Chester in the Summer of 1803*, written as a series of letters, described the shingle beach: '...a natural rampart of pebbles, which rises in four or five successive stages from the surface of the sea at low water. With every tide the exterior parts of this shifting wall assume some different situation; are sunk either higher or lower, or are driven to the east or west, according to the strength and direction of the wind. At low water, considerable spaces of fine, hard sand are visible...At the head of this shingly rampart, a broad commodious walk, which is called 'The Beach' has been constructed, and furnishes a delightful promenade'.[15]

An 1810 guide gave an account of Sidmouth: 'As a watering-place it is now much frequented, the company every season generally amounting to three hundred. The inhabitants are remarkable for their healthy appearance, and for their longevity. Such, indeed, might be naturally expected, from the suitability of the air, the fine dry soil, and a situation the most delicious, open to the oceans, yet not subject to fogs, and screened from all but the southern winds. The rides and walks about Sidmouth are very pleasant, and at every turn present a variety of romantic and beautiful views'.[16]

Queen Victoria

Sidmouth became famous in 1819 as the childhood home of the Princess Victoria. Brought here as a baby, she narrowly escaped being accidentally shot by a boy firing pellets at sparrows, but she survived to become Queen of England for 64 years. Her holiday home is now the Royal Glen Hotel. In 1824 the town was badly damaged by a storm, the same one that wrecked The Cobb at Lyme Regis and washed a ship over Chesil Beach.

A Sidmouth Diary

In the following year the diarist, Peter Orlando Hutchinson, came to live here. He produced five volumes of unpublished handwritten notes, sketches and newspaper cuttings, compiled between 1870 and 1881, and held by the Devon County Council Library in Exeter, with a copy in Sidmouth. He recalled arriving in Sidmouth in January 1825: 'a few months after the great storm of the previous November; and my earliest recollection of the place is that all the sea front of the town was a blank desolation of sand and gravel, the waves having rushed into all the houses on that side, beating in the doors and windows and carrying the shingle along with them. As I grew to manhood I began to take an interest in the antecedents of the parish, and subsequently to commit to paper such circumstances as seemed worthy of record'.[17] The outcome is a remarkable picture of nineteenth century events in and around the town.

Sidmouth Novels

Sidmouth appears incidentally (as 'Baymouth') in Thackeray's *Pendennis*. The young Arthur Pendennis had galloped down to 'Baymouth' one morning in search of the tutor, Mr. Foker, in whose company he had been the evening before, at the theatre, captivated by the beautiful Irish actress known as Miss Fotheringay. Now he must see Mr. Foker to learn more about her – but to his disappointment, the tutor had not come home to 'Baymouth': 'Pen went down the rock, and walked about on the sand, biting his nails by the shore of the much-sounding sea. It stretched before him bright and immeasurable. The blue waters came rolling into the bay, foaming and roaring hoarsely: Pen looked them in the face with blank eyes, hardly regarding them. What a tide there was pouring into the lad's own mind at the time, and what a little power had he to check it! Pen flung stones into the sea, but it still kept coming on. He was in a rage at not seeing Foker. He wanted to see Foker. He must see Foker'. And he did see Foker, and in due course he met Miss Fotheringay, who was actually Emily Costigan, daughter of a wild and tipsy Irish Captain - but the rest of the History of Pendennis was set inland, away from 'Baymouth'.[18]

Sidmouth became 'Idmouth' in Thomas Hardy's story, 'The Romantic Adventures of a Milkmaid', but this was written originally (1882-3) with the Frome valley in mind, and later transposed to the Exe valley and Sidmouth; consequently, the Devonshire setting is thin, and not worth quoting. Sidmouth may also have been the model for 'Sanditon' in Jane Austen's last (unfinished) novel, but she gave the location as the Sussex coast, and we quoted from that book in the Sussex chapter of *Writers on the Coast.*

'In Sidmouth', wrote Bryn Frank, 'the seafront is dominated by sandstone cliffs and small hotels with fretted wooden balconies, quite a number of them blue-and-white, with lots of ironwork and yellow AA signs. As you glance into the dining rooms, there are no sauce bottles on the tables, so you know that these are a cut above ordinary guesthouses. Instead, there are restrained alabaster table lamps with neatly coifed napkins of linen, silverware, potted plants in the dimly lit lounges.

'There was quite a little enclave of fishermen at the eastern end of the promenade, where you can buy crabs and other shellfish, and, not least, turn your car round, for the seafront is too narrow to allow that in any comfort. It occurred to me that there was a surprising amount of activity for off-season, mainly provided by suede-coated senior citizens with labradors in matching colours'.[19]

A Poor Man's House

This is the conventional portrait of Sidmouth, but in 1908 Stephen Reynolds published *A Poor Man's House*, a sociological exposé of the conditions of life of impoverished fishermen living alongside the genteel. Reynolds abandoned Edwardian middle class society to live and work with the Woolleys, a poor Devon fishing family who lived in Egremont Villas in Alexandria Square, in the little town of 'Seacombe' (i.e. Sidmouth). He shared their problems, and wrote about them to show Edwardians 'how the other half lived'. The summer of 1906 was particularly grim: 'The sea is merely grinding against the shingle. The fishermen themselves appear less picturesque and salty than they used to do. It is a slack time after a bad herring season. They are dispirited and lazy, and very likely hungry'.

Reynolds liked to work with 'Uncle Jake', who took the family boat, *Moondaisy*, along the shore on fishing and gathering forays: 'Once I backed the boat ashore for Uncle Jake to go and look at one of the numerous holes under the cliff, in every one of which he has wreckage stored up for firewood against the winter.

He can at least depend on having warmth'. Finding food was a continual problem.

'At eight in the morning we made sail with the wind just north of east. The little *Moondaisy* was full of sacks, old boots and gear. Past Refuge Cove we sailed, past Dog Tooth Ledge, and across the out-ground of Landlock Bay, which holds the last long stretch of pebble beach for some miles down. Uncle Jake pointed to the western end of it. "If ever yu'um catched down here by a sou'wester, yu can al'ays run ashore just there - calm as a mill-pond no matter how 'tis blowing". Similar bits of lore or reminiscence did he give me about every few yards of the coastline'.

'We ran the *Moondaisy* ashore at Brandy Keg Cove – a little beach running up into a deep gloomy cave where the smugglers used to store their cargoes and hand them up over the cliff. "Us can walk down to Lobster Ledge, an' west from there to Tatie Pool". As we walked along the rocks he placed above high-tide mark what bits of wreckage he could find, and kept a sharp look-out for any rabbits which might have fallen over the cliff. The only two we found, however, had been partially eaten by sea gulls and rats. "Let 'em have 'em an' welcome", said Uncle Jake, "The winter's coming. I can't think how they poor gulls lives when all the sea round is a hustle o' froth. I al'ays feeds 'em when I can. Don't yu think that *they* gets hungry tu?".

'At Lobster Ledge – a jumble of peaked rocks with pools between, he left the sack conspicuously on the top of a high stone, and hopped – seemed to hop – down to a pool. "They're here!" he cried. Underneath the stone, clinging to it and lying on the bed of the pool were so many large winkles that instead of picking them out, I found it quicker to sweep up handfuls of the loose stuff and then to pick out the refuse from the winkles. I soon got to know the likely stones - heavy ones that wanted coaxing over – and discovered also that the winkles hide themsleves in a green rather gelatinous weed, fuzzy like kale tops, from which they can be combed with the fingers. They love, too, a shadowed pool which is tainted a little, but not too much, by decaying vegetation. Uncle Jake likes the stones turned back and then replaced "as you finds 'em" '.[20]

Alexandria Square was apparently Bedford Square in Sidmouth, but the 'poor man's house' has long since gone. Reynolds himself succumbed to the 1919 influenza epidemic at the age of 28.

Vaughan Cornish and Coastal Scenery

Up on the cliff to the east is a stone commemorating the geographer, Vaughan Cornish (1862-1948), who wrote on the beauty of English scenery and the need to conserve it, and thereby contributed to the evolution of Nature Conservation and National Parks in Britain, and in due course the Countryside Commission and the Heritage Coasts concept. He was the younger brother of C.J. Cornish, whose work we have quoted previously. Among other things, he advocated the making of an open pedestrian broadway a hundred yards in width all along the cliffs of Southern England, so that people could enjoy their scenic heritage.

'The full grandeur of the scene from the summit of a cliff depends upon the maintenance of an open space on the landward side to balance the expanse of the sea. Thus not only is a cliff path required, but its users should not be cramped by a high fence or paling on the landward side.

'Cliff lands are only perfect in their charm when they present a pastoral scene, downland where the shepherd and his flocks are wandering, or meadows where the cattle are at graze, or arable where the ploughman and his team are furrowing in the field. These most picturesque of all occupations cannot be seen to advantage when the summit of a cliff is a public play ground with seats and shelters; a show place, accessible by car, with the usual accompaniments of notice boards and litter baskets.

'Cliff scenery has the same superiority over an inland landscape as sculpture in the round compared with bas-relief. It is also pre-eminent in its contribution to the scientific understanding of the origin and nature of the ground we tread. The cliffs from Lyme Regis to Sidmouth so clearly show the structure of the plateau which they terminate that they led the pioneers of geology to write certain chapters in the physical history of the world. The losses of a cliff are always lamented, but consolation should be found in the fact that the continual renewal of surface maintains the freshness and richness of colour which is so great an asset in cliff scenery. The red cliffs of the Sidmouth coast do so much to redeem the dullness of the English winter that they provide some compensation for the sunshine of the Mediterranean shore'.[21]

The Cornish family came from this part of Devonshire: 'Since I first knew the Sidmouth district in the days of childhood I have been a pilgrim of scenery in many lands, but no aspect of the world from Arctic to Equator has diminished my admiration for this peaceful spot on the south coast of Devon'.[21] He bequeathed South Combe Farm to public use as an open space in 1937, and is buried in the churchyard at Salcombe Regis.

A Sidmouth Picture

In 1949 Rising Bray wrote of Sidmouth: 'In olden days when canvases were dear, artists often used an old picture as a base on which to paint a new one. Time always uses old canvases for his new pictures. Here in Sidmouth I want you to clean away the new and discover the old.

'Stand on our sea front, clean away the picture of the houses you see there, wipe off the line of the sea wall and you will discover a picture of Sidmouth in the days of the Regent; you will see the wide bank of shingle with its rolled walk and a few houses facing the sea, with the cliffs and hills very much as in the first.

'Then clean that away: there is no library upon the front, fewer houses still, different from any you have seen in the previous picture. There will be many fishermen and boats, storehouses for gear, curing houses for fish, and on the hills the fields will not reach quite so far up towards the tops, there will be fewer hedges.

'Clean that away: you will see the beach more desolate: the hills and the sea remain, but east and west the land by river mouth and Chit reach farther out to sea; on the hills there is more woodland.

'Clean that away: you see ships, long boats, a galley beached on the shore, sheltered by the high lands east and west.

'Clean that away: but to see this picture you must stand out to sea. All the shore land stands high, there are no valleys reaching down to sea-level; the line of cliff is broken only by shallow dips, the beginnings of valleys yet to be. The cliffs are not sheer as they are to-day, for the sea has not yet cut away so much of the seaward slopes.

'Clean that away: you see land newly risen. You are not looking at it from the sea, but as from an inland point. You are standing on a wide plain where now the English Channel ebbs and flows; the great plateau rises high and stretches as far as the eye can see. Britain has risen from the azure sea, but not as two islands; its lands are part of a great continent'.[22]

Budleigh Salterton

Peak Hill and High Peak are prominent cliffs of red sandstone west of Sidmouth, whence the coast declines past Ladram Bay, with its sandstone stacks and pinnacles, to the Otter valley. Budleigh Salterton, a discreet resort, was the site of Sir John Millais' painting 'The Boyhood of Raleigh' (the sea wall depicted in it is still standing), and retains the house where Millais lived. Sir Walter Raleigh was born in 1552 at Hayes Barton, a little way inland. The beach has large ovoid cobbles that have been washed out of the red cliffs which cuts across a desert wadi that formed here more than a hundred million years ago. Salterton refers to the salterns or salt pans that were once used in the River Otter.

Victor Clinton-Baddeley set one of his stories, *No Case for the Police*, here, calling it 'Tidwell St. Peter's'. It featured Dr Davie, the academic detective who, revisiting the town, 'walked across the garden to the path on the edge of the low cliff – low here, but on the right, mounting steeply to the beacon. Below, in the great circle of the bay, lay the beach – the famous stone beach.

'Once upon a time a grassy slope had stretched down nearly to the sea, but early in the nineteenth century, as a result of a tremendous storm, these stones had arrived from somewhere beneath the English Channel – round flat stones as big as an open hand, quite unlike any other stones in neighbouring bays. The people of Tidwell St. Peter's used them to build their garden walls, to edge their flower beds, or singly as door stoppers. More than anything else it was this beach which had preserved the village from the tripper. You can't run races, play cricket, or wield a bucket and spade on stones. It was not the people so much as the place itself that was exclusive.

'Davie turned to the left and wandered along the path towards the parade.

Presently he reached the broad sea wall with the end-piece shaped like a mushroom. [He] sat down on one of the green benches and looked across the parade at the beach. Boats, lobster pots, ropes, windlasses, discreet rows of bathing cabins. A few late bathers. Gulls. Everywhere the gulls. And out in the tranquil bay two small boats, It was nearly all as he remembered it – except for one thing. Long ago there had been six bathing machines. "Machines" – no one had thought anything odd about that eighteenth-century word, and they were indeed eighteenth-century conceptions with two great wheels, originally intended to be drawn down to the sea by a horse'.[23]

It was in this setting that Davie was to solve the mystery of a local murder.

Budleigh Salterton

Exmouth

A huge caravan site dominates the cliffs at Sandy Bay. These diminish towards Exmouth, which in the eighteenth century became a seaside resort with some fine Georgian buildings: Lady Nelson lived at No.6 The Beacon and Lady Byron at No.19, a few doors away.

'Exmouth', wrote Dr. Richard Pococke in 1750, 'situated near the place where the River Exe empties itself into the sea is chiefly inhabited by fishermen and publicans, it being a place to which the people of Exeter much resort for diversion and bathing in the sea. The situation is so pleasant, having beautiful little hills to the east finely improved, and a view of the fine country on the other side, that some persons of condition have come to live at the place'.[24]

J.H. Wade found Exmouth 'a pleasant, well-ordered but rather conventional watering-place. It will delight those who like to take their airing in the vicinity of a bandstand, for it has some fine sands, a spacious promenade, a pier, and all the rest of it. A terrace-crowned cliff, the scarp of which has been ingeniously converted into a pleasure garden, preserves the shore from the flat monotony of many popular sea-side resorts'.[25]

The Exe Estuary
The Exe estuary has intricate shoals and channels when the tide ebbs, but is wide and spacious water at high tides. One channel leads to the old port of Topsham, another up into the River Exe and the city of Exeter, which was called 'Chatteris' by Thackeray in his novel *Pendennis*.

Lympstone
According to Mary Insull the site of Lympstone 'is explained by the fact that Lympstone Lake, the deep-water channel in the estuary branches from the main channel, runs close to the shore at Sowden End and continues as far as Parsonage Style where it peters out well within a hundred yards of the shore. It is possible that this deep-water lake, centuries ago, approached still closer to the shore and gave access to the smaller vessels to Lympstone harbour even at low water. It may also have been the natural end of early trackways used by the dwellers on the high ground of Woodbury Common when they came down to the water to fish'.[26]

Topsham
'Topsham', wrote W.G. Hoskins, 'is one of those ancient, decayed estuary ports which are perhaps the most fascinating kind of town that England can show, with their colour, smells, and the strong sense of past life everywhere in the streets and alleys and along the water-fronts. It consisted formerly of one long main street with a number of short streets running at right angles to it down to the foreshore of the Exe, where its life and navigation lay'.[27]

George Gissing had 'a very great liking for Topsham, and that churchyard overlooking what is not quite sea and yet more than a river, is one of the most restful spots I know'.[28] Dr John Willing, a local author, claimed that Topsham should be pronounced 'Tops-ham' or 'Tops-hm', rather than 'Top-sham'. He recalled that 'James, Duke of Monmouth, received a warm welcome from the inhabitants in 1685. It was from a first floor bay window in New Street, later renamed Monmouth Street in his honour, that he declared:

> *Topsham thou'rt a pretty town*
> *I think thou'rt very pretty*
> *And should I ever wear a crown*
> *I'll make of thee a city.*

But Monmouth was soon to lose his head, so his promise was never fulfilled'.[28]

Tryphena Sparks, whose name has been romatically linked with Thomas Hardy, married Charles Gale and came to live in Topsham. After her death in 1890, Hardy and his brother cycled over from Dorchester to lay a wreath on her grave, and met her daughter Nellie, who inspired Hardy's poem 'To a Motherless Child' as well as perhaps a chapter in *Jude the Obscure* and the theme of *The Well-Beloved.*

Exeter Quay

The estuary narrows upstream into the River Exe, and The Quay which is the port of Exeter. There is a seventeenth century Custom House, and a collection of a remarkable variety of boats from all over the world in the Exeter Maritime Museum, opened in 1968 and occupying the head of the canal that was cut in the sixteenth century. It is said that in the 13th century the Countess of Devonshire, annoyed at a refusal by the Mayor of Exeter to pay her customary tithes, arranged for a weir to be built across the River Exe. Certainly there was a weir, built to power a mill, which impeded navigation up to Exeter and so favoured Topsham as a wool port, until a canal was built to provide ship access to Exeter. W.G. Hoskins, who wrote much about Devon and Exeter, noted that this was 'the first true canal' cut in England, 'with locks and a towpath, constructed by the municipal authorities of Exeter between 1564 and 1567 to allow barges to pass around the weirs on the river and to reach the city. It was a small undertaking, only sixteen feet wide, three feet deep, and about three miles long, but it was a remarkable work for its time, all the more so because it was a municipal enterprise. Since then it has been three times enlarged in width, length and depth. It became a favourite walk in the eighteenth century for the citizens of Exeter, and remained so until recent years. Perhaps it still is, for it winds peacefully between the elm-shaded meadows of the Exe valley past congenial inns'.[29]

There are traces of the old city wall nearby, and a new precinct has been built, harmonising well with the older buildings.

Exeter has long had literary associations. The Exeter Book is a tenth century manuscript of elegiac Old English poems, including *The Wanderer* and *The Seafarer*, given to the Cathedral by Bishop Leofric, and much prized as evidence of the literary achievements of the Dark Ages.

The Atmospheric Railway

On the western shore of the Exe estuary is Starcross, notable for mementos of the inventive engineer Isambard Kingdom Brunel, who in the 1840s designed and built a chain of ten coal-fired pumping stations to enable trains on the Exeter to Teignmouth railway, following the coastline, to be drawn along by a piston in a depressurised pipe. One of these pumping stations survives beside the Starcross railway station. The 'Atmospheric Railway' through to Newton Abbot was inaugurated in February 1848, and had passenger trains noiselessly reaching 60 miles per hour, but it was closed because of a multiplicity of technical and operational problems.

Starcross Pumping Station

'History makes us all travellers in time', wrote Charles Hadfield, imagining a journey from Exeter in the spring of 1848, when he took a ticket for Teignmouth on one of the broad-gauge atmospheric trains of the South Devon Railway, leaving Exeter on the run to Newton Abbot.

'The train of three carriages is waiting, and a number of men are pushing the piston carriage past them to take its place at the front. It is backed on and coupled up, and the driver in his greatcoat carrying the South Devon Company's initials climbs to his platform. If we peer underneath we can see the piston pointing to the mouth of the main tube at the near end of Exe bridge.

'Our signal clears, the station bell rings, the guard blows his horn, and a porter opens the valve to admit air to the 8-inch tube. The driver pulls in the bar to drop the starting rope, there is a bang beneath our carriage as the train piston passes the entrance valve of the main tube, and with a surge the train accelerates as it is driven forward.

'At Countess Wear, three miles from Exeter, we see the engine-house on the up-side, with its reservoir behind it. Bang! The piston leaves the first section of the tube. Bang! It enters the next.

'We suddenly slow down. Evidently Starcross is having engine trouble, and has failed to get its proper vacuum. More slowly we run beside the Exe, till we hear the piston leave the tube: we stop at Starcross station. Passengers for the ferry to Exmouth get out, and one or two locals. Clouds of smoke are coming from the engine-house on the up-side just beyond the station: the Starcross engineman is determined that he will have full vacuum for the coming up train.

'We watch for the train. Six or seven minutes later we can see it coming – smokeless, nearly silent, without a locomotive, the driver standing at the front of the six-wheeled leading carriage, his hand on the brake handle. His passengers are behind a partition, with others in the following carriages. As the express shoots past at over 60 m.p.h. we hear the echoing rumble of air rushing into the opened valve, and then the sharp rattle of the smooth steel pressing wheel to close it again. Then it is gone, and to all appearances the tube and valve are as before.

'We [resume our journey, and] are taking the Warren curve fast, and flash along behind the sea-wall until the driver begins to screw down his brake for Dawlish. Again the train is started with a rope. Away through the tunnels, winding round by beach and cove, to emerge on the sea-wall before swinging away to the station at Teignmouth'.[30]

Dawlish Warren

Dawlish Warren is a dune-capped spit at the mouth of the Exe estuary, and in 1910 Sidney Heath described it in his coastal book: 'an inner and an outer warren, with a lake between them and the railway at the back.

Formerly, and indeed until quite recently, this was a deserted and waste piece of land, and on it, alas! grew many plants dear to the heart of the botanist. Here the sea-holly, the yellow-horned poppy and the large sea convolvulus flourished, and also did the *Trichonema columna*, a little crocus like plant with purplish flowers, having a yellow tinge; a rare botanical species that has been found in few places besides this once deserted and sandy shore, where quantities of it could formerly be found. For picnics it was an ideal spot where one could ramble in all directions, scamper down sand-hills, with no other companions but the native rabbits and flocks of birds, among them some rare species. Here might be seen herons, terns, several varieties of gulls, flocks of little sandpipers, and here year after year came the Little Stint'.[31] Sidney Heath went on to lament the intrusion of a golf course and the spread of bungalows, but the spit still has dunes and salt marshes, and is a Nature Reserve.

To the south the red cliffs revive to dominate the Dawlish coastline.The 1810 guide book, which we have already quoted, described Dawlish as 'delightfully situate in a valley, on all sides surrounded by high grounds, except towards the east, which opens to the cerulean expanse; fronting which, on the strand, are some good lodging-houses. The bathing-machines are numerous, and well-conducted. The beach in front of the lodging-houses has a gentle descent to the sea, which is generally pure and clear. The promenade is kept in excellent repair, and extends in a straight line across the strand. It may be lengthened at pleasure by a ramble under the cliffs which are here bold, precipitous and of a tremendous height'.[16]

Soon after this was written, the Great Western Railway was built along the esplanade, separating the town from its beach. The railway dominates the coastline from here to Teignmouth, tunnelling through successive headlands of red sandstone and passing the the prominent rock formations of the Parson and Clerk, off Hole Head.   Times have certainly changed: imagine the outcry now if a proposal were made to build such a railway – for example along the coastline from Seaton to Exmouth!

Charles Dickens set the beginning of *Nicholas Nickleby* on a small farm near Dawlish, but did not mention the coast.

Teignmouth

Teignmouth in the eighteenth century was exporting granite blocks for the construction of London Bridge (which was later purchased by the Americans – some say they thought they were acquiring Tower Bridge – so that it now spans an artificial lake in Arizona).

Fanny Burney was in Teignmouth, writing her diary, in 1773: 'We all went on Monday evening to the sea-shore, to see the seine drawn: this is a most curious work, all done by women. They have a very long net, so considerable as to cost them thirteen or sixteen pounds. This they first draw into a boat, which they go off the shore in, and row in a kind of semicircle, till they land at some distance. All the way they spread this net, one side of which is kept above water by corks. Then they land and divide forces; half of them return to the beginning of the net, and half remain at the end; and then with amazing strength both divisions at the same time pull the net in by the two ends. Whatever fish they catch are always encircled in the middle of the net, which comes out of the water the last; and, as they draw towards each other, they all join in getting their prey. When once they perceive that there is fish in their nets, they set up a loud shout, and make an almost unintelligible noise in expressing their joy and in disputing at the same time upon their shares, and on what fish escaped them. They are all robust and well-made, and have remarkably beautiful teeth, and some of them are really very fine women. Their dress is barbarous; they have stays half-laced, and something by way of handkerchiefs around their necks; they wear one coloured flannel or stuff petticoat; no shoes or stockings, notwithstanding the hard pebbles and stones all along the beach; and their coat is pinned up in the shape of a pair of trousers, leaving them wholly naked to the knee. Mr. Western declares he could not have imagined such a race of females existed in a civilised country; and had he come thither by sea, he should have almost fancied he had been cast on a newly discovered coast. They caught this evening at one time nine large salmon, a john dory, and a gurnet. On Tuesday evening we went again, and saw them catch four dozen of mackerel at a haul'.[32]

John Keats lived in Northumberland Place, Teignmouth in 1818, where he completed his poem 'Endymion'.

Gerard Manley Hopkins

A nineteenth century visitor, Gerard Manley Hopkins, described waves on the coast to the south of Teignmouth: 'Heavy seas: we walked along the seawall to the Kennaway Tunnel to watch them. The wave breaks in this order – the crest of the barrel "doubling" (that, a boatman said, is the word in use) is broken into a bush of foam, which, if you search it, is a lace and tangle of jumping sprays; then breaking down these grow to a sort of shaggy quilt tumbling up the beach; thirdly this unfolds into a sheet of clear foam and running forward in leaves and laps the wave reaches its greatest height upon the shore and at the same time its greatest clearness and simplicity; after that, raking on the shingle and so on, it is forked and torn and, as it commonly has a pitch or lurch to one side besides its backdraught, these rents widen: they spread and mix and the water clears and escapes to the sea transparent and keeping in the end nothing of its white except in long dribble bubble-strings which trace its set and flow. The shore here is not pebbly but sand and in some places a fine red grit hardly to be called sand, when wet of a rich maroon, fallen from the red cliffs, which are richly tapestried with bramble, traveller's joy I think, and ivy and other things. The colour of the breakers registered the nature of the earth they were over – mostly brown, then a wandering streak or stain of harsh clayey red'.[33]

Kipling at Maidencombe

The Great Western Railway turns inland along the Teign estuary to Newton Abbot, but the pine-clad cliffs and woody combes continue along the coast southwards, without a railway, to Torquay. The main road runs a short way inland, behind Babbacombe Bay and past the village of Maidencombe, where Rudyard Kipling and his wife leased Rock House in the autumn of 1896, after returning from the United States:

'We found a house for our needs that seemed almost too good to be true. It was large and bright, with big rooms each and all open to the sun, the grounds embellished with great trees and the warm land dipping southerly to the clean sea under the Marychurch cliffs'.[34]

In his biography of Kipling, Lord Birkenhead described the situation: 'Kipling looked from his work-table on to the decks of the fishing boats which came in to tend their lobster pots, and upon the sea, sometimes aquamarine in the sun and so clear he could see the smooth white stones upon the bottom, sometimes ruffled dark purple when a rising sea stirred the listless palms, and always, as he wrote, was in his ears the monotonous rise and fall of the "lazy, plunging sea". Their beach was a tiny cove reached by an almost perpendicular lane – a place, he thought, for the smuggling days – and a flight of rude stone steps. Three miles south was the rocky nose that covered Torquay harbour, and there were dangerous shoals outside, half-tide rocks slimy and razor-toothed, where the whiting and pollock congregated in shoals. No one went to the little bay except the fishermen and Kipling, but now and then he found footprints in the sand and the mark of a row-boat's keel.

'Down in the cove, where the cliffs towered on either side, the air was heavy as in a greenhouse, the silence broken only by the forlorn scream of sea birds and the beat of the waves on the sand. Over all the place was a lush redness. The grass and trees grew to the water's edge, but the dominant note was red: the soil was a deep red, and there was a splendid mixture of red, green foliage and blue sea and sky.

'At first it seemed that Kipling would be happy here, in this sub-tropical "un-English" place, which resembled rather some wooded cleft in the Italian coast asleep in the noonday heat. He had arrived auspiciously in the splendour of a storm, an equinoctial, when the glass fell an inch and oscillated wildly, and the wind took hold and whipped the Channel into lather. Kipling exulted, as always, in the sudden anger of the sea and the wind. He watched the top twisted out of a big poplar on the lawn, then an elm torn up by the roots. He saw a trawler blown out to sea, a rag of brown sail in the flying spume, and heard the whistle of a steamer. The scud was thick over the sea and from a secluded corner in the kitchen garden he looked down on the waters boiling like a tub of yeast. Off Brixham the fishing fleet were holding on under the lee of the land, with everything down that could bite bottom. It was an exhilarating welcome'.[35]

Rock House is still there, a grey mansion with turretted gateposts, but Kipling did not much like the Torquay area in the wet winter of 1896-7. He started to write *Stalky & Co.*, here, but it has no local references.

Oddicombe

The South Devon Coast Path skirts Babbacombe Bay, past Watcombe Beach and Petit Tor to Oddicombe, which Edmund Gosse described: 'Far below us, in an immense arc of light, there stretched the enormous plain of waters. We had but to cross a step or two of downs, when the hollow sides of the great limestone cove yawned at our feet, descending, like a broken cup, down, down to the moon of snow-white shingle and the expanse of blue-green sea.

'In these twentieth-century days, a careful municipality has studded the down with rustic seats and has shut its dangers out with railings, has cut a winding carriage-drive round the curves of the cove down to the shore, and has planted sausage-laurels at intervals in clearings made for that aesthetic purpose. When last I saw the place, thus smartened and secured, with its hair in curl-papers and its feet in patent-leathers, I turned from it in anger and disgust, and could almost have wept. I suppose that to those who knew it in no other guise, it may still have beauty. No parish councils, beneficent and shrewd, can obscure the lustre of the waters or compress the vastness of the sky. But what man could do to make wild beauty ineffectual, tame and empty, has amply been performed at Oddicombe'.[36]

The parkland atmosphere is still there, but the coast is too bold to be really tamed. There is a cliff railway dating from 1926 from Oddicombe up to Babbacombe, which is now a suburb of Torquay.

Babbacombe Bay

Gerard Manley Hopkins sat down above Babbacombe Bay to describe the scene: 'The sea was like blue silk. It seemed warped over towards our feet. Half-miles of catspaw like breathing on glass just turned the smoothness here and there. Red cliffs, white ashy shingle, green inshore water, blue above that, clouds and distant cliffs dropping soft white beams down it, bigger clouds making big white tufts of white broken by ripples of the darker blue foregound water as if they were great white roses sunk in a blue dye'.[33]

Torquay

Torquay is one of England's most popular resorts, because of a mild climate: palm trees and sub-tropical plants grow well behind its three beaches: Torre Abbey Sands, Corbyn Beach and Livermead Sands.

Elizabeth Barrett lived in Torquay and wrote to Mary Russell Mitford in 1838: 'Here we are immediately *upon* the lovely bay – a few paces dividing our door from its waves – and nothing but the 'sweet south' and congenial west wind can reach us – and *they* must first soften their footsteps upon the waters. Behind us – so close as to darken the back windows – rises an abrupt rock crowned with the slant woods of Beacon Hill – and thus though the North and East wind blow their fiercest, we are in an awful silence and can only guess at their doings'.[37]

The 1859 edition of Murray's *Handbook for Devon and Cornwall* dwelt upon the recuperative qualities of Torquay: 'This watering-place, reputed to possess a moist but one of the most equitable climates in England, and much resorted to by invalids with delicate lungs, is for the most part of very modern growth. The general effect of the white houses, the grey limestone cliffs, and the foliage and greensward forming the ground of the whole, is unusually pleasant and picturesque, and calculated to soothe, as far as scenery can soothe, the lassitude and depression of ill-health.'[38]

After the branch railway line from Newton Abbot reached it in 1848, Torquay grew quickly into a sprawling town, which now merges with Paignton, and has suburbs overlooking Tor Bay. Kipling, as we have said, disliked it. In an 1896 letter to Charles Eliot Norton he wrote: 'Torquay is such a place as I do desire acutely to upset by dancing through with nothing on but my spectacles. Villas, clipped hedges and shaven lawns; fat old ladies with respirators and obese landaus. The Almighty is a discursive and frivolous trifler compared with some of 'em'.[39]

Tennyson's poem, 'Audley Court', written in 1838, seems to have been inspired by Torre Abbey, built in 1196, which looks out over lawns to the seafront south of the town: 'Torquay was in the old days the loveliest sea-village in England', he wrote, 'and it is now a town. In those old days, I, coming down from the hill over Torquay, saw a star of phosphorescence made by the little buoy appearing and disappearing in the dark sea, and was at first puzzled by it

> .....'ere night we rose
> *And saunter'd home beneath a moon that, just*
> *In crescent, dimly rain'd about the leaf*
> *Twilights of airy silver, till we reach'd*
> *The limit of the hills; and as we sank*
> *From rock to rock upon the glooming quay,*
> *The town was hush'd beneath us: lower down*
> *The bay was oily calm; the harbour buoy,*

Sole star of phosphorescence in the calm,
With one green sparkle ever and anon
Dipt by itself, and we were glad at heart.[40]

In 1908, Rupert Brooke holidayed in Torquay, and wrote his early sonnet 'Seaside':

Swiftly out from the friendly lilt of the band,
The crowd's good laughter, the loved eyes of men,
I am drawn nightward: I must turn again
Where, down beyond the low untrodden strand,
There curves and glimmers outward to the unknown
The old unquiet ocean. All the shade
Is rife with magic and movement. I stray alone
Here on the edge of silence, half afraid,
Waiting a sign. In the deep heart of me,
Black swaying waters surge to greet the moon
And all the tides set seaward. From the band,
Sudden and careless, the throb (or snatch) of an old tune
Leaps lightly forth, and blows along the sand
And dies between the sea-wall and the sea.[41]

Tickner Edwardes, walking and hitch-hiking in Devon in the early years of the present century, was enthusiastic about Torquay: 'The town lies in a pool of wellnigh unbroken sunshine, wedged in between a barrier of great rocky hills and the sea. Foreign-looking villas are dotted about everywhere in the greenery of the encircling heights. The fish-quays with their rows of lines and sauntering crowds, the fussy little harbour, the straggling house-fronts, each painted a different hue, are all undisguisedly continental. The public gardens might have been imported intact from any town on the Riviera. Palms and queer exotic shrubs shadow the winding ways at every turn. Among the people, even among the well-to-do, there is a love of bright raiment wholly Italian in spirit.

'But most foreign of all is the climate – the soft, sleepy, indolent air of South Devon, that pervades the whole place. You may bring to it the liveliest energy. You may be the most earnest, go-ahead soul that ever lamp-lightered through Cheapside or the Strand. But once you have settled down in Torquay, and the place has got its slothful, golden grip upon you, it is good-bye to all your upstart, aeroplaning moods. In a little while you will have forgotten time and London almost as completely as the gently stirring multitudes around you'.[43]

The Swimming Detective

About this time, Agatha Christie was a young girl in Torquay, enjoying sea-bathing: 'Bathing as I remember it was strictly segregated. There was a special Ladies' Bathing-Cove, a small stony beach, to the left of the Bath Saloons. The beach was a steeply sloping one, and on it there were eight bathing machines in the charge of an ancient man, of somewhat irascible temper, whose non-stop job was to let the machine up and down in the water. You entered your bathing machine – a gaily painted striped affair – saw that both doors were safely bolted, and began to undress with a certain amount of caution, because at any moment the elderly man might decide it was your turn to be let down into the water. At that moment there would be a frantic rocking, and the bathing machine would grind its way slowly over the loose stones, flinging you from side to side. In fact the action was remarkably similar to that of a Jeep or Land Rover nowadays, when traversing the more rocky parts of the desert.

'The bathing machine would stop as suddenly as it had started. You then proceeded with your undressing and got into your bathing-dress. This was an unaesthetic garment, usually made of dark blue or black alpaca, with numerous skirts, flounces and frills, reaching well down below the knees and over the elbow. Once fully attired you unbolted the door on the water side. If the old man had been kind to you, the top step was practically level with the water. You descended and there you were, decorously up to your waist. You then proceeded to swim. There was a raft not too far out, to which you could swim and pull yourself up and sit on it. At low tide it was quite near; at high tide it was quite a good swim, and you had it more or less to yourself. Having bathed as long as you liked, which for my part was a great deal longer than any grown-up accompanying me was inclined to sanction, you were signalled to come back to shore – but as they had difficulty in getting at me once I was on the raft, and I anyway proceeded to swim in the opposite direction, I usually managed to prolong it to my own pleasure.

'There was of course no such thing as sunbathing on the beach. Once you left the water you got into your bathing machine, you were drawn up with the same suddenness with which you had been let down, and finally emerged, blue in the face, shivering all over, with hands and cheeks died away to a state of numbness'.[43]

Torbay

South from Torquay is the Livermead Cliff Hotel, where Charles Kingsley once lived. He thought that 'Torbay is a place which should be as much endeared to the naturalist as to the patriot and to the artist. We cannot gaze on its blue ring of water, and the great limestone bluffs which bound it to the north and south, without a glow passing through our hearts, as we remember the terrible and glorious pageant which passed by in the glorious July days of 1588, when the Spanish Armada ventured slowly past Berry Head, with Elizabeth's gallant pack of Devon captains (for the London fleet had not yet joined) following fast in its wake, and dashing into the midst of this vast line, undismayed by size and numbers, while their kin and friends stood watching and praying on the cliffs, spectators of Britain's Salamis.

'And as for the scenery, though it can boast of neither mountain peak nor dark fiord, and would seem tame enough in the eyes of a western Scot or Irishman, yet Torbay surely has a soft beauty of its own. The rounded hills slope gently to the sea, spotted with squares of emerald grass, and rich red fallow fields, and parks full of stately timber trees. Long lines of tall elms run down to the very water's edge, their boughs unwarped by any blast; here and there apple orchards are bending under their loads of fruit, and narrow strips of water-meadow line the glens, where the red cattle are already lounging in richest pastures, within ten yards of the rocky pebble beach. The shore is silent now, the tide far out; but six hours hence it will be hurling columns of rosy foam into the sunlight, and sprinkling pasengers, and cattle, and trim gardens which hardly know what frost and snow may be, but see the flowers of autumn meet the flowers of spring, and the old year linger smilingly to twine a garland for the new'.[44]

Paignton

Paignton is another seaside resort on the A379. Darrell Bates said in his *Companion Guide to Devon and Cornwall*: 'It used to be spelled Paington but when the railway was extended to the town in 1859 and it began to be developed as a less exclusive sort of Torquay, the spelling was changed by the railway company in case the look of the first four letters discouraged visitors'.[45]

It was perhaps in this area that John Le Carré's *A Perfect Spy* began: 'In the small hours of a blustery October morning in a south Devon coastal town that seemed to have been deserted by its inhabitants, Magnus Pym got out of his elderly country taxi-cab, and, having paid the driver and waited till he had left, struck out across the church square. His destination was a terrace of ill-lit Victorian boarding-houses with names like Bel-a-Vista, The Commodore, and Eureka. A strong sea wind lashed at his city suit, salt rain stung his eyes, balls of spume skimmed across his path. Pym ignored them. Reaching the porch of a house marked "no vacancies" he pressed the bell and waited, first for the outside light to go on, then for the chains to be unfastened from inside. While he waited a church clock began striking five. As if in answer to its summons, Pym turned on his heel and stared back at the square. At the graceless tower of the Baptist church posturing against the racing clouds. At the writhing monkey-puzzle trees, pride of the ornamental gardens. At the empty bandstand. At the bus shelter. At the dark patches of the side streets. At the doorways one by one'.[46]

Magnus Pym, a spy, had "disappeared", and was about to write his complicated memoirs. He had first come here several years before, by train from

Paddington, changing to another train at Exeter, and so to a destination from which he caught a bus, until the conductor said "Far as we go, sir".[46] The seaside town is not identified – the televised version used Dawlish, but the description mentions no coastal railway. It could fit any of several south Devon towns, but our guess is somewhere in Torbay.

Brixham

The coast curves on past Roundham Head towards Brixham, which has been for centuries a fishing port, using various kinds of nets and lines to catch herring. In the nineteenth century an improved boat design for trawling nets along the sea floor became known as the Brixham Trawler. Brixham is still a busy fishing port, though yachting is increasing. There is a full-size replica of the *Golden Hinde* in the harbour. The statue on the quay is William of Orange, who landed at Brixham in 1688. His fleet, sailing for Torbay, had been blown off course towards Plymouth, where a landing was impossible without confronting the local garrison. Then, according to the eminent historian, Thomas Macaulay: 'the wind changed: a soft breeze sprung up from the south: the mist dispersed: the sun shone forth: and, under the mild light of an autumnal noon, the fleet turned back, passed round the lofty cape of Berry Head, and rode safe in the harbour of Torbay.

'Torbay, when the Dutch fleet cast anchor there, was known only as a haven where ships sometimes took refuge from the tempests of the Atlantic. Its quiet shores were undisturbed by the bustle either of commerce or of pleasure; and the huts of ploughmen and fishermen were thinly scattered over what is now the site of crowded marts and of luxurious pavilions.

'The peasantry of the coast of Devonshire remembered the name of Monmouth with affection, and held Popery in detestation. They therefore crowded down to the seaside with provisions and offers of service. The disembarkation instantly commenced. Sixty boats conveyed the troops to the coast [and] the Prince soon followed. He landed where the quay of Brixham now stands. The whole aspect of the place has been altered. Where we now see a port crowded with shipping, and a marketplace swarming with buyers and sellers, the waves then broke on a desolate beach; but a fragment of the rock on which the deliverer stepped from his boat has been carefully preserved, and is set up as an object of public veneration in the centre of that busy wharf'.[47]

Berry Head

A large 19th century fortification dominates Berry Head, a fine viewpoint. The lighthouse is the highest and lowest in Great Britain being 200 feet above sea level and just 6 feet high. J.L.W. Page was here in 1895: 'The summit of Berry Head is a good wide table-land covered with turf when it is not covered with furze brake. Open and breezy though it be, it is rather a melancholy spot, for it is laden with ruins – the ruins of forts erected at the time of the threatened French invasion.

These buildings succeeded earlier fortifications, dating from Roman times, or perhaps earlier still. A misty tradition states that Berry Head was the spot where Vespasian and Titus landed. This is impossible as the cliffs are much too precipitous

'The fortifications at the extremity of the Head are less ruinous than those of the older battery and much more extensive, covering quite three times the area. One or two of the buildings are still kept in repair, and the one near the gate is a refreshment house much affected by the people of Torquay and Brixham, for whom, on a summer day, Berry Head is a happy hunting ground. And, indeed, the bracing air of this wind-swept bluff must be like a draught of champagne after the relaxing atmosphere of "the queen of watering places," not to speak of the view. For, although Sharpham Point cuts off the prospect towards Dartmouth, the panorama northwards has few rivals anywhere. Let us seat ourselves upon the turf by the signal station and look about us. So abruptly does the rock wall sink to the waves below, that if you are suicidally inclined you may actually sit upon the edge, and look straight down upon the breakers. But a seat safer and more dignified will be found a few paces further inland, whence it is still possible to see the rocks and watch the long line of Brixham trawlers creeping past two hundred feet below, their red sails contrasting strongly with the pearly grey of the limestone'.[11]

Dartmouth

South of Torbay the red rocks come to an end, and give place to the grey slates, which outcrop along the rocky shore south to, and beyond, the estuary of the River Dart. Kingswear has ferries across the deep estuary to Dartmouth, where the fifteenth century castle guards the entrance from the sea.

Chaucer visited the town in 1373 when he was a customs officer at a time when the wine trade with Bordeaux was thriving, along with smuggling and piracy. In the Prologue to *The Canterbury Tales* one of the pilgrims may have been modelled on John Hawley, the chief ship-owner in his day, and whose brass is now in St. Saviour's Church:

> *A Shipman was ther woning fer by weste*
> *For aught I woot he was of Dertemouthe.*[48]

Daniel Defoe was here in 1724: 'The opening into Dartmouth Harbour is not broad, but the channel deep enough for the biggest ship in the royal navy. The narrow entrance is not much above half a mile, when it opens and makes a basin, or harbour able to receive 500 sail of ships of any size, and where they may ride with the greatest safety, even as in a mill-pond, or wet dock. I had the curiosity here with the assistance of a merchant of the town to go out to the mouth of the haven in a boat to see the entrance, and castle, or fort that commands it; and coming back with the tide of flood, I observed some small fish to skip, and play upon the surface of the water, upon which I asked my friend what fish they were; immediately one of the rowers or seamen starts up in the boat, and throwing his arms abroad, as if he had been bewitched, cried out as loud as he could bawl, "a school, a school". The word was taken to the shore as hastily as it would have been on land if he had cried fire; and by the time we reached the quays, the town was all in a kind of uproar'.[49]

The fish were pilchards, Defoe's servant bought seventeen for a halfpenny and 'the cook at the inn broiled them for us...with pepper and salt, which cost us about a farthing, so that the two of us, and servant dined, and at a tavern too, for three-farthings, dressing and all'.[49]

In 1897 Arthur H. Norway thought Dartmouth 'strangely situated. The old town lies at the water's edge and the hills sink down so straight and deep that they do in fact resemble walls, rendering other fortifications on the landward side almost needless. And now the entrance, the sight of which was blocked by the jutting town of Kingswear on the further bank, comes full in sight, a deep and narrow gorge, with a castle low down upon a rocky point, whence in old days a chain was drawn nightly to the other shore, blocking the entrance against all vessels. For there are here no intricacies of channel to perplex an enemy'.[50]

Jonathan Raban sailed into Dartmouth at sunset one evening in 1982: 'By night, Dartmouth was a dazzling incandescent city. It blazed on the water, a mile-long pool of blinding reflections so hard and bright that you could nearly hear them clink. They shattered and regrouped in the criss-cross wakes of fishing boats and ferries – a Manhattan of lights on the hop. I left *Gosfield Maid* chained to a buoy in midstream, rowed through the middle of the loud reflections, found a seafood restaurant on the waterfront and basked in my luck at happening on such unexpected splendour.

'But day broke on Boots the Chemists and on Barclays Bank. It disclosed an English seaside town, bunched and squat, with too much pastel pebbledash and too much teashoppe half-timbering. The jam of traffic in the streets was as quiet as sludge, patiently shifting a few feet at a time, through narrow conduits of low brick villas and tall advertisements for low-tar cigarettes. On the green hill of razored lawns to the south of the town, the Britannia Royal Naval College lorded it over Dartmouth. I studied it through binoculars. No one seemed to be at home, although some wheeled cannons were parked on the gravel near the front door. The college didn't look a very friendly place. Its bland white facade and banks of bare uncurtained windows gave it the supercilious expression of an officer staring fixedly over the tops of the heads of the Other Ranks. Searching the grounds I found a gardener marching a motor mower uphill, another cannon, pointed strategically at Marks & Spencer's in the town, a bed of obedient and well-drilled roses, a blue naval Land Rover and a horse. Perhaps everyone had gone to the Falklands'.[51]

The coastal cliffs resume past Stoke Fleming to Slapton, where a long beach of fine shingle encloses a reedy lagoon, Slapton Ley, which some local people pronounce as 'Lea'. Occasionally, as in 1978, and again in 1990, easterly gales drive huge storm waves over the beach into this lagoon.

Slapton Beach was the site, in 1944, of manoeuvres in preparation for the Allied landings in Normandy. Ken Small told what happened: 'Once the landing beaches on the French coast had been selected, it was essential that stretches of coastline in Britain with similar features be made available for training. So it was that, on 4th November 1943, the chairman of the Devon County Council, Sir John Daw, received a telephone call from the War Office informing him that a considerable part of the land under his authority was being requisitioned and had to be totally evacuated by 20 December. A total evacuation of 30,000 acres was to take place at once, involving parts of six parishes, 3,000 people, 180 farms, village shops and other dwellings, affecting 750 families in all.

'The evacuation completed, the South Hams was occupied by 30,000 US troops who camped in and around the deserted villages, and prepared for intensive rehearsals for the invasion landings. Their prime site of interest was Slapton Sands, not just because of its already battered appearance, but most importantly because it was a stretch of coast that closely resembled the area of Normandy coast code-named Utah Beach'.[52]

Sherman Tank at Slapton Sands

There was, however, a major disaster when, on 28 April, a group of landing-craft practising for the D-day landings, without any protective air or naval cover, were intercepted offshore and sunk by a flotilla of German E-boats, with the loss of 946 American servicemen. This fiasco was called Exercise Tiger. It is commemorated by a monument beside the carpark just north of Torcross, consisting of a Sherman tank dredged from the sea floor and preserved in black acrylon. A granite monument was earlier erected by Americans as a presentation to the people who had to leave their homes in 1943.

Slapton Ley

Slapton Ley is a local nature reserve, much used by students and others who come to the nearby Field Studies Centre to take courses in geology, botany, zoology, and many other subjects. Mark Wallington was here with his mongrel Boogie in 1982: 'For a while I managed to lose myself amongst the reeds of Slapton Ley, where I caught up with a party of naturalists out collecting specimens, butterflies, I think. They all had nets and notebooks open, and were clearly of the mind that insects were omnipotent and just biding their time until they made their move for world domination. "Look everyone!", cried a little man with a big moustache, "a green fritillary", and he dived gleefully into the undergrowth'.[53]

The lagoon contains perch and pike and, according to J.L.W. Page, writing in 1895: '...is so full of reeds that the owner is said to make as much as two hundred pounds a year by the sale of them. They are used for thatching. The upper end beyond Slapton Bridge is almost a solid mass; indeed, it is difficult to distinguish the water at all – it is a sea of reeds. Along the top of the bank dividing the lea from the sea runs the Dartmouth road. The lea is only a few feet below it on the one hand, and the sea, at high water, approaches very near it on the other. There is a story that the waves, driven before an easterly gale, once washed right over it into the lea, killing all the fish. I can well believe it, having seen the sea very near it myself. Enormous breakers thundered upon the shingle, and the spray flying across hid the distant line of road in a white mist. I was on the top of the Dartmouth coach at the time, and the guard coming forward spread over us water-proof aprons. He made no remark, and was evidently continually in the habit of thus protecting the passengers from the briny rain'.[11]

Hallsands

At the southern end of Slapton Ley the village of Torcross, with its grey cottages, stands alongside the main road that swings inland towards Kingsbridge. Hallsands, to the south, was a fishing village on a rocky ledge beneath the coastal slopes and behind a wide shingle beach until, late in the nineteenth century, 650,000 tons of gravel were dredged from here to be used in the building of Devonport dockyard. The beach was depleted, and without its protection erosion began, culminating in 1917 with a storm that destroyed all but one of the fishermen's cottages. Now there are only ruins and foundations to remind coastal managers of the fragility of the coastline, and make them wary of proposals to exploit coastal resources.

Hallsands

Raymond Cattell, sailing in this area in the *Sandpiper* in the nineteen-thirties, came to 'ocean-battered Hallsands. These strange ruins tell a touching story of human love, courage and stupidity. The fishermen built their homes beside their boats, clinging to the foot of the cliff, with only a narrow shingle beach between themselves and the hungry sea. On winter nights the storms would send the surf to the doors of the houses.

'In the stout wall and intersecting ramparts before these ruined houses you can see how this village tried valiantly to defend itself against the storms which each year came further. We are told that the landlady of the inn was serving tea (probably expressing her views on scaremongers) when the side of the house fell out. The onshore gale and spring tides wiped out the whole village in a couple of days. You will find only a number of broken walls and fallen roofs, looking exactly like a derelict war village blasted by a deluge of shell'.[54]

Start Point

Start Point is a high rocky spur with a neat lighthouse. Hilaire Belloc was cruising in the *Nona* off here when the First World War was imminent in 1914: 'When I set out from Plymouth there was nothing but rumour, nothing certain. The Fleet had dispersed already some days past from the great review at Spithead, and was, as we were told, in the Atlantic at manoeuvres. A night, a day, and now another night had passed; I had heard no news.

'Nothing was further from my mind than war and armament as the sun rose on that glorious July morning, right out of a clean horizon, towards which the wind blew fresh and cool. It was a light but steady wind of morning that filled my sails as I sat at the tiller with a blanket about me, and laying her head to the north.

'We had just rounded the Start at dawn. My companion went below to sleep. I watched, over the quarter, the Start Light flashing pale and white in the broadening day, and at last extinguished. Then the sun rose, as I have said. Immediately after its rising a sort of light haze filled the air to eastward. It was denser than it seemed to be, for it did not obscure the low disc of the sun, nor redden it, but, as you will read in a moment, it performed a mystery. The little ship slipped on, up past the Skerries Bank, and I could see far off the headland which bounds Dart Bay. There was no sail in sight. I was alone upon the sea; and the breeze neither freshening nor lowering, but giving a hearty line of course (along which we slipped, perhaps, five knots or six) made the water speak merrily upon the bows and along the run of our low sides. In this loneliness and content, as I sailed northward, I chanced to look after an hour's steering or so, eastward again towards the open sea – and then it was that there passed me the vision I shall remember for ever, or for so long as the longest life may last.

'Like ghosts, like things themselves made of mist, there passed between me and the newly risen sun, a procession of great forms, all in line, hastening eastward. It was the Fleet recalled.

'The slight haze along that distant water had thickened, perhaps, imperceptibly; or perhaps the great speed of the men-of-war buried them too quickly in the distance. But, from whatever cause, this marvel was of short duration. It was seen for a moment, and in a moment it was gone.

'Then I knew that war would come'.[55]

Salcombe River

The rugged coast west from Start Point past Prawle Point to Bolt Head is interrupted by the Salcombe River, a deep, branching, steep-sided estuary. John Seymour, who sailed in here in his lantern-rigged Northumberland coble, commented: 'The harbour is encumbered with a bar, which makes entry difficult and dangerous at low tide, or at any tide when a southerly or south-easterly is blowing. This is the bar which inspired Tennyson to write 'Crossing the Bar', which he did after a bumpy passage in the yacht *Sunbeam*, when he was staying with James Anthony Froude, the historian'.[14] There is also a claim that he actually composed it on the Lymington ferry, in Hampshire, but Lymington has no such bar. Off Salcombe harbour the sound of waves breaking over the bar as storms approach may have given rise to the legend of the 'moaning of the bar', a bad omen for departing sailors. Salcombe River is a popular sailing area, with wide water at high tide up to Kingsbridge.

John Masefield was certainly inspired by the Salcombe bar:

O, the gold glints bright on the wind-vane as it shifts above the squire's house,
And the water of the bar of Salcombe is muttering about the bows.
O, the salt sea tide of Salcombe, it wrinkles into wisps of foam,
And the church-bells ring in Salcombe to ring poor sailors home.[56]

Salcombe

Burgh Island

The steep coast continues from Bolt Head, a grim rocky cliff to Bolt Tail, to Bigbury Bay, where Burgh Island stands beside the mouth of the Avon estuary. The painter J.M.W. Turner visited Burgh Island, when he explored the area with friends. Eric

Shane has told how they 'made a memorable boat journey down the coast to Burgh Island in Bigbury Bay, ... an extremely rough trip with high seas running. Other members of the party were violently seasick, but Turner was delighted by it all [and was] observed studying the movement of the waves with intense concentration, muttering "that's fine – fine!". When they finally arrived at the island Turner wasted no time in making some sketches whilst freshly caught lobsters (the object of the expedition) were being prepared'.[57]

John Grimson also described Burgh Island, which 'carries on its back a sizeable hotel and a genuine smugglers' haunt, the [fourteenth century] Pilchard Inn. The island may be walked to at low tide but, at any state of the tide, the crossing can be made on a weird sort of "bus-on-stilts" which rolls across the sand on four huge tyres, with its passengers seated on an elevated deck well above the water'.[6]

Hercule Poirot

In the nineteen-thirties Agatha Christie used to spend writing holidays on Burgh Island. It has been suggested that Nigger Island, in *Ten Little Nigger Boys*, was based on Burgh Island, but it was described as being well offshore, and accessible only by boat from the fishing village of Sticklehaven, whence the ten guests were ferried across to meet their successive ends. A more convincing adaptation of the setting appears in *Evil Under the Sun*, where Burgh Island becomes Smugglers' Island, and Bigbury Bay is disguised as Leathercombe Bay. An accompanying map confirms the outline and location, but shows an imaginary causeway across the connecting sand bar. A house, said to have been built on the island by Captain Roger Angmering in 1782, had been converted into the Jolly Roger Hotel in 1922, and enlarged in 1934, a few years before the story began: 'There was one very important person (in his own estimation at least) staying at the Jolly Roger. Hercule Poirot, resplendent in a white duck suit, with a panama hat tilted over his eyes, his moustaches magnificently befurled, lay back in an improved type of deck-chair and surveyed the bathing beach. A series of terraces led down to it from the hotel. On the beach itself were floats, lilos, rubber and canvas boats, balls and rubber toys. There was a long springboard and three rafts at varying distances from the shore.

'Of the bathers, some were in the sea, some were lying stretched out in the sun, and some were anointing themselves carefully with oil.

'There was a path that led off round the cliff on the south-west side of the island. A little way along it, a few steps led down to a series of recesses cut into the cliff and labelled on the hotel map of the island as Sunny Ledges. Here cut out of the cliff were niches with seats in them.'

Further round was Pixy Cove, and on the eastern shore, Gull Cove. There was time for Poirot to meet each of the other hotel guests before one of them, Arlena Marshall, was found strangled in Pixy Cove. In due course Hercule Poirot unravelled the clues, and identified the murderer.[58]

The film version of *Evil Under the Sun*, starring Peter Ustinov, transferred the location from South Devon to Majorca.

Bigbury Bay

'In Bigbury Bay', wrote John Grimson: 'the course of rugged cliffs is broken only by two more drowned valleys which form the estuaries of the Erme and Yealm. For the most part, its cliffs and coves are remote and lonely, its waters so clear that the sea-bed remains visible a hundred yards offshore and displays a changing variety of watery tints, ranging from the sombre brown of the weed-strewn shore through the pale glacier greens of the shallows and out into the ultramarine of the sea'.[6]

In Thomas Hardy's *A Pair of Blue Eyes*, Elfride Swancourt and Henry Knight are on board the steamship *Juliet*: 'All up the coast, prominences singled themselves out from recesses. Then a rosy sky spread over the eastern sea and behind the low line of the land, flinging its livery in dashes upon the thin airy clouds in that direction. Every projection on the land seemed now so many fingers anxious to catch a little of the liquid light thrown so prodigally over the sky. The bluff and bare contours of Start Point caught the brightest, earliest glow of all and so also did the sides of its white lighthouse, perched upon a shelf in its precipitous front like a mediaeval saint in a niche. Their lofty neighbour Bolt Head on the left remained as yet ungilded, and retained its gray.

'Then up came the sun, as it were in jerks, just to seaward of the easternmost point of land, flinging out a Jacob's-ladder path of light from itself. The inferior dignitaries of the shore – Froward Point, Berry Head and Prawle – all had acquired their share of illumination ere this, and at length the very smallest protruberance of wave, cliff, or inlet, even to the innermost recesses of the lovely valley of the Dart, had its portion; and sunlight, now the common possession of all, ceased to be the wonderful and coveted thing it had been a short half hour before.

'After breakfast, Plymouth arose into view, and grew distincter to their nearing vision, the Breakwater appearing like a streak of phosphoric light upon the surface of the sea'.[59]

Newton Ferrers and Noss Mayo

Newton Ferrers is a pretty village on a deep yachting ria, facing across to Noss Mayo, to which it is linked by a causeway exposed at low tide. Jonathan Raban sailed into the Yealm estuary in 1982, using Keble Chatterton's *Yachtsman's Pilot* of 1933, which had described it as "one of the most secluded and lovely spots to be found in Southern England": 'In search of loveliness, I motored east through the grey swell and found Chatterton's first set of marks – a church spire followed by a pair of white-painted wooden triangles on posts, one on the shore inside the estuary mouth, the other high up on a hill behind. So far, so good.

'I waited while the triangle on the shore moved slowly rightwards to join the triangle on the hill, then swung the boat round and squeezed it by within feet of Yealm Head, where the sea slopped and piled on the rocks, blackening the lichens and leaving the exposed granite* looking like wet moleskin. The course zig-zagged through high bluffs of trees and bracken, going east, then northeast, then southeast, then northeast again, then finally northwest into a deep wooded cleft containing a mile-long pool of dark water like a secret lake. A Victorian hotel stood on a sandy point, half hidden in pines. A dozen early season yachts swung on their moorings. The noise of my engine, echoing in the hollow, disturbed a wading heron, which flipped off up into the woods on boxy wings'.[55]

Noss Mayo sounds Irish, but thirteenth century records show it as Nesse Matheu, the promontory of Matthew, a local lord of the manor.

Devon Sailors

Plymouth Sound is sheltered by a mile-long breakwater designed by John Rennie, built of granite and limestone, and completed in 1840. Plymouth has a long nautical history. In 1562 John Hawkins embarked from here on an expedition to collect black slaves from West Africa and take them to the West Indies, to be traded for gold and sugar. A few years later another Devonian, Francis Drake sailed out to plunder the Caribbean, Panama and Peru, and circumnavigate the globe, returning to Plymouth on 26 September 1580. Richard Grenville sailed from here on 9 April 1585 with a small fleet to establish an English colony on Roanoke Island, in what is now North Carolina: it quickly failed. Walter Raleigh was a Devon man who organised this venture, in an era when England's somewhat piratical ships sailed from Plymouth into confrontations with the growing Spanish empire. Francis Drake, led attacks on northern Spain, Spanish colonies in the West Indies, and the port of Cadiz as war broke out between England and Spain.

The Spanish Armada

'On Plymouth Hoe', wrote Nigel Calder, 'on July 29 1588 Drake and the other commanders were playing at bowls when word came that the [Spanish] Armada had been sighted off the Lizard, away to the west. If Drake really did say "There's time to finish the game and beat the Spaniards too", he would have had good reason. The tidal current was setting into Plymouth at the time, and an onshore wind meant that there was no hope of moving the fleet until nightfall. Some of the ships were beached, having the summer growth of weed and barnacles scraped from their bottoms. So while signal fires were carrying the news of the Armada's sighting all across the kingdom, the fleet was a scene of fretting men and immobile ships.

'As the Spanish did not mean to attack Plymouth, the delay did not matter; in fact it helped the English fleet to station itself upwind of the Armada. In the long chase up the Channel the average speed was two knots. Although they

---

* Yachtsmen are rarely geologists: the 'granite' near Yealm Head is a Devonian metamorphic rock.

barked like terriers with their long-range guns, the English did little harm to the Armada until the culminating fight off Gravelines'.[60]

In *The Master Mariner*, Nicholas Monsarrat evoked Plymouth as it had been just before Sir Francis Drake confronted the Armada, seen through the eyes of Matthew Lawe, Drake's coxswain: 'At his back lay Sutton Pool, the inner harbour of Plymouth; this Pool and the nearby Cattewater, and the whole Sound itself, was one forest of ships, a woven pattern of drying sails, steep oaken hills, rocking masts, and flags and banners streaming in the brisk southerly wind. Before him lay the town, clamorous and astir with men, and the green slopes of Plymouth Hoe. But Matthew Lawe was precoccupied with the smaller things, and his main gaze rested on the tide-mark: the rime of flotsam on the sand, the seaweed, the chippings of wood, the pale husks of shrimp and crab, the rope-strands, the polished shells of periwinkle-blue, blood-red, dawn-yellow.

'By day the ship-boats, cockboats and pinnaces sped to and fro, bearing men and weapons; the fly-boats loaded with provisions went about their dutiful business, the powder-hoys with their red flags of danger wove carefully through the fleet; on shore, the shipwrights and the sailmakers and the armourers toiled against the run of the clock to fashion whatever the captains and the sailing-masters and the gunners demanded – whether it was new spars, flaxen ropes, brass culverin and basilisk, fresh-water casks or cross-bar shot for the cannon-royal.

'By night these same men wandered ashore, crowding past the corbelled houses, thronging the Barbican, drinking in the taverns at the sign of the Turk's Head in St Andrews Street and the Mitre and the Pope's Head in Looe Street, where the Vice-Admiral himself had his household'.[61]

The Pilgrim Fathers

Plymouth was also the final port of departure for the *Mayflower* with the Pilgrim Fathers in 1620, commemorated by the Mayflower Stone and Steps in Sutton Harbour. *Speedwell*, which had left Southampton with *Mayflower* in August, sprung a leak, and the two ships called at Dartmouth for repairs; their voyage then got as far as the Isles of Scilly before more leaks in *Speedwell* forced a return to Plymouth. Her passengers transferred to *Mayflower*, which left alone on 6 September. Shirley Harrison continued the story: 'One hundred and one men, women and children were to embark on that Atlantic crossing divided into 'Saints' and 'Strangers'. The 'Saints' were the residue of the Leyden Community who were hoping for great things for their children in the New World. The 'Strangers' were ordinary passengers, servants and a group of men who had indentured themselves for seven years to pay for their passage. No one came from Plymouth.

'Down on the quay that day the little ship was watched sadly by a small group of those who had to be left behind and a collection of local people. Edward Winslow, one of the Pilgrims, wrote in his diary: "Wednesday 6th September. The winds coming east-north-east, a fine smalle gale. We loosed from Plymouth having been kindly entertained and courteously used by diverse friends there dwelling."

'And so began the voyage which was at the time unremarkable, but was in fact to prove the most significant expedition in British colonial history'.[62] *Mayflower* made her way across the Atlantic to Cape Cod, and eventually anchored off the Massachusetts coast to found another Plymouth.

Plymouth Sound

The Royal Dockyard, on the shores of the Tamar estuary, was founded in 1691, and a few years later, in 1724, Daniel Defoe came here: 'I was at Plymouth, and walking on the Hoo, which is a plain on the edge of the sea, looking to the road, I observed the evening so serene, so calm, so bright, and the sea so smooth, that a finer sight, I think, I never saw; there was very little wind, but what was, seemed to be westerly; and, about an hour after, it blew a little breeze at south-west, with which wind there came into the Sound, that night, and the next morning, a fleet of fourteen sail of ships, from Barbadoes; richly loaden, for London. Having been long at sea, most of the captains and passengers came on shore to refresh themselves and the ships rode all in the Sound on that side next to Catwater.

'The next day the wind began to freshen, especially in the afternoon, and the sea to be disturbed, and very hard it blew at night, but all was well for that time;

but the night after it blew a dreadful storm, not much inferior, for the time it lasted, to the storm [that in the previous year] blew down the lighthouse on the Eddystone; about midnight the noise indeed was very dreadful, what with the roaring of the sea, and of the wind, intermixed with the firing of guns for help from the ships, the cries of the seamen and people on shore, and, which was worse, the cries of those, which were driven onshore by the tempest, and dashed in pieces. In a word, all the fleet, except three, or thereabouts, were dashed to pieces against the rocks, and sunk in the sea, most of the men being drowned. One ship in the dark of the night, the men not knowing where they were, run into Catwater, and run on shore there, by which she was however saved from shipwreck.

'This was a melancholy morning indeed; nothing was to be seen but wrecks of the ships, and foaming furious sea, in that very place where they rode all in joy and triumph, but the evening before'.[49]

Other notable departures from Devon's Plymouth were Captain Cook on the *Endeavour* in 1768 and Charles Darwin on the *Beagle* in 1831. It was from here, too, that Sir Francis Chichester set out on his lone sailing adventures, including his round-the-world voyage in *Gipsy Moth IV* in 1966: 'Gipsy Moth IV lay to a mooring off Mashford's Yard at Cremyll for a thousand and one last-minute jobs to be done. The time of departure was drawing very close. It was good to be at Mashford's again, the starting point of all my singlehanded ocean sailing. Sheila and Giles helped me to sail *Gipsy Moth IV* from the mooring at Mashford's to the Royal Western Yacht Club's normal starting line off Plymouth Hoe. I crossed the line as the gun fired and was off on my 14,000-mile sail [to Sydney]. It was a sparkling sunny morning and I added my big staysail and the mizzen as I made my way out of Plymouth Sound. Eighty-eight minutes after the start, Eddystone Lighthouse was abeam'.[63]

Eddystone Lighthouse

The first lighthouse on these dangerous rocks was Henry Winstanley's Tower, completed in 1698, but it disappeared (together with Winstanley and several other men) in the Great Storm of 26 November 1703. A second was destroyed by fire, and in 1754 John Smeaton completed a solid Tower of Portland Stone. Unfortunately, fissures appeared in the underlying rock, and another (the present) lighthouse was added in 1852. Part of Smeaton's Tower was then dismantled, and rebuilt on The Hoe. Sir Arthur Quiller-Couch reflected in 'The Lighthouse Seat':

> *Here from the Lighthouse garden seat*
> *I watched the steamers trailing West;*
> *Almost I hear their engines beat*
> *And take their pulsing to my breast.*

So still the evening silken-spread!
  So soft the twilit Channel heaves!
As soft the lantern overhead
  In skeins of light its warning weaves.[64]

Plymouth

Early in the century, Ernest Radford mused on Plymouth from the Bay of Naples:

Oh! what know they of harbours
Who toss not on the sea?
They tell of fairer havens,
But none so fair there be

As Plymouth town outstretching
Her quiet arms to me,
Her breast's broad welcome spreading
From Mewstone to Penlee.

And with this home-thought, darling,
Come crowding thoughts of thee;
Oh! what know they of harbours
Who toss not on the sea?[65]

Thomas Hardy's first wife, Emma Gifford, came from Plymouth, but Hardy didn't return there until after her death, when in 1913 he began this poem:

A very West-of-Wessex girl
  As blithe as blithe could be,
Was once well-known to me,
  And she would laud her native town,
And hope and hope that we
  Might sometime study up and down
Its charms in company.

But never I squired my Wessex girl
  In jaunts to Hoe or street
When hearts were high in heat,
  Nor saw her in the marbled ways
Where market-people meet
  That in her bounding early days
Were friendly with her feet.

> *Yet now my West-of-Wessex girl,*
>   *When midnight hammers slow*
> *From Andrew's, blow by blow,*
>   *A phantom draws me by the hand*
> *To the place – Plymouth Hoe –*
>   *Where side by side in life, as planned,*
> *We never were to go!*[66]

Hardy was also thinking of Emma Gifford when he described Plymouth in another poem:

> *I reach the marble-streeted town,*
>   *Whose 'Sound' outbreathes its air*
>   *Of sharp sea-salts;*
> *I see the movement up and down*
>   *As when she was there.*
> *Ships of all countries come and go,*
>   *The bandsmen boom in the sun*
>   *A throbbing waltz;*
> *The schoolgirls laugh along the Hoe*
>   *As when she was one.*[66]

Geoffrey Grigson included this poem in an anthology, and offered a sequel:

> *Revisiting your marble-paved sea-perfumed town*
> *I find it, like the middle-class family of that*
> *Girl you married, much run down.*
>
> *I know, bombs fell; but years ago.*
> *Bombs smashed the Regency facades*
> *Which led you uphill to the Hoe.*
>
> *Whereon later no aching comfort could be found*
> *In pacing the daisied ground, in a drizzle*
> *Vapouring as usual from the Sound.*
>
> *Now out of irregular rubbly open spaces*
> *Dirt concrete rises and replaces your town's*
> *Stuccoed dignities and maritime graces,*
>
> *And only in a neglected dead-end lane*
> *I've seen, striped black or rose, a slab or two*
> *Of your old marble glittering in the rain.*

The other slabs are uniformly matt and grey
As if your town were now re-paved with all
The more aching recollections of your stay'.[67]

The Bombing of Plymouth

Plymouth was severely damaged by bombing in the Second World War. R.A.J. Walling told how, in March 1941 'the King and Queen had come on a visit to see what the city had already suffered, to meet the people who were doing the work, to speak words of encouragement. They had taken tea with the Lord Mayor and the Lady Mayoress at their house on the Hoe, and at six o'clock they drove away.

'Less than three hours later the enemy roared over in darkness, raining fire, destruction and death from the sky. Going from east to west along that three miles of crescent, in seven nights he methodically destroyed everything. Everywhere his fire-bombs reduced stores, shops, houses, streets, whole districts to gaunt and blackened ruin. He killed over a thousand men, women and children among the civilian population; he wounded five times as many. He razed to the ground the dwellings of 10,000 people; he made many more uninhabitable; he damaged the houses of 70,000.

'There was that fine square – Church, Guildhall, Post Office, Council Chamber – the focal point of religious and social life, the omphalos of the city; at the end of three days it was no more. The noble tower under which Drake had walked into church the day they elected him mayor still stood. But the church behind it was a mere shell. The streets around, the formerly crowded, gaily coloured, busy shopping streets – Old Town Street, Bedford Street, George Street – were levelled to the ground. Charles Church was a roofless, sooty skeleton.

'Those who knew Plymouth before the blitz (and among them nearly every man in the British navy and thousands of visitors from overseas who landed and passed through it) could hardly recognize a physical feature of the place'.[68]

Plymouth was soon rebuilt when the war ended, a modern glass and concrete city rising upon the ruins, and like its counterpart, Brest in Brittany, it is still very much a naval place. Plymouth Dockyard, which had been re-named Devonport in the nineteenth century, has continued to prosper.

The Royal Albert Bridge

The majestic bridge that carries trains across the Tamar and into Cornwall was designed by Isambard Kingdom Brunel, whose many other engineering works included Paddington Station, the Suspension Bridge over the Avon Gorge at Bristol, and the steamship *Great Eastern*. His intention was to provide a 'triumphal arch' for the Great Western Railway entering Cornwall. Derrick Beckett described it under construction: 'The floating out of the first arch/chain span took place on 1 September 1857, and the whole operation was directed by its designer from a platform in the centre of a truss. Even allowing for the fact that Brunel had the advantage of observing the floating and lifting of Robert Stephenson's Britannia Tubular Bridge girders [over Menai Strait in Wales] some seven years previously, the event, witnessed by thousands, can only be described as heroic. By means of an elaborate system of signals, the truss was moved out into the river and then swung into position between the piers. The whole operation took two hours and was conducted in complete silence. This was followed by a vocal response which would now be reserved for kicking a ball in a net'.[69]

Sadly Brunel was ill and unable to attend the official opening of the bridge by Prince Albert on 3 May 1859, but he was able to visit it shortly before his death. He had said that he expected it to last a hundred years, and then to no longer be needed; but he underestimated on both counts. It is still in use, and in 1961 was parallelled by a new suspension bridge, with an 1100 foot span, built to carry road traffic and replace the Saltash Ferry, which for more than six centuries had plied to and fro across the Tamar between the Devon and the Cornish shores.

Sea Kale

S O U T H
C O R N W A L L

Saltash

The terraced slate-roofed cottages and little quays of Saltash look back eastward across the Tamar into Devonshire, but we have crossed the frontier, and are now in Cornwall. In 1905 Philip Porter described the prospect from Saltash: 'The grandest view of the River Tamar is to be obtained from the delightful acclivity on which St. Budeaux Church rests. Standing just on the north side of the Tower, we are instantly charmed with a panorama of the wide spreading river, its numerous creeks at our feet, and the great Cornish hills retreating illimitally in the distance beyond. Saltash is built upon a hill, and its picturesque environs are of that undulatory nature peculiar to the West of England; gentle slopes and swelling hills alternate with sunny valleys and fertile coombs. River and harbour, hill and dale, ancestral mansion and lowly cot, swelling fields and sombre wood, comprise a perfect panorama of beauty'.[1]

Saltash and shellfishing were commemorated in the poem 'A Cockle Woman', quoted by Philip Porter:

> *Where Tamar's waters roll along*
> *O'er muddy banks and rocks,*
> *The ancient Town of Saltash stands,*
> *Well known for pickle cocks.*
>
> *It claims the right to shrimp and dredge,*
> *Within the headlands round,*
> *From Shagstone up to Ogle Tor,*
> *The Bay and Plymouth Sound.*[1]

St. German's River leads westward into branching, narrowing valleys, and to the south, in a peaceful setting, is Antony House, designed by Thomas Repton and built in 1712-21. Naval installations and warships dominate the Hamoaze, off Torpoint, where the Tamar estuary is broad and deep. St. John's Lake and Millbrook Lake are wide waters at high tide, but seaweedy mudflats emerge when

111

the tide falls, and the bold promontory of Mount Edgcumbe slopes down to the little village of Cremyll, quiet in contrast with the bustling docks and city of Plymouth across the water.

Mount Edgcumbe was formerly the 'stately home' of the Earl of Mount Edgcumbe, whose wife, Lady Ernestine, wrote in 1897: 'The first sight that greets the sailor returning from a three years' commission, or of a soldier returning from India, is this peninsula, woods crowning its red cliffs, the trees growing down so close to the water's edge that they almost dip their boughs into the blue waves (for they *are* blue), and the deer park with its hills and valleys diversified by clumps of pinasters and Scotch firs, and old thorn trees in blossom, or, if the season be autumn, the bracken glowing red and gold in the sunshine'.[2]

Originally a Tudor mansion, the house was destroyed by bombs in 1941, but it has been rebuilt and stands in 800 acres of varied gardens and woodlands in what is now Mount Edgcumbe Country Park.

Tamar Suspension Bridge and Brunel Railway Bridge at Saltash

Cawsand

In the next bay is the little village of Cawsand, of which Nigel Calder wrote: 'Cawsand's picturesque cottages lead in narrow streets down to a quay and a pleasant beach that faces the morning sun. Even to-day it is an out-of-the-way spot; anyone approaching by land has to make a grand tour around Plymouth harbour to reach it. Yet Cawsand offers a sheltered bay in a strategic position beside the Channel, concealed by Picklecombe Point from Plymouth town and the King's men. As a result, this village was a prime centre for smuggling in the early nineteenth century.

'In March 1824 a Cawsand smuggling cutter called *Two Brothers* arrived here from France on a moonless night. A revenue cruiser spotted her approaching the shore, and chased her on to the uncompleted Plymouth breakwater. At daylight the smugglers were found clinging to the wreckage of their boat, along with more than a hundred tubs of French brandy. Other tubs had broken open in the wreck. It was one minor incident in the never-ending war between the seafarers of the English Channel and the officials who want to tax their cargoes and stop the running of contraband'.[3]

Rame Head

From Cawsand the road curves up the side of the hill and over to Rame Head. This is one of the several bold Channel headlands mentioned in sea shanties, and looks out towards Eddystone Lighthouse, which can be seen in clear weather on its rocks 8 miles offshore. It is bordered by the long curve of Whitsand Bay, where the Atlantic swell breaks on a rocky shore with sandy coves, and the view west is towards Tregantle Fort, built as a National Monument after the Napoleonic War. Crowning the Head is the ruined fourteenth century chapel of St. Michael. The coastal footpath then skirts rocky shores and diminutive coves towards the mouth of the Looe River.

Looe

Wilkie Collins walked this way in 1860, and found Looe: 'one of the prettiest and most primitive places in England. The river divides it into East and West Looe; and the view from the bridge, looking towards the two little colonies of houses thus separated, is in some respects almost unique.

'At each side you see high ranges of beautifully wooded hills; here and there a cottage peeps out among the trees, the winding path that leads to it being now lost to sight in the thick foliage, now visible again as a thin serpentine line of soft grey. Midway on the slopes appear the gardens of Looe, built up the acclivity on stone terraces one above another; thus displaying the veritable garden architecture of the mountains of Palestine magically transported to the sides of an English hill. Here, in this soft and genial atmosphere, the hydrangea is a common flower-bed ornament, the fuchsia grows lofty and luxuriant in the poorest cottage garden, the myrtle flourishes close to the sea-shore, and the tender tamarisk is the wild plant of every farmer's hedge. Looking lower down the hills yet, you see the houses of the town straggling out towards the sea along each bank of the river, in mazes of little narrow streets; curious old quays project over the water at different points; coast-trade vessels are being loaded and unloaded, built in one place and repaired in another, all within view; while the prospect of hills, harbour, and houses thus quaintly combined together, is beautifully closed by the English Channel, just visible as a small strip of blue water.

'Then, when you have at last threaded your way successfully through the streets, and have got out on the beach, you see a pretty miniature bay, formed by the extremity of a green hill on the right, and by fine jagged slate-rocks on the left. Before this seaward quarter of the town is erected a strong bulwark of rough stones, to resist the incursion of high tides. Here, the idlers of the place assemble to lounge and gossip, to look out for any outward-bound ships that are to be seen in the Channel, and to criticise the appearance and glorify the capabilities of the little fleet of Looe fishing-boats, riding snugly at anchor before them at the entrance of the bay'.[4]

Geoffrey Grigson was born near Looe, and reminisced: 'The Looes were never meant to be big. Two streams come down two deep valleys to the tidal water. Five minutes walk from the sea, the two valleys merge into one. At low tide the floor of the valley is left almost dry; so it was easy in the Middle Ages to build a bridge a hundred and twenty eight yards long, joining east to west. The bridge (nearer the sea than the modern bridge) lasted from the fifteenth century until 1855. Above the bridge on the west there is no room for anything but the mill and the mill pool. On the east, the narrow space between hill and water leaves only room for the railway and the road. It is only within my own memory that shops have crept up to the bridge in East Looe, the heart of which still beats between the sea and the modern guildhall.

'The beach is not very long. Its capacity for bathers, sleepers, paddlers and the architects of the sand castle is another limitation to the swelling and the absolute transformation of Looe. And man's work on either side of the harbour is most of it fitting and decent enough. The quays, the nineteenth century warehouses, the banjo pier (made for use and not pleasure) speak with a Cornish or at least a maritime accent. The bridge is solid and human. The streets wiggle like the ancient footpaths they have replaced. Even the railway from Liskeard cannot run straight.

'But the valley is still wild; and it keeps its wildness because its sides are mostly too steep for cultivation, because the floor of the valley is poorly drained and seldom much more than a hundred yards across, and because the roads – there are few of them – cross down one hillside and up the other. No road penetrates right up the valley parallel to the little trout, sea trout, salmon, dipper, and kingfisher and sandpiper river, which runs down under the alders and over stones of red-veined quartz to the wider tidal portions above the sea and below the limekiln.

'To get to know such a valley as one knows the furniture in a room or the body of a woman, one must know it and possess it at all hours and in all months from childhood'.[5]

West Looe has hotels and guest houses looking back eastward to Rame Head along the Seaton-Downderry coast, and out towards Looe Island, which the Luftwaffe bombed in the Second World War, evidently mistaking it for a battleship. They failed to sink it.

In 1964 Evelyn Atkins and her sister bought Looe Island. She described the trip they made when they first acquired it: 'The weather being fair and the sea calm, we hired a boatman to take us across. First we sailed right round our future home taking photographs. Although only twenty two and a half acres the island, with its indented coastline, appeared much larger. The west coast wild and rugged and remote looked like a Land's End in miniature. Here, above the forbidding cliffs of rock and caves, the island rose to a height of 150 feet. On the north and east the wooded hillside sloped steeply down to cliffs above shelving beaches of rock, sand and shingle. The south coast, like the west, was buttressed with perpendicular rocky cliffs, but sloped down to a promontory on the south-eastern tip where it was joined to the little island by a stony bridge. It was here that the tabernacle for the flagstaff that we had mistaken for a rival purchaser stood, a lonely sentinel against the skyline. The trees that bordered the cliffs of the eastern shore and climbed the slopes of the hill that crowned the island were a blaze of reds, oranges and gold as the leaves gleamed in the autumn sunlight.

Looe

'We landed for a short time and were amazed to find outdoor tomatoes ripening, the trusses heavy with fruit; butterflies fluttering among huge clusters of blackberries along the hedgerows and, incredibly, we had to take off our jackets and walk in short-sleeved summer dresses as we walked down the cliff path to the little island. And this was late afternoon near the end of October. We had stepped into another world. We were in time to see a most spectacular sunset

115

from the bridge. The lichen-covered rocks below us and the dramatic cliffs of the southern coastline glowed gold, purple and wondrous shades of rose in the rays of the setting sun far out in the Atlantic'.[6]

Modern Looe is the headquarters of a shark fishery, of which Darrell Bates wrote: 'Despite its other occupations Looe has always remained a substantial fishing port, and it is partly for this reason perhaps that shark fishing was first developed here in 1952 as an added attraction for visitors in the summer. It has been similarly developed in many other towns on the south coast of Devon and Cornwall and at Newquay. It is not cheap but it is now so well arranged that you will be unlucky if you don't come back with something. No skill or experience is needed on the part of the visitor, and as young boys and girls are almost as likely to bring in a 100 lb shark as a seasoned fisherman it makes an excellent family outing. The boatmen usually go out for ten or twenty miles and attract the shark with a trail of chopped-up mackerel or pilchard. The most common catch is the slim, dark-blue blue shark which grow up to twenty feet in length but tend to average about sixty pounds in weight. Thicker and heavier porbeagle sharks may also be caught, and even larger mako sharks which run to four or five hundred pounds have been found farther west off Falmouth Bay and the Lizard.'[7]

Polperro

Along the coast is Polperro, a fishing village in a cove at the mouth of a deep valley; it was another place damaged severely in the great storm of 1824. Jonathan Couch, in his 1871 *History of Polperro*, wrote: 'The vale or rather *coomb* in which it [Polperro] is situated is long and narrow, winding singularly, so that where one hill recedes, the opposite advances to fill up the vacancy; and its steep sides look as if they had been torn asunder by some violent convulsion of nature, and still bore marks of the disruption. At Crumplehorn, a hamlet some three furlongs up the valley, is the confluence of two coombs, each with its attendant rill. Converging they form Polperro valley. The sides of the precipitous hills, on either side, are roughened by bare rocks rising tier above tier, or in almost vertical ridges.

'The harbour of Polperro, locally termed *haven*, opens into the ocean in a south-easterly direction, and runs up into the land a furlong. It is guarded on its western extremity by a natural breakwater jutting out from the base of the Chapel Hill. The *Peak*, as this rocky barrier is named, forms a bold and picturesque object of no ordinary character; its craggy pinnacles rising in two huge masses, to the height of 90 feet. On the eastern side, the mouth of the haven is bounded by the hills' abrupt descent into the sea, ending in a ledge of irregular wave-worn rock. The inward sweep of the wave is broken by two piers, both thrown out from the foot of the south-western hill, and built of the blue and red schist of the neighbour-hood'.[8]

Nigel Calder found Polperro: 'the very model of a smuggling village. The nearer headland, with a small white lighthouse, is called Spy House Point. The harbour, 150 metres wide, dries out, and at low tide sightseeing launches lie toppled on the mud. Polperro, remember, was where the revenue men were said to row like ploughboys. Here, and all along England's south coast, the locals titillate visitors with reminders of the heyday of free trade. The inns and coves and caves are real enough, but don't mistake these basking days of summer for smugglers' weather. The best time for a run was a dirty, starless night in midwinter, when the rocks fountained with spray and the revenue men collapsed over their oars from exhaustion and hypothermia.'[3]

In summer Polperro is crowded with ambling tourists. The streets narrow to mere pathways on either side of the harbour and there are many gift shops selling piskies and other trinkets. Paul Theroux walked through in 1982: 'Polperro was in such a deep ravine the sun did not strike it in the morning. I walked through the damp dark village – straight overhead the sky was blue – and climbed out of the little harbour on to the cliffs, just as a bright mist descended. It hung lightly over the rocky shore and the purple sea, and created luminous effects of live creatures appearing and disappearing near the tumbledown cliffs, and dripped morning light on the waves. The whole cliff was green, from the top to the sea, full of ivy and meadow grass and brambles.

'On the path to Fowey the cliffs were like steep meadows. The bramble bushes and the gorse made a mild reflection in the water; the trailing ivy gave a delicacy to the sea, and the foliage muffled the wind. The air was sweetened by all this greenery'.[9]

Polruan

Fowey River opens into a broad estuary, with the small port of Polruan on its eastern side and ferries to the town of Fowey. This little village has steep, narrow streets running down to the quay and was a favourite spot for writers: Sir Arthur Quiller-Couch called it 'Ruan' or 'quaint Penpoodle'; Leo Walmsley referred to it as 'Porthkerris' and it was 'Plyn' in Daphne du Maurier's *The Loving Spirit*.

Fowey

Fowey is protected by another of Henry VIII's fortifications, St. Catherine's Castle. Arthur H. Norway described in 1897 how 'The town and river of Fowey lie so deeply in the valley that nothing is seen of either till the road has merged upon an open hillside almost overhanging the convolutions of the estuary; and the suddenness with which this view discloses itself adds immensely to the effect. One moment there is nothing to be seen but the windings of an unlovely road. The next there has opened far below a dark green highway, broad and spacious, branching among hills. Deep down at the foot of the descent lie the roofs and cottages of Bodinnick, with its heavy ferry boat lumbering across to Fowey, of which quaint hillside town more and more is seen at every winding of the road. The salt air mingles strangely with the scent of violets as we descend the hill, and the sweet odour of the woodlands unites with a decided savour of tarry rope. One could drop a pebble on the roofs of the four or five houses which stand about the higher end of the sloping pier, pretty white-washed cottages, of that neat aspect which sometimes enables the Cornishman to recognise the dwellings of his own people in other countries.

'The dusk has fallen while we are waiting for the ferry boat. The few vessels lying in the harbour have lit their lanterns. Across the water come the faint noises of a wheezy hurdy-gurdy, and the cries of children. We are landed on a dark and slippery jetty, and go through the dim old town too weary to notice more than that its streets are steep and tortuous, and that through many openings and courtyards we see the dark water washing to and fro.'[10]

Sir Arthur Quiller-Couch, widely known as 'Q', lived here from 1892 until his death in 1944, and wrote several novels set in and around Fowey, disguised as *Troy Town*. In his autobiography he recalled arriving at Fowey as a schoolboy about to go up to Oxford: 'I stood and gazed on the harbour, the track of the moon on its water, the riding lights of two or three small schooners at anchor in the shadow of the farther shore, and decided that this were no bad place in which to live'. Later, 'the most and best part of my Long Vacations found me ever at Fowey 'like faithful hound returning.'[11]

Sir Arthur became the first Professor of English at Cambridge University, but made his home in Fowey. He enjoyed being Commodore of the Regatta, and Mayor of Fowey. He was a prolific writer and anthologist, and had some donnish fun with English spelling in *The Harbour of Fowey*:

> O, the Harbour of Fowey
>   Is a beautiful spot,
> And it's there I enjowey
>   To sail in a yot;
> Or to race in a yacht
>   Round a mark or a buoy-

Such a beautiful spacht
  Is the Harbour of Fuoy!

When her anchor is weighed
  And the water she ploughs,
Upon neat lemoneighed
  O it's then I caroughs;
And I take Watt's hymns
  And I sing them aloud
When it's homeward she skymns
  O'er the waters she ploud.

But the wave mountain-high,
  And the violent storm,
Do I risk them? Not Igh!
  But prefer to sit worm
With a book on my knees
  By the library fire
While I list to the brees
  Rising hire and hire.

And so, whether I weigh
  Up the anchor or not,
I am happy each deigh
  In my home or my yot;
Every care I resign,
  Every comfort enjoy,
In this cottage of mign
  By the Harbour of Foy.

And my leisure's addressed
  To composing of verse
Which, if hardly the bessed,
  Might be easily werse.
And, the spelling I use
  Should the critics condemn,
Why, I have my own vuse
  And I don't think of themn.

Yes, I have my own views:
But the teachers I follow
Are the Lyrical Miews

And the Delphic Apollow.
Unto them I am debtor
For spelling and rhyme,
And I'm doing it bebtor
And bebtor each thyme.[12]

A Day in Troy

Quiller-Couch spent a great deal of time in Fowey, and his deep affection for the place was frequently expressed. In the Prologue to *The Delectable Duchy*, for example, he told the story of a journalist friend who came to spend a day in 'Troy':

'A week ago, my friend the Journalist wrote to remind me that once upon a time I had offered him a bed in my cottage at Troy and promised to show him the beauties of the place. He was about (he said) to give himself a fortnight's holiday, and had some notion of using that time to learn what Cornwall was like. He could spare but one day for Troy, and hardly looked to exhaust its attractions. By anticipation he spoke of my home as a "nook". Its windows look down upon a harbour wherein, day by day, vessels of every nation and men of large experience are for ever going and coming; and beyond the harbour, upon leagues of open sea, highway of the vastest traffic in the world.

'I answered his letter, warmly repeating the invitation; and last week he arrived. I learned that he had already seen half the Duchy, in seven days. I began to feel that I lived in a nook, and to wonder how I could spin out its attractions to cover a whole day: for I could not bear to think of his departing with secret regret for his lavished time. In a flash I saw the truth: that my love for this spot is built up of numberless trivialities, of small memories all incommunicable, or ridiculous when communicated; a scrap of local speech heard at this corner, a pleasant native face remembered in that doorway, a battered vessel dropping anchor – she went out in the spring with her crew singing dolefully; and the grey-bearded man waiting in his boat beneath her counter till the custom-house officers have made their survey is the father of one among the crew, and is waiting to take his son's hand again, after months of absence. Would this interest my friend, if I pointed it out to him? Or, if I walk with him by the path above the creek, what will he care to know that on this particular bank the violets always bloom earliest – that one of a line of yews that top the churchyard wall is remarkable because a pair of missel-thrushes have chosen it to build in for three successive years? The violets are gone. The empty nest has almost dissolved under the late heavy rains, and the yew is so like its fellows that I myself have no idea why the birds chose it. The longer I reflected the more certain I felt that my friend could find all he wanted in the guide-books.

'None the less, I did my best: rowed him for a mile or two up the river; took him out to sea and along the coast for half a dozen miles. The water was choppy, as it is under the slightest breeze from the south-east; and the Journalist was seasick; but seemed to mind this very little, and recovered sufficiently to ask my boatman two or three hundred questions before we reached the harbour again. Then we landed and explored the Church. This took us some time, owing to several freaks in its construction, for which I blessed the memory of its old successive builders. We went on to the Town Hall, the old Stannary Prison (now in ruins), the dilapidated Block-houses, the Battery. We traversed the town from end to end and studied the barge-boards and punkin-ends of every old house. I had meanly ordered that dinner should be ready half an hour earlier than usual, and, as it was, the objects of interest just lasted out'.

'After dinner, the Journalist sought leave to go and write an article on Troy for his newspaper: this, it seemed, was a working holiday in Cornwall.

'He finished his coffee, lit a fresh cigarette, and strolled off to the little library where I usually work. I stepped out upon the veranda and looked down at the harbour at my feet, where already the vessels were hanging out their lamps in the twilight. I had looked down thus, and at this hour, a thousand times; and always the scene had something new to reveal to me, and much more to withhold – small subtleties such as a man finds in his wife, however ordinary she may appear to other people. And here, in the next room, was a man who, in half a dozen hours, felt able to describe Troy; to deck her out, at least, in language that should captivate a million or so breakfasting Britons.

'In an hour's time the Journalist came sauntering out to me, and announced that his [article] was written. We went indoors, and he read it over to me. It was a surprisingly brilliant piece of description; and accurate, too. He had not called it "a little fishing-town" for instance, as so many visitors have done in my hearing, though hardly half-a-dozen fishing boats put out from the harbour. I corrected a date and then sat silent. It amazed me that a man who could see so much, should fail to perceive that what he had seen was of no account in comparison with what he had not; or that, if he did indeed perceive this, he could write such stuff with such gusto. "To be capable of so much and content with so little!" I thought; and then broke off to wonder if, after all, he were not right. To-morrow he would be on his way, crowding his mind with quick and brilliant impressions, hurrying, living, telling his fellows a thousand useful and pleasant things, while I pored about to discover one or two for them.'[13]

April the First

'Q' is commemorated by a granite monolith on the spur on Hall Walk, looking down the harbour and out to sea. Fowey is still a compact little town, with its triangular Trafalgar Square, the Town Quay, and a Market Street. Q's stories of 'Troy' are rich in character:[14]

'Next morning, almost before the sun was up, all Troy was in possession of the news; and in Troy all that is personal has a public interest. It is this local spirit that marks off the Trojan from all others.

'In consequence, long before ten o'clock struck, it was clear that some popular movement was afoot; and by half-past eleven the road to the railway station was crowded with Trojans of all sorts and conditions – boatmen, pilots, fishermen, sailors out of employ, the local photographer, men from the shipbuilding yards, makers of ship's biscuit, of ropes, of sails, chandlers, block and pump manufacturers, loafers – representatives, in short, of all the staple industries: women with baskets, women with babies, women with both, even a few farmers in light gigs with their wives, or in carts with their families, a sprinkling from Penpoodle across the harbour – high and low, Church and Dissent, with children by the hundred. Some even proposed to ring the church bells and fire the cannon by the harbour's mouth; but the ringers and artillery men preferred to come to see the sight. As it was, the "George" floated proudly from the church tower, and the Fife and Drum Temperance Band stood ready at the corner of East Street. All Troy, in fact, was on tiptoe'.

They were on their way to meet someone off the train. A passenger disembarked, and the Admiral, fancying it must be the new tenant for *The Bower*, sought to greet him with a formal welcome. But it was "April the fust", and the baffled new arrival was a stranger, Mr Philip Fogo, who did not know what it was all about. 'The whole deluded town turned and cast its April folly, as a garment, upon the Admiral's shoulders. It was in vain that he stamped and raved and swore. They only held their sides and laughed the louder'.

Before long 'Troy had resumed its work-day quiet. By two o'clock nothing was to be heard but the tick-tack of mallets in the shipbuilding yards, the puffing of the steam-tug, the rattle of hawsers among the vessels out on the harbour, and the melodious "Woo-hoo!" of a crew at capstan or windlass. Troy in carnival and Troy sober are as opposite, you must know, as the poles. Fun is all very well, but business is business, and Troy is a trading port with a character to keep up: for who has not heard the byword: "Working like a Trojan?"'[14]

The Wind in the Willows

Kenneth Grahame, author of *The Wind in the Willows* was a frequent visitor to Fowey, and it is surely Fowey that was in mind when he wrote of the Sea Rat beguiling the Water Rat with his stories of voyaging and adventure:

"And now" he was softly saying "I take to the road again, holding on southwest for many a long and dusty day; till at last I reach the little grey sea town I know so well, that clings along one steep side of the harbour. There through dark doorways you look down flights of stone steps, overhung by great pink tufts of valerian and ending in a patch of sparkling blue water. The little boats that lie tethered to the rings and stanchions of the old sea-wall are gaily painted – the salmon leap on the flood tide, schools of mackerel flash and play past quaysides and foreshores, and by the windows the great vessels glide, night and day, up to their moorings or forth to the open sea. There, sooner or later, the ships of all seafaring nations arrive; and there, at its destined hour, the ship of my choice will let go its anchor. I shall take my time, I shall tarry and hide, till at last the right one lies waiting for me, warped out into midstream, loaded low, her bowsprit pointing down harbour. I shall slip on board, by boat or along hawser; and then one morning I shall wake to the song and tramp of the sailors, the clink of the capstan, and the rattle of the anchor-chain coming merrily in. We shall break out the jib and the foresail, the white houses on the harbour side will glide slowly past us as she gathers steering-way, and the voyage will have begun! As she forges towards the headland she will clothe herself with canvas; and then once outside, the sounding slap of great green seas as she heels to the wind pointing South!" '

The Water Rat was entranced; and when the Sea Rat asked him to come along he very nearly did so: only the determined Mole prevented him from leaving.[15] In Peter Green's account of the world of Kenneth Grahame it was suggested that the setting of the first chapter of *The Wind in the Willows*, 'The River Bank' is not simply, as many have supposed, the Thames in Berkshire, but has elements derived from a boat trip up the Fowey River to Golant. This, it seems, could have been where the Water Rat met the Mole; where they went "messing about in boats"; where they picnicked from a fat, wicker luncheon-basket; where the Wild Wood lay, and beyond it the Wide World; and where they first came to Toad Hall.[16]

Gribbin Head and Menabilly

A broad promontory leads out to Gribbin Head, with a square tower 84 feet high, painted in red and white, to guide mariners. Menabilly Barton, a short way inland, was the home of Daphne du Maurier, who set her novel *Rebecca* largely here, with Menabilly disguised as the house Manderley. It was here that Maxim de Winter brought his young second wife:

'We were not far from the house now, I saw the drive broaden to the sweep I had expected, and with the blood-red wall still flanking us on either side, we turned the last corner, and so came to Manderley. Yes, there it was, the Manderley of my picture postcard long ago. A thing of grace and beauty, exquisite and faultless, lovelier even than I had dreamed, built in its hollow of smooth grass-land and mossy lawns, the terraces sloping to the gardens, and the gardens to the sea.

'The peace of Manderley. The quietude and the grace. No one would ever hurt Manderley. It would lie always in its hollow like an enchanted thing, guarded by the woods, safe, secure, while the sea broke and ran and came again in the little shingle bays below'.

But at the climax of the story, when they are driving back from London, Mrs de Winter saw a glow in the sky: "It's in winter you see the northern lights, isn't it?" I said. "Not in summer?"

"That's not the northern lights," he said, "That's Manderley".

'I glanced at him and saw his face. I saw his eyes.

"Maxim", I said. "Maxim, what is it?"

'He drove faster, much faster. We topped the hill before us and saw Lanyon lying in the hollow at our feet. There to the left of us was the silver streak of the river, widening to the estuary at Kerrith six miles away. The road to Manderley lay ahead. There was no moon. The sky above our heads was inky black. But the sky on the horizon was not dark at all. It was shot with crimson, like a splash of blood. And the ashes blew towards us with the salt wind from the sea.'[17]

So Manderley burned down; but Menabilly House, happily, survives just inland, private and inaccessible, beside the deep wooded valley that opens to Polridmouth, behind The Gribbin.

Par Sands

At Par there is a wide sandy beach with a caravan site and a pool in the dunes. Nearby china clay is processed beside the dusty white harbour from which it is exported. Daphne du Maurier set another of her stories, *The House on the Strand*, at nearby Tywardreath, close to Par. Her hero, Richard Young, imbibed a drug concocted by his biophysicist friend, Magnus Lane, which carried him back six centuries, to the era just before the Black Death. The first of these trips began as he walked through the Tywardreath countryside, and found himself in the fourteenth century:

'The first thing I noticed was the clarity of the air, and then the sharp green colour of the land. There was no softness anywhere. The distant hills did not blend into the sky but stood out like rocks, so close that I could almost touch them, their proximity giving me that shock of surprise and wonder which a child feels looking for the first time through a telescope. I was walking downhill towards the sea, across fields of sharp-edged silver grass that glistened under the sun, for the sky – dull, a moment ago, to my ordinary eyes – was now cloudless, a blazing ecstatic blue. I remembered that the tide had been out, the stretches of flat sand exposed, the row of bathing huts, lined like dentures in an open mouth, forming a solid background to the golden expanse. Now they had gone, and with them the rows of houses fronting the road, the docks, all of Par – chimneys, roof-tops, buildings – and the sprawling tentacles of St Austell enveloping the countryside beyond the bay. There was nothing left but grass and scrub, and the high distant hills that seemed so near; while before me the sea rolled into the bay, covering the whole stretch of sand as if a tidal wave had swept over the land, swallowing it in one rapacious draught. To the north-west the cliffs came down to meet the sea, which, narrowing gradually, formed a wide estuary, the waters sweeping inward, following the curve of the land and so vanishing out of sight.

'When I came to the edge of the cliff and looked beneath me, where the road should be, the inn, the café, the almshouses at the base of Polmear hill, I realised that the sea swept inland here as well, forming a creek that cut to the east, into the valley. Road and houses had gone, leaving only a dip between the land which rose on either side of the creek. Here the channel ran narrowly between banks of mud and sand, so that at low tide the water would surely seep away, leaving a marshy track that could be forded, if not on foot, at least by a horseman.'[18]

A horseman duly appeared, and the adventures with the past began.

Par is a china clay port, and there has indeed been much change here in recent centuries, because of the deposition of sand and clay washed downstream from tin and copper mines, as well as kaolin from the clay pits of Hensbarrow Down, the upland north of St Austell. Ruth Manning-Sanders commented on the mining landscape:

'The high white pyramids of refuse from the workings are familiar in the landscape. These workings have been described as "depressing reminders of the price of exploiting Nature"; but that, surely, is seeing with a jaundiced eye. For, in truth, the china-clay quarries with their gleaming white pits, ice-green water, and steep-sided chalky "dumps", so quickly and so lovingly diapered with natural growths, are really very beautiful. See them on a summer day, with the white pyramids rising against a serene blue sky, and the white cliffs mirrored

in the green of the pools; or see them, far off, under the cloud-piled skies of spring and autumn, their tentlike stacks cresting the high moors as though an army of giants bivouacked there - and who shall say that these are a "depressing reminder" of anything? This exploit of man's, Nature here accepts for her adorning, and lacking it the country would be poorer.'[19]

Nowadays the white conical tip-heaps are less obtrusive than they were then, many of them having been reduced to elongated ridges and stabilised with vegetation.

Charlestown

China clay used to be loaded on to ships from the beach at Charlestown until 1791, when a new harbour was commissioned by Charles Rashleigh, an 18th century squire and mining investor, and designed by John Smeaton, builder of one of the Eddystone lighthouses, as an outport for St Austell. Charlestown was used in the filming of the television series 'The Onedin Line', and also for some of the scenes in the other popular television serial based on Winston Graham's *Poldark* novels.

Noël Coward used to spend boyhood summers here, staying with his Aunt Laura: 'The Cornish seas were much more exciting than the refined Sunny South Coast variety. Here were no neat breakwaters and trim stone esplanades, no rompered children patting at sand castles, while fat mothers lolled near-by in deck-chairs reading novels and knitting; there was no discreet band music here to interfere with the sound of the waves. The waves had it all their own way in Cornwall; grey and formidable, they hurled themselves endlessly against the rocks and swirled into the little sandy coves, leaving yellow suds of foam high up on the beach among the crushed shells and thick ridges of brown seaweed. There were sea-birds, too: cormorants and gulls in hundreds, wheeling and squawking round their nests on the cliffs, and diving for fish far out beyond where the waves curled and broke. I was happy by myself in those days. I spent many hours wandering along the cliffs, frequently returning drenched to the skin to eat large teas in my aunt's kitchen. Dripping-toast and splits and saffron cake, this last bright yellow and delicious.'[20]

Black Head – Trenarren

Towards Black Head, to the south, is Trenarren, the home of A.L. Rowse, historian, poet, and man of letters. His interest in local geography, as well as history, was evident in the first volume of his autobiography, *A Cornish Childhood*, an account of his early life in the village of Tregonissey, up the hill to the north of St Austell. He made frequent visits to: 'Polkerris – that delicious little cove [on] the Gribbin peninsula: a tiny fishing village, now almost deserted by its fishermen, with its pier and a few nets and crab-pots lying in the sun, the air filled with the thick scent of honeysuckles and fuchsias and veronicas in summer, a dog or two scratching themselves lazily in the one little street. An almost Italian scene, facing the eye of the western sun'.

He also went often to Crinnis Beach, 'that magnificent great stretch of white, glistening sand almost a mile long, with the red-brown tin-and-copper-stained cliffs enclosing it', but his memories of Crinnis picnics were 'by no means unalloyed bliss. One of them stands out in a lurid glow like the brazen thunderous day on which it took place: August Bank Holiday 1914, the day when word went round that war was going to be declared. It was a lowering sulphurous day: as the news went round the beach people began quietly and gloomily to pick up their things and go home. That day was a great dividing line. It had a strange significance for me, which is not wholly explicable. It was a symbolic day. For the first time I became aware of the outer world, the world beyond the village and the town. I was ten years old.'[21]

Later Rowse came to live in a house on the headland at Trenarren, with a garden that he had known and envied since he was a schoolboy. In 1963, in the Prologue to *A Cornishman at Oxford*, he described the scene in the spring that followed a long, cold winter:

'Yet never have I seen the garden here at Trenarren look more beautiful. Colours: bright gold of the swathes of daffodils on the bank opposite the upper study where I write, from which I can see the cherry-red of one rhododendron, the crimson, pale pink, magenta, waxy cream, a rosy white of others. There are the butter-yellows and lavender-pink of primroses, white of narcissi, saffron of those trumpeting or ox-eyed daffodils, a myriad greens, the deep sea-blue of grape-hyacinths. The sea itself through the retarded, reluctant trees (after a long winter of ice and snow) is of a rare, pale blue – last evening under a rain-cloud there were different bands of thunder-purple-blue and a clear cerulean; now this moment, the morning relenting, the bay glistens summery under the sun.'[22]

Then, a year later he wrote (in the Prologue to *A Cornishman Abroad*): 'Never have I known a more beautiful summer (except the fatal summers of 1914 and 1940), or Trenarren in greater beauty. The last two days – the last of August and the first of September – there have been hot sun and a high south-easterly gale. At this moment the heat-hazy blue bay is running white horses in full career, hurrying along, crested manes flowing, breaking at the Point. Not a boat out in these sizzling summer seas, though frequently I have looked up from work this August to see Shelley-white sails spreading wings across the crystalline-blue bay. Or I have come down the narrow neck of lane from Lobb's Shop (who was Lobb? a common enough Cornish name – evidently a blacksmith with smithy annexed: neither shop nor smithy now) to see the inset of the bay from Silvermine and Gwendra to Porthpean and beyond. At this moment a whole crew of seagulls are making their difficult way inland in high wind across the valley. I watch the frantic spiralling upwards of a leaf caught in the summer gale; a moment later, a superb Red Admiral borne along the terrace.'

Another time the bay was 'as still as a mill-pool, with the iridescent sheen of mother-of-pearl, milky white-grey-blue, set off by a foreground of brilliant plots of scarlet geranium, and a pink-and-lavender screen of sweet peas hanging over the evening sea.'[23] The sea was milky white-grey-blue because of china clay pollution, when white water sluiced from the Hensbarrow claypits flowed down the local rivers, but this has since been brought under control and the bay is blue again.

Pentewan

Pentewan has a harbour infilled by sandy waste washed down by the river from the mining areas in the hinterland. E.V. Thompson set some of his historical novels, notably *The Restless Sea* and the two Polrudden books, on the coast between Pentewan (formerly Pentuan) and Mevagissey. Polrudden Manor is based on the farm on the hill to the north of Pentewan. In another book, *Ben Retallick*, reference is made to the Happy Union tin-streaming excavation, active in the Pentewan Valley in the 1820s:

'Ben and his father set off for work together at dawn. The diminutive harbour at Pentuan was less than a mile away. The Happy Union Mine was half a mile further on. At the foot of the hill a small river met the sea on a beach of smooth sand. The Happy Union 'mine' proved to be very different from those in which Ben had worked, farther west in Cornwall. The 'levels' were not tunnels deep in the ground, but trenches dug in the hillside to form an intricate interconnecting pattern. Water was pumped to the highest level and used to wash the ore-carrying gravel down to the lowest. Here it was picked out and crushed to extract the tin'.

The mine extended well below sea level, and so was at risk from flooding: 'For days a south-easterly gale had pounded Cornwall. It was particularly severe along the stretch of coast about Pentuan and Mevagissey. In Mevagissey the sea-wall was breached and heavy seas sank many of those boats that could not be quickly drawn up to the safety of the narrow water-washed streets.

'At Pentuan things were even more serious. The village was little more than a cluster of houses huddled in the lee of a hill, protected from the sea by a wide bar of sand that stretched across a gap between the cliffs. This sand also prevented the sea from running up the wide valley to where the Happy Union tin-streaming mine was situated. During the day of the storm, this natural barrier took an unprecedented battering. Driven by winds of near-hurricane force, the waves from the bay roared up the beach, attacking the protective ridge. Each wave, as it made a grumbling retreat, took with it tons of irreplaceable sand. Not until the highest tide of the year was expected, and the storm showed no signs of abating, did the residents of Pentuan suddenly realise the very real danger they were in. By now, only a thin strip of sand stood between the village and the sea'.[24] And soon this was breached by the waves.

A.L. Rowse recalled Sunday School picnics here: 'In early childhood there was the excitement of Sunday School outings to Pentewan. Not a far cry: three miles down the valley from St. Austell to the little china-clay harbour with its large beach and 'Winnick' – grass-covered towans [sand dunes], a splendid playplace. But the excitement was increased a hundredfold by the fact that we went down the valley, not by the road, but by the diminutive railway that carried the china clay to the harbour and coal back to the town. The trucks were cleaned out for this annual event, and filled with Sunday School forms: we were a small, shrieking, gesticulating, singing trainload, children, parents – as child-like as the children – Sunday School teachers very prim and lady-like. But what violent pleasure it was: we couldn't have been more excited and tingling with expectancy if we were making a journey into Darkest Africa. And actually when we left the obviousness of the roadway behind us and the track took us beside the river skirting King's Wood, the river might have been the Limpopo and the wood equatorial forest, it was all so exotic and thrilling. The overhanging vegetation plucked your cap off before you knew where you were; the dragon-flies darted gorgeously by on the wing; the honeysuckles reached their fingers into the truck and tickled your neck; there was a rank vegetation of every sort of flower, yellow and purple and red, alongside the track; there were moorhens flitting in and out the flags of the swamps; and as we arrived at our destination, the little ponds that fed the dock-basin were the splendidest of lakes for me.

'When we were decanted there were the dangers of the beach with the white river to be warned against: so-and-so had been drowned here so many years before. We paddled; hardly anybody bathed in those days: I wouldn't have bathed for anything. We ran about the Winnick, played games and quarrelled. And then we had tea: each of us an enormous, round, golden saffron bun, corrugated with currants and flavoured with lemon-peel. Never were there such saffron buns as those![21]

Mevagissey

High rocky cliffs and coves continue from Pentewan to Mevagissey, long a fishing port, with its pilchard fleet. Mary Lakeman, recalling her *Mevagissey Childhood*, wrote of another annual Cornish picnic on Polstreath Beach: 'Polstreath was our Mecca, that long silvery beach on the north side half a mile from the village. It is approached along the coast from the battery by the Coastguard post, across a high field, and along a narrow path offering a descent in two places which we called the short and the long. You chose by the state of the path, treacherous or safe according to the severity or otherwise of the preceding winter.

'Polstreath Cliffs are high, and to use a word of my mother's, verdant. Marguerite daisies, thrift, honeysuckle, willow herb, bladderwort, wild rose and blackberry claim a habitat in different parts, and bracken turns the face into a golden expanse when the year declines.

'If these cliffs had consciously decided to arrange their base for our convenience, they could not have obliged us more handsomely. Indentations offer small harbours which provide shelter and privacy, and we could always find a smooth perpendicular piece of rock as a support for our backs. Soft sand, diversified by small pebbles and thin blue stones, covers the beach. Ridges of rock enclosing seaweedy pools are exposed when the tide is low. It recedes so as to reveal two rocks in the centre, the cow and the calf, and when spring tides ebb the water round this pair is not more than a few inches deep.[25]

Mevagissey

John Amis had a musician's anecdote from this same beach. The composer (now Sir) Michael Tippett had served a prison sentence as a conscientious objector during the Second World War: 'On 21 August 1943 Michael came out of jug and had breakfast with Pears and Britten. That evening he, Tony Hopkins, Alison Purves and I took the crowded night train to Cornwall. We got off at St Austell and, by previous arrangement, went to have breakfast with A.L. Rowse. After the excitements of the previous day and a sleepless night we were exhausted, but the sharpness of Rowse's conversation revived us like a cold shower. We then went to Mevagissey where we found a café with rooms, just off the harbour, where we put up. Michael for some reason had neither his ration card nor his identity card returned to him.

'A few days later we found ourselves in a secluded bay with the weather suddenly getting warm. There being no one in sight we decided to bathe despite the fact that we hadn't any bathing costumes, although Alison decided to keep her very brief pants on. Imagine our naked amazement when a small rowing boat came round into the bay with a large man in it: a coastguard. He ordered us ashore then went up to Alison, topless but still panted, and solemnly asked her if she had her identity card on her. He then asked us our address in Mevagissey.

'That evening we were eating fresh mackerel just out of the sea – is there anything more delicious? – and in comes the local copper, demanding to see our identity cards. OK for three of us but we had visions of Michael being hauled off to gaol again. Whereupon Michael whispered "Marx Brothers" and we re-enacted a scene from a film in which documents were rapidly handed back and forth, together with a stream of wisecracks and chit-chat. This we did with our three identity cards in the fortunately not very well lit café room, giving a card to the constable and then snatching it away saying "Sorry, you've seen that one, try this one" until eventually the copper went away thoroughly confused by the young witty folks into thinking he had seen four cards when he had seen only three.'[26]

Mevagissey was the setting for a swashbuckling story of Cornish and Breton fishermen, 'Johnny Frenchman', filmed by Ealing Studios in 1944. Cliffs and coves continue south to Bodrugan's Leap, where Sir Henry de Bodrugan, in trouble with rival Cornish neighbours for fighting on the wrong side at Bosworth Field, escaped pursuit by leaping his horse over the cliff, landing on the shore and swimming out to a boat waiting to take him to France.

Gorran Haven

Cliffs and sandy coves continue south towards Gorran Haven, a small fishing harbour. Colin Wilson came to live in this area in the nineteen-fifties: 'You could follow the brook down to the valley, over three or four fields to the sea. If you turn right at the beach, and walk uphill towards Gorran Haven, you see some of the finest cliff scenery in southern Cornwall. There are long sheer drops down to the sea, and the usual jagged rocks pointing up at you. If you walk down to Gorran Haven and continue along the cliff path, you have to walk waist-deep in ferns for a quarter of a mile and you find yourself on another beach, Vault, one of the longest in this part of the world. Because it is so inaccessible that it is impossible to drive a car closer than a quarter of a mile away, this remains fairly deserted; even in the height of the tourist season there are seldom more than a few dozen people along its enormous length. And if you care to plod over its yielding pebbles to the far end, you can reckon on total solitude, beyond the reach of the noisiest transistor radio.

'Assuming you do not want to spend the day on the beach, you can turn right up the hill just before you reach it and emerge, after a steep climb over a couple of fields, at Lamledra Farm. It is now possible to follow the shore-line along a narrow asphalted road above Vault beach. Headlands stick out on both sides. The magnificent gorse-covered promontory on the right is the Dodman, an ominous-sounding name which actually means a snail. You can walk right out to the point of the Dodman, if you don't mind some rough going, to the great stone memorial cross which overlooks the sea.'[27]

Dodman Point

The Dodman, with its great granite cross erected in 1896, is a bold headland of hard, contorted, dark grey rock rising 373 feet above the sea: it is feared by mariners and figures in sea shanties. Just inland, high on the plateau, was the Gorran School, about which Anne Treneer wrote 'Except in thick mist or in high summer I hardly remember still air at Gorran. The wind either played or howled round our house; it rarely died altogther. It was a constant companion, in one's hair and in the leaves and in the telegraph poles, whirling the smoke down the chimneys, rattling the sash windows, and bringing the middle door to with a bang if the front or back were suddenly opened. When I was told the story of Jacob wrestling with God I saw him struggling to open our heavy door in the wind.

'It was bare country; no trees sheltered the house. There were two stranded thorns at the foot of the garden, but they looked as though they had tried to run away and had been caught by the heels, and retained the slanting attitude of those ready to race. The wind streamed round us straight from everywhere. From whatever direction it blew it met house and swept on and round it like a sea-swirl over and around rocks. Winter gales were glorious. The School House and High Lanes were the windiest spots in Gorran.

'The high hedges which bordered the roads and divided the fields were shelter for beasts and men. Cattle, seeking the hedges in wet windy days would stand, their hind-quarters in comparative comfort, looking with melancholy eyes over the fields. Except for the moor-like stretches round Dodman and the Grebe, all Gorran was field and hedge. At Hemmick the poppies and corn and a lovely blue flower – I think succory - grew to the cliff edge, so that the summer wind could be heard in the waves on the one hand and in the wheat or oats or barley on the other... to hear it rustle the ripe oats is the luxury of summer.'[28]

The Roseland Peninsula

West from the Dodman, past Hemmick Beach and the rocky outcrops of the Grebe, the cliffs decline to Porthluney, a wide sandy cove. Close by is Caerhays Castle, designed by John Nash and built in 1808. The coastal footpath crosses successive rocky promontories on past Portloe to Portscatho on the Roseland peninsula. Laurence O'Toole told the story of the little harbour at Portscatho: 'For centuries the only protection for the fishermen had been the narrow drang that ran between two ridges of rock, and ended on a broad stretch of sand. This gave adequate protection from every direction except the eastward, but it meant that only such boats as could be hauled up the slip were able to be there with safety at all times. Bigger boats had to be prepared to run round to the shelter of the creek at Percuil.

'Then came the great blizzard of March 1891, when Cornwall and the west country was battered by gales of wind and snow from the east. Many vessels were wrecked on these coasts, among them a German steamer called the *Carl Hirschberg*. She was driven helplessly across Gerrans Bay, and finished on the rocks at Pencabe. The crew were rescued by local men, but the steamer stayed high and dry for a month. All efforts to tow her off failed. At length the sailors proposed to blast the top off the rocks in order to drag her clear. But to do this would remove the shelter of the porth, and local fishermen only agreed when the Board of Trade promised to build a sea wall.

'The rocks were blasted, the *Carl Hirschberg* was towed away, and in time the harbour wall was built. But it was too small, and built too close in, and the man-made harbour gave less shelter than the old natural one.

'So a small extension was built on, and though none of the older men was ever satisfied, there it stands today.'[29]

Morgawr

For centuries there have been legends about a sea monster in these waters, known to local people as Morgawr, which is Cornish for 'sea giant'. In 1876 the West Briton published a brief report: 'The sea serpent was caught alive in Gerrans Bay. Two of our fishermen were afloat overhauling their crab-pots about 400-500 yards from the shore, when they discovered the serpent coiled about their floating cork buoy. Upon their near approach it lifted its head and showed signs of defiance, upon which they struck it fiercely with an oar, which so far disabled it as to allow them to proceed with their work, after which they observed the serpent floating about near their boat. They pursued it, bringing it ashore yet alive for exhibition, soon after which it was killed on the rocks and most inconsiderately cast again into the sea'.

Graham McEwan, having quoted this report in his book on *Mystery Animals of Britain and Ireland*, mentioned several subsequent sightings of a large marine creature in the waters of Gerrans Bay, Falmouth Bay and the Helford River. One was from a headland near Portscatho, on the calm evening of 10 July 1985, by a group of four people, including one of the compilers of this book.[30]

Towan Beach

Many have been saddened by the gradual spoliation of beautiful places on the Cornish coast by tourists. Just south of Portscatho, at Towan Beach on the Roseland Peninsula, Winston Graham had an unusual experience: 'Towan is a lovely small, rock and sand beach where there is no surf but endless brilliant rock pools, seaweed grown, anemone starred, and full of tiny fishes and shells. It is also one of the few places in Cornwall where cowries can be found. The cliffs gently slope, green almost to the sea. And there are no houses of any sort. When we left Cornwall it was just beginning to be spoiled. Caravans encroached on the sandy field leading to the cove. There were a few more every year. It was only a matter of time before an ice-cream kiosk came, and a hut hiring out deck chairs and selling teas.

'For a reason I cannot now remember it was five or six years before we returned to it, dreading what we might find. What we found was all the caravans gone, an arrow pointing to a fairly distant car park, and the one or two people on the beach outnumbered by the Friesian cows which sat around chewing by the water's edge. We rubbed our eyes. This was an instance of the clock being put *back!* How could it be?

'The answer was in fact simple. The National Trust had got it. What we in England, and people in Cornwall especially, owe to the National Trust is beyond computation.'[31]

St. Anthony Lighthouse

St. Mawes

Roseland culminates in Zone Point, beside the entry to Carrick Roads, a wide branching inlet extending up to Truro. On the eastern side Percuil River comes in beside St Mawes. 'The old road to the sea alters little', wrote Laurence O'Toole, 'The ebb-tide still runs green and swift at Percuil, past the bows of anchored vessels, and beyond St Mawes into the Channel. But where the black-hulled trawlers lay, the moorings are closely packed with yachts. Jack Webb's Boatyard dominates the beach where the storage sheds stood. For a couple of months in the year the old slipway is busy again, but now with comings and goings of dinghies. A thriving sailing club holds its races on summer evenings and at weekends. No doubt the old salt-house mariners would have approved of so much activity, though they would be astonished that anyone should go to sea for pleasure.'[29]

Those who know Arthur Ransome's books for children will recall that at the end of *Missee Lee* the Swallows, Amazons and Captain Flint, after sundry adventures on the coast of China, arrived back in England: 'And you may, yourselves, have read how the people of St. Mawes, in Cornwall, woke one morning to find a little Chinese junk, with a monkey at the masthead, anchored off their harbour mouth.'[32]

Tresillian Creek

W.P. Hodgkinson in *The Under-Road*, took one of his solitary walks along 'a winding lane which threads its way along the edge of Tresillian Creek, a mile above Malpas – the traditional meeting-place of Tristan and Isolde. There is a seat there to which I often go alone and meditate; hushed by the wind in the pines, and soothed by the lap of little waves against the rocks at my feet, I find it easy to step inside the gates of heaven, and without any difficulty at all to become utterly at peace with the world. My seat is formed by the tangled roots of an old oak whose branches, like all exposed trees in Cornwall, make exaggerated and dramatic gestures against the skyline. Beside me, the purple sea-asters and the tufts of pink thrift mingle with the delicate amethyst of the sunlit mud-banks. Here, looking towards Lamorran and St.Just-in-Roseland, I lean back to listen to the lamentations of innumerable curlews and the guttural cries of the gulls.'[33]

Falmouth

The waterways of Carrick Roads lead inland to a maze of creeks and rivers, including the Fal, the Truro and the Tresillian. Near the entrance is the magnificent natural harbour of Falmouth, sheltered by Pendennis Point. Susan Gay, a local historian, wrote in 1903, that 'Three hundred years ago Falmouth consisted of a little handful of primitive houses, not far from the old Manor House of Arwenack, home of the Killigrews. In 1646 the house was set on fire by the troops at Pendennis Castle – the last [in Cornwall] to hold out against the Cromwellian forces, in order that it should not be occupied by the latter.

'An old fort, Pendennis was heard of a thousand years ago, but the development of the fort with a Castle dates no earlier than the time of Henry VIII, who was bent on defending his sea-coast, and built the round tower. The town of Falmouth, like Topsy, grew in its own fashion. Antagonised by Penryn, Truro and Helston, the Killigrews fought successfully on its behalf. [It had been] known as Smithick from 'Smith's Creek', a smith who lived in the valley. The nickname of 'Penny-come- quick' is to be found in old documents. Many assert that it was a corruption of *Pen-y-cwm-quic*, 'the head of a narrow valley'. That shrewd old sailor, Sir Walter Raleigh, on his return from Guiana [at the end of the sixteenth century] saw in a moment the necessity for the creation of a town on account of the requirements of vessels.'[34]

According to Nigel Calder 'The pirates of the Killigrew family built and named

Falmouth town in the seventeenth century. Before then, towns farther up the rivers had the trade, Pendennis and St. Mawes possessed the castles, and the Tudor naval dockyard was at Mylor. But Falmouth's harbour, the most westerly of any great size, was an excellent base for preying on shipping at the entrance to the English Channel. The seafarers of Falmouth then found more respectable work as transatlantic mailmen.

'If you had an urgent message for the American colonies, you did not want it beating to and fro for weeks in a ship trying to go down-Channel from London or Portsmouth in the teeth of the prevailing winds, and exposed to attack by the French *corsaires*. So you sent it by mounted courier overland to Cornwall, and dispatched it by the appropriate Falmouth packet boat. Starting as a mail packet station with a service to Lisbon in 1688, Falmouth acquired worldwide fame as a communications centre'.[3] The original John Bull was born in Falmouth in 1772, and captained the Post Office packet *Grantham*.

A plaque erected by the Falmouth Civic Society on Fish Strand Quay, records how news of the naval victory at Trafalgar in 1806, brought into Falmouth by a ship returning from the fray, was carried by post-chaise to London in only 38 hours: 'News of Trafalgar: On 4th November 1805 Lieutenant John Richards Lapenotière, Captain of H.M. Schooner *Pickle*, landed near here with official despatches from Vice-Admiral Collingwood. These announced the victory at the Battle of Trafalgar and reported the death in action of Admiral Lord Nelson. By noon Lapenotière had left by post-chaise for London where he reported to the Admiralty some 38 hours later. Normal stage coach services took a week for this journey. J.R Lapenotière, born at Ilfracombe in 1770, joined the Royal Navy in 1780, rose to the rank of Captain, and died in Liskeard in 1834.'

Falmouth's port stands in the lee of Pendennis Point on the western shore, its waterfront lined by several quays and mooring areas. In Howard Spring's novel, *There is no Armour*, the young artist Edward Pentecost came here in 1904: 'Falmouth's old grey buildings were expiring in the heat of summer. An exhilarating languor lingered in the narrow ways that led off from the main street to the waterfront. It was one of these narrow ways that I was seeking. "You can't miss it", my mother had said, "It's right opposite the steps that come down from the parish church". I was above the church now, and here were the steps twisting downhill behind it, a narrow gulch with iron railings on either hand. Right in front was the short narrow lane leading to the waterfront. The whole extent of Falmouth harbour, glistening under the sun, lay before me. To the right Pendennis Castle crowned its headland, and before me, across the water, the castle of St Mawes seemed to dip its feet in the tide. I could see the Carrick Roads running up to St Just, and on that windless day the blue expanse was full of ships standing on the water as though they were models exhibited on glass. From a splendid barque anchored in the offing to the red and green and white yachts scattered like dainty toys, there was no movement anywhere, save for a dinghy here and there being lazily rowed over the water, and the gulls clamouring above garbage heaved overside.'[35]

According to Ida Procter, Beatrix Potter was staying in the Pendennis Hotel in 1894 when she wrote to one of her former governess's children:

'There are a great many ships here, some very large ones, and a French one unloading at the Quay. Some of the sailors have little dogs, and cocks and hens on the ships. I have read about the owl and the pussycat, who went to sea in a peagreen boat, but I never saw anything of that kind till to-day. I was looking at a ship called *The Pearl of Falmouth* which was being mended at the bottom because it had rubbed on a rock, when I heard something grunt! I went up a bank where I could see onto the deck and there was a white pig with a curly tail walking about. It is a ship that goes to Newfoundland, and the sailors always take a pig. I daresay it enjoys the voyage, but when the sailors get hungry they eat it. If that pig had any sense it would slip down into the boat at the end of the ship and row away.'[36] This was the inspiration for Little Pig Robinson, published much later, in1930, about a pig who did have the sense to row away.

Along the waterfront is Greenbank Hotel, where Kenneth Grahame was staying when he began to write the letters to his son in which the adventures of Toad began to take shape for *The Wind in the Willows*. The town has spread across the promontory to seaside hotels and guest houses on the southern shore, from which the coast curves away towards Rosemullion Head. The coastal footpath climbs to Pennance Point, where a granite monument is dedicated to No.1 (Falmouth) Company, Home Guard 'who during 1940-44, after their daily work, nightly patrolled this coast, armed and vigilant against German landings. Thus they watched 1000 dawns appear across the great waters which form our country's moat'. Further on, a steep track descends through bracken to a shingly cove where the impressionist painter, Henry Scott Tuke, painted his naked boys: it is known locally as Arthur's Cove, perhaps after Arthur White, who posed for these paintings.

Falmouth Bay

Helford River

Helford River is a deep marine inlet branching into several valleys. It is the scene of another Daphne Du Maurier novel: 'When the east wind blows up Helford river the shining waters become troubled and disturbed, and the little waves beat angrily upon the sandy shore. The short seas break above the bar at ebb-tide, and the waders fly inland to the mud-flats, their wings skimming the surface, and calling to one another as they go. Only the gulls remain, wheeling and crying above the foam, their grey feathers glistening with the salt spray.

'The long rollers of the Channel, travelling from beyond Lizard point, follow hard upon the steep seas at the river mouth, and mingling with the surge and wash of deep sea water comes the brown tide, swollen with the last rains and brackish from the mud, bearing upon its face dead twigs and straws, and strange forgotten things, leaves too early fallen, young birds, and the buds of flowers.

'The river was little known, save to a few mariners who had found shelter there when the south-west gales drove them inshore from their course up-channel, and they found the place lonely and austere, a little frightening because of the silence, and when the wind was fair again were glad to weigh anchor and set sail.

'Today there are many voices to blunder in upon the silence. The pleasure steamers come and go, leaving a churning wake, and yachtsmen visit one another, and even the day-tripper, his dull eye surfeited with undigested beauty, ploughs in and out among the shallows, a prawning net in hand.

'The river flows on, the trees rustle in the summer wind, and down on the mud flats the oyster-catchers stand at ebb-tide scanning the shallows for food, and the curlews cry. The solitary yachtsman who leaves his yacht in the open roadstead of Helford, and goes exploring up-river in his dinghy on a night in midsummer, when the night-jars call, hesitates when he comes upon the mouth of the creek, for there is something of mystery about it even now, something of enchantment. Being a stranger, the yachtsman looks back over his shoulder to the safe yacht in the roadstead, and to the broad waters of the river, and he pauses, resting on his paddles, aware suddenly of the deep silence of the creek, of its narrow twisting channel, and he feels – for no reason known to him – that he is an interloper, a trespasser in time'.[37] This is Frenchman's Creek.

Hereward the Wake

Charles Kingsley imagined Hereward the Wake arriving in the Helford River in the eleventh century 'The next place in which Hereward appeared was far away to the west, upon the Cornish shore. He went into port on board a merchant ship carrying wine, and intending to bring back tin. The merchants had told him of one 'Alef', a valiant 'regulus' or kinglet, living at Gweek, up the Helford River. {He] had increased his wealth, not only by the sale of tin and of red cattle, but by a certain amount of 'summer-leding' (*i.e.* piracy between seed-time and harvest) in company with his Danish brothers-in-law from Dublin and Waterford; and Hereward, who believed with most Englishmen of the East Country, that Cornwall still produced a fair crop of giants, some of them with two and even three heads, had hopes that Alef might show him some adversary worthy of his sword.

'He sailed in, therefore, over a rolling bar, between jagged points of black rock, and up a tide river which wandered and branched inland like a landlocked lake, between high green walls of oak and ash, till they saw at the head of the tide Alef's Town, nestling in a glen which sloped to the southern sun. They discovered, besides, two ships drawn up on the beach, whose long lines and snake heads, beside the stoat carried on the beak-head of one and the adder on that of the other, bore witness to the piratical habits of their owner. The merchants, it seemed, were well known to the Cornishmen on shore, and Hereward went up with them unopposed; past the ugly dykes and muddy leats where Alef's slaves were streaming the gravel for tin ore; through rich alluvial pastures spotted with red cattle; and up to Alef's town'. It was to be a brief but lively visit, during which he slew a giant, succoured a princess, and left with dawning notions of chivalry.[38] From the description, Alef's town could have been Gweek, now a little village in the wooded valley at the head of the Helford River, with a Seal Sanctuary nearby.

A.E. Copping sailed this way in 1907:'And the day came when the *Betty* passed from heaving waters of the open sea, and glided into a river that was broad and still and beautiful – a perspective of repose and velvet hills where, travelling through green reflections, we were among the little singing birds.

'This was Helford River, the western limit of our voyage – a fairy region with foregrounds of fern and purple rocks; and beyond a headland smoothly clothed with oak trees we found an ancient ruin of turreted masonry, grey and peaceful. All other things were also tranquil: elms and their cawing population; three homely houses with frontages of sunshine, limewash, and ivy; a little white boat that lay on the shore; and five pink pigs.'[39]

The land rises south from Helford River to the Lizard Peninsula, a plateau bordered by steep cliffs and stormy seas. Its rugged eastern shores are disfigured by abandoned stone quarries near Porthallow and Porthoustock, known locally as Prallow and Prowstock. Many ships have been wrecked on the jagged Manacles offshore.

Coverack

Frank Baines described the coast near Coverack 'A funny thing must have happened to our coast in remote geological ages. It was most evident at Penjerrick and Trevean. And I suppose all the Lowland Point and the Manacles owed their configuration to it. The sea had receded. You could see this quite clearly when you put out half a mile from Godrevy. Trevean farm and buildings stood in a clump of trees on the rocky coast of the old promontory, and from the farmyard a precipice fell away one hundred and fifty feet. The ruined farm at Gillie High Rocks was situated similarly. Between them, everywhere the old cliff dropped vertically, severed by cow paths and intersected by little gullies. At the foot of these cliffs a desolate scree, littered with small avalanches and encumbered with boulders, sloped for two hundred yards to the shore. The real cliffs were only fifty feet high, of mud, and embedded in them were more of the boulders. This scree was the loneliest and wildest place I have ever known. Hundreds of little springs, bursting out from the foot of the old cliffs, made the bog, which the half-wild store cattle tramping about in their search for winter fodder converted into a quagmire. At its foot was Godrevy Bank, a place very difficult to get to by boat. The passage in and out between seething, half submerged fine-grained blue boulders to which no weeds or limpets adhered, was hair-raising.'[40] Another ideal place for smugglers.

Goonhilly Downs

Up on the heathy plateau of Goonhilly Downs stands the Satellite Earth Station, transmitting and receiving messages from satellites poised over the Equator. Sheila Bird described how 'The awe inspiring futuristic clutter of dishes projecting heavenwards on Goonhilly Downs, amidst the standing stones, hut circles and tumuli left by our early ancestors, combines the mystery of the distant past, our responsibility for the present, and the wonder of the future, where earth knows no bounds.'[41] Such refinements come in succession, for in 1901 at nearby Poldhu, on the Lizard's western shore, the first transatlantic radio messages were sent.

Church Cove, Landewednack

C.C. Rogers came to Church Cove where:'The old church stands hidden from the world, half-way down a winding lane that runs to the sea. All the way down the lane there is a tangle of campion and hedge-parsley on either side, until passing three deserted cottages and an old life-boat house, one comes suddenly to the

Cove, a little beach with fishing-boats drawn up, and a triangle of the bluest sea framed by a bluff or cliff to right and left. Following an upward instinct one climbs the steeper cliff path on the left. The close-cropped grass is springy to the tread. In April it was covered with the vernal squill as with a blue mist, for the dainty little flowers, blue-grey on a ruddy stem, were starred in profusion everywhere. Now only the transparent seeds are left, standing two inches high, like tiny silver ghosts.

'There on top of the cliff, with sky and water for one's world, the thoughts aroused in that little grey church return; thoughts of mortality and longings after immortality. And then the breaking waves of that infinite sea, relentless yet somehow reassuring, bring a message of death in life and life in death. The wave ends, but the sea remains and will remain.'[42]

The Lizard

In *Vanishing Cornwall*, Daphne du Maurier commented: 'The rugged cliffs of West Penwith and Kerrier [i.e. between the Lizard and Land's End], thinly populated, the small fishing-villages little more than hamlets clustered above high water in the coves were remote from the law and order which ruled inland. Weather-bound in winter, existing on a bare subsistence of salted fish, the inhabitants saw no evil in plundering a foundered ship if the contents helped to fill their bellies or put clothes upon their backs. Dead men told no tales, and a drowning man was as good as dead, more so if a stranger.'[43]

Wilkie Collins, walking here in 1860, recounted the grim story of a mass burial of shipwrecked soldiers in Pistol Meadow, not far from the lighthouse at Lizard Point. The meadow was so called because many firearms were found in it. A century later Daphne du Maurier searched for the site: 'Near to the lighthouse a man pointed out Pistol Cove west of the point, but the meadow was more difficult to place, for the cliff walk above the cove was bounded with wire for safety's sake – there had been a recent fall of earth – and then the path wound to the left to the further headland and a look-out hut beyond. Here was no meadow with sweet-smelling wild flowers and waving grass blowing peacefully over the mounds of the dead, as described by Wilkie Collins. The rough ground sloped directly to the cliff, intersected by a stream, the mounds I trod on were natural hillocks sprouting gorse, until - could this be it? A small enclosure, set about with stumpy willows grotesquely shaped by the prevailing wind, the ground hussocky and rough. It was peaceful, untroubled, better than many another resting-place for sleeping soldiers.'[43]

The Lizard is the southernmost point on the Channel coast. Its intricate geology includes mottled serpentine, a striped blue, green, red and black rock, which has been carved into lighthouses and other ornaments sold to tourists. The coast seems unchanging, but from time to time there are landslides, as Wilkie Collins described from the Lizard: 'As we passed before the front of the large and massive

[Lizard Lighthouse] our progress was suddenly and startlingly checked by a hideous chasm in the cliff, sunk to a perpendicular depth of seventy feet, and measuring more than a hundred in circumference. This chasm – melodramatically entitled by the people, "The Lion's Den" – was formed in an extraordinary manner, not many years since. In the evening the whole surface of the down above the cliff was smooth to the eye, and firm to the foot – in the morning it had opened into an enormous hole. The men who kept watch at the Lighthouse heard no sounds beyond the moaning of the sea – felt no shock – looked out on the night, and saw that all was apparently still and quiet. Nature suffered her convulsion and effected her change in silence. Hundreds of tons of soil had sunk down into depths beneath them, none knew in how long or how short a time; but there the Lion's Den was in the morning, where the firm earth had been the evening before.

'The explanation of the manner in which this curious landslip occurred, is to be found by descending the face of the cliff, beyond the Lion's Den, and entering a cavern in the rocks called "Daw's Hugo" (or Cave). The place is only accessible at low water. Passing from the beach through the opening of the cavern, you find yourself in a lofty tortuous recess, into the farthest extremity of which, a stream of light pours down from some eighty or a hundred feet above. This light is admitted through the Lion's Den, and thus explains by itself the nature of the accident by which that chasm was formed. Here, the weight of the upper soil broke through the roof of the cave; and the earth which then fell into it was subsequently washed away by the sea.'[4]

Pentreath Beach and Kynance Cove

J.C. Trewin had childhood memories of the west coast of the Lizard: 'Farther on, beyond Caerthillian, is the broad scarf of Pentreath where, at low evening tide, one could go launcing in the moonlight: not a country dance but the pursuit of a tiny streaking sand-eel: an exercise once recorded by a Lizard artist, Sydney Hart. Farther yet are the elaborations of Kynance Cove, moulded and colour-veined in serpentine, the Gull Rock, the Steeple and Asparagus Island, the Lion massively on its haunches: all disposed by an expert director, not to mask each other. Kynance, with the Rill Head (from which the crescent moon of the Spanish Armada was sighted on a July evening in 1588) was the first picture I saw every morning on waking in my attic.

'In stormy, or "coarse", January weather, each cliff and beach has its individual note: a dynamiting, pile-driving boom against the full face of Old Lizard Head; the boiling hiss, as of a sea serpent, among the rocks and pools of Pistol Cove; a growl, swooping yet protracted, as wave upon wave drove, white to the lips, across the shelving sand of Pentreath. There were places, too – the crest of Rocky Lane was one - where the sea appeared to be running downhill to meet you. You were level then with the horizon. By the time you reached Pistol Meadow, the stile with its serpentine slabs and the hummocked grass, water should have been pouring over you in a cascade. But it never did.'[44]

Wilkie Collins came to Kynance Cove in 1850: 'What a scene was now presented to us! It was a perfect palace of rocks! Some rose perpendicularly and separate from each other, in the shapes of pyramids or steeples – some were overhanging at the top and pierced with dark caverns at the bottom – some were stretched horizontally on the sand, here studded with pools of water, there broken into natural archways. No one of these rocks resembled another in shape, size, or position – and all, at the moment we looked on them, were wrapped in the solemn obscurity of a deep mist.'[4]

A few years later, Charlotte Mason saw Kynance Cove 'a snow-white beach washed by a blue sea, a background of cliffs, green, and purple, and red; pebbles of gorgeous colours strewed on the white sand; the cliffs pierced by caverns with polished walls of all beautiful colours, fresh and glowing from a a sea-bath.'[45]

H.D. Rawnsley composed 'The Gull Rock' here:

> *If all the seas that ever sucked the hue*
> *From midmost heaven, about dark rocks were rolled,*
> *If all the winds that ever gathered gold*
> *From out sea-air, upon their foreheads blew,*
> *If all the wings of oceanbirds that flew,*
> *Milk-white upon the ledges dropped to fold –*
> *Then, Kynance, would thy wave-bound fortress hold*
> *Blue-girt, gold-washed, wing whitened, rise to view.*
> *Dear to the wanderers as they westward rove,*
> *Landewednack's cape, Landewednack's double eye;*
> *But, from Carthethra to St. Levan's bound,*
> *No rocks so magical as those that lie*
> *The Tawny lion-guards of Kynance Cove.*[46]

High cliffs continue past Mullion Cove, with its outlying island, and Poldhu Point, where the first radio messages were transmitted across the ocean in 1901. A morse code message (dot-dot-dot) sent from here bounced off the ionosphere and was received by the initiator of the experiment, Giugelmo Marconi, in St. Johns, Newfoundland. A cliff-top monument records this achievement.

In the 1840s the Reverend C.A. Johns explored the coasts of the Lizard Peninsula, describing geology, fisheries and landscapes: 'It was at the close of a very hot day in July, still and cloudless, and I was walking from Mullion to Helston, having quickened my steps to be in time to see the sun go down from the Halzaphron cliffs, as they are called. When I reached this point the sun was within a few degrees of the horizon, but shining brilliantly here and over several miles of sea to the westward: but beyond this all was impenetrably wrapped in mist. Where I stood the air was clear, bright and still; what little motion of the wind had been perceptible during the day was from the east and south. Towards the Land's End the sun slowly descended behind a mass of dense mist, which, as he disappeared, assumed the deepest of all possible blue-purple hues, with a narrow half-defined edge of gold, or rather of liquid yellow fire. In a few seconds every bright tint had vanished, the whole mass of the clouds, for such they had now become, were of a dull whitish-grey character. A few seconds more, and a chilling north wind blew in my face, and accompanied me during the remainder of my walk.'[47]

Gunwalloe Cove

As the cliffs decline towards Gunwalloe a long shingle beach begins. Sir Compton Mackenzie recalled a holiday here in 1908: 'The weather became so hot in July that I suggested the children should celebrate it by learning to swim. The first bathing expedition was one warm and misty Saturday morning in a sea of oxidized silver, but these children who had spent all their lives on the brink of the Atlantic were horribly frightened of entering it when the moment came. Each one urged the other to go in first; but nobody would advance beyond his or her knees. As far up as that their bodies were familiar with the sea when they went washing feet, which was what they called paddling; the moment the scarcely heaving water rose an inch higher all the children leapt back as if they were going to be bitten by a savage fish. No reproaches of mine for their timidity were of any avail until Alec Bolitho decided to set an example at Charlie Wearne's expense by suddenly giving him a push in the back which sent him face-downwards with a splash into the water. Fired by her brother's action Bessie did the same thing to her sister Beattie. On the way back to dress in the caves there was much bragging about their bravery. By the end of the summer most of them could swim.'[48]

Loe Pool

Along the cliffs to the west the track descends towards Loe [pronounced Low] Pool, where a white cross bears the inscription: "Sacred to the memory of about 100 officers and men of HMS Anson, who were drowned when their ship was wrecked on Loe Bar 29th Dec,1807, and buried hereabout. Henry Trengrouse of Helston was so impressed by this tragedy that [in 1808] he invented the Life Saving Rocket Apparatus which has since been instrumental in saving thousands of lives".

Sabine Baring Gould described Loe Pool as: 'The largest lake in Cornwall; the only other is Dozmare [on Bodmin Moor]. It is a beautiful sheet of fresh water cut off from the sea by a pebble ridge, which it was wont to overflow, but a culvert has been bored through the rocks to enable the [River] Cober to discharge without, as formerly, rising and inundating the land below Helston. It is really marvellous to see how the mesembryanthemum flourishes here, throwing up masses of pink

144

and white blossom. In the neighbourhood it is fondly dreamed that this was the tarn into which Arthur had Excalibur cast.'[49] In the words of Tennyson, from 'The Passing of Arthur' in *Idylls of the King*:

> *On one side lay the ocean, and on one*
> *Lay a great water...'*
> *.....To left and right*
> *The bare black cliff clang'd round him, as he based*
> *His feet on juts of slippery crag, that rang*
> *Sharp smitten with the dint of armed heels –*
> *And on a sudden, lo! the level lake,*
> *And the long glories of the winter moon.'*[50]

'Hither came the dusky barge that was to bear Arthur away to the isles of the blessed. This is very pretty; the lake, the black serpentine rocks agree well enough, but how was the fairy barge to get over the pebble ridge? Mr. Rogers had not then cut the culvert. No doubt it was brimming, but it must have been risky over the bar. I do not believe a word of it. Arthur was never down there!'[49]

Loe Bar and Pool

Folliott Stokes also described this area: 'We descend by a path to the broad expanse of sand, or rather shingle (for it is composed of minute rounded stones) known as Loe Bar. After walking a few yards across its level surface, a most magnificent sight confronts us. The coast hills have suddenly receded, and enclose between their wooded flanks a broad sheet of water. This is Loe Pool, the largest lake in the South of England. It is about a mile and a half long and half a mile wide. Tall reeds line its banks, flocks of wild fowl are scattered over its surface, in which the foliage of the overhanging trees is faithfully reflected, and out of which great trout occasionally rise at the flies. A scene of peaceful rural beauty, and yet only this strip of shingle, on which we are standing, separates it from the Atlantic, which we can hear thundering a hundred yards or so behind us. For this bar is no more than a hundred and fifty yards wide at its broadest part. Being formed of small stones it acts as a sort of filter, through which the flood water, being at a higher level, percolates to the salt water, thus maintaining the lake at a more or less uniform height, the percolation being about equal to the volume of water received by the Cober brook and a few other smaller streams. In times of heavy rains this bar used to be cut, in order to let the water off and prevent the lake from flooding the surrounding valleys. Now a culvert carries off the surplus.'[51]

Helston

A short way inland is Helston, which W.G. Maton described at the end of the eighteenth century as 'situated on the banks of the Loe. It is a populous decent town and a borough, and its trade has long been good. Several tin-ships take their lading at its port, which is commodious and provided with a tolerable quay.'[52]

Several early accounts mention Helston as an old port, and it seems that the Loe Bar was less of a barrier to shipping in the past than it has been over the last century or so, but there seems to be a conflict with John Skinner's account of his visit to Helston at about the same time.

John Skinner came to Helston on 13th November: 'We found good accommodations at the Inn, and we left it after tea on 14th November in order to visit Looe Pool, which is a beautiful piece of water belonging to Mr. Rogers. This gentleman's house, called Penrose, is situated in the midst of a finely wooded scene about two miles from the Town on the borders of the Lake which is everywhere a fine object from his grounds. When the waters extend so far as to obstruct the working of the mills at Helston and Carminouse, the miners apply to Mr. Rogers, as Lord of the Manor, and presenting him with two leather purses, each containing three halfpence, solicit his permission to open the Bar. This being granted, workmen are employed by the Mayor of Helston, to cut a passage through the pebbles; and the opening is no sooner made, than the whole body of water rushes through the aperture with wonderful force and impetuosity. Indeed the conflict between the wave and the river at these times constitutes an extraordinary spectacle, and this is often visible six or eight miles from the shore; yet such is the peculiar situation of the place, and force of the rolling surge, that the bar of pebbles is formed again in a few days.'[53] How, we wonder, did ships carrying tin ore get in and out through a wide shingle ridge like the Loe Bar?

The Furry or Flora Dance

Helston is notable for its Flora Day each 8th May. In 1850, Wilkie Collins wrote that 'this festival is said to be of very ancient origin, and is called "The Furry" – an old Cornish word signifying a gathering; and at, Helston particuarly, a gathering in celebration of the return of spring. The Furry begins early in the morning with singing, to an accompaniment of drums and kettles. All the people in the town immediately leave off work and scamper into the country; having reached which, they scamper back again, garlanded with leaves and flowers, and caper about hand-in-hand through the streets, and in and out of all the houses, without let or hindrance. Even the 'genteel' families allow themselves to be infected with the general madness, and wind up the day's capering consistently enough by a night's capering at a grand ball.'[4]

Overcoming some doubts, Winston Graham was finally persuaded 'by a Helston lady to share her window overlooking the main street. Of course it is a show. Of course it is self-conscious. Of course it is a tourist attraction. But under it all there is a deep sense of pagan ritual which continues to pervade the dance - and fascinates, and sometimes hypnotizes. The band plays the tune with endless repetition - only about sixteen notes in all - as an early nineteenth century newspaper put it: music of more antiquity than variety. The band guards its score jealously.

'There is more in this music than meets the ear. On the surface it is a charming celebration of summer. Below the surface it is very ancient and very earth-bound and rather haunted.'[31]

The beach enclosing the Loe Pool runs on to the fishing village of Porthleven with its inner and outer harbours, a place frequently damaged by Atlantic storms. Rocky cliffs continue past Rinsey Head, where the engine house and chimney of the old Wheal Prosper copper mine stands boldly on the coast, and on to Marazion, where St Michael's Mount is linked to the mainland by a stone causeway submerged at high tides.

St. Michael's Mount

Alphonse Esquiros, a Frenchman who wrote books explaining the English to his countrymen, came to Cornwall in the summer of 1863: 'The characteristic features of the mineralogy of the country is the presence of copper, and, before all, of tin. The abundance of the two metals has favoured in Cornwall, since time immemorial, the development of the mining industry. Diodorus Siculus states that the ancient Britons loaded tin on wicker boats covered with leather and carried it thus to the island of Ictis. Where is this Ictis? Persons have fancied that they found it in St. Michael's Mount, an island at high water and a peninsula when the sea retires. In history, the St. Michael's Mount of Cornwall has been frequently confounded with Mont Saint Michel, near St. Malo. Both are alternately separated from the coast, and rejoined to it by the tidal movement, and both have been a monastery, but the English Mont Saint Michel, more fortunate than ours, has never been a prison.

'Timoeus, the historian, who lived in the time of Pliny, tells us also that these same Britons tore tin out of the rocks, and carried it to the neighbouring islands at low water. The tin was loaded to Phoenician ships, which conveyed it to Tyre and Sidon. It is supposed that the bronzes of Assyria and Egypt were made of this metal, which was employed at a very early stage in the arts.'[54]

The idea that St Michael's Mount may in the third century B.C. have been a Phoenician tin port was also indicated by the Greek explorer Pytheas, quoted by Nigel Calder as saying 'They beat the metal into half cylinders and carry it to a certain island lying off Britain, called Ictis. During the ebb tide the space between dries out, and they carry abundant tin over into this island in their wagons.'[3]

The landscape painter, Joseph Farington, recorded a day at St Michael's Mount on 8 September 1810: 'Before breakfast made a finished sketch of St Michael's Mount from the Star Inn. I next hired a boat with two fishermen to take me round the island, which they undertook to do and to allow me time for making sketches, for a reward of four shillings. The weather was very fine, and the sea sufficiently smooth to enable them to keep the boat nearly stationary wherever I chose to remain. This rock, with its castle, is a noble subject for a painter. The west front of it which faces the ocean is the most rugged and precipitous, The form and the colour of it is beautiful, and all the parts are so much in unison; the castle is in all respects in such harmony with the rock upon which it stands, as almost to seem a natural part of it. The general colour of the rock is grey of various degrees; such also is that of the castle; but in both there is a mixture of other tints which by their opposition give greater effect to the whole. The herbage which forms a part of the surface is of a mild and subdued colour, well agreeing with the grave hue of the castle and rock.

'I passed a considerable time in contemplating the island from various points and in sketching; and my boatmen being satisfied with the bargain they had made, and being young and cheerful, they sung while I pursued my purpose.'[55]

John Davidson wrote a poem about it:

> *St. Michael's Mount, the tidal isle,*
> *In May with daffodils and lilies*
> *Is kirtled gorgeously a while*
> *As ne'er another English hill is:*
> *About the precipices cling*
> *The rich renascence robes of Spring.*[56]

Here is a more recent description from James Turner. 'St. Michael's Mount has to be seen, in sunlight, from the town of Marazion, when light flashes from the glass of the church on the top. Now is the Archangel sharpening his bright sword and you can believe in the host of heaven. The strand which joins the island to the mainland is bright with shells and seaweeds, with Oarweed and Bladderwrack, or the red seaweed from which women used once to make lipstick and rouge. And small cowrie shells, and the piddock shell which is phosphorescent at night, giving forth a pale-blueish white light, and the limpet and purple mussels, those small strong shells with their effective armour. When the tide is full over the strand and the Island is isolated, then is the time for the anemones to open their colours from pink through yellows and whites to a pinkish brown, the Beadlet, the Strawberry, the Daisy, the Dahlia and the Snake Locks anemone, poisoning their prey before pulling it into a central mouth.'[57]

Mount's Bay

Raleigh and Spenser landed in Mount's Bay in 1589, on their return from Ireland, Spenser describing their approach to the shore, past Land's End and St. Michael's Mount in 'Colin Clout's Come Home Again':

> *The first to which we nigh approchèd, was*
> *An high headland thrust far into the sea,*
> *Like to an horne, whereof the name it has,*
> *Yet seemed to be a goodly pleasant lea:*
> *There did a loftie mount at first us greet,*
>
> *Which did a stately heape of stones upreare,*
> *That seemd amid the surges for to fleet,*
> *Much greater then that frame, which us did beare:*
> *There did our ship her fruitfull wombe unlade,*
> *And put us all ashore.*[58]

Penzance

Pen Sans is Cornish for 'holy headland', the town being a port and seaside resort at the beginning of the Land's End peninsula. It has a long history, and is a cultural centre for the far south-west. It was the birthplace in 1778 of Sir Humphry Davy, poet and inventor of the miners' Safety Lamp: his statue, in a quite elegant pose, stands upon granite blocks at the top of Market Jew Street. The poet John Davidson lived the last year of his life in Penzance, before drowning himself in Mount's Bay in 1909.

Thomas Hardy set his short story 'A Mere Interlude' partly in Penzance, which he called 'Pen-Zephyr'. Baptista Trewthen, daughter of a farmer in St. Maria's, one of the Isles of Lyonesse (*i.e.* Scilly), and graduate of a Teachers' Training College at Tor-upon-Sea (*i.e.* Torquay), arrived in Pen-Zephyr just too late for the Saturday steamboat, and had to pass the time there until the next one on

DAVY

Tuesday: 'The town and the walks in this land of strawberries, these headquarters of early English flowers and fruit were then, as always, attractive. From the more picturesque streets she went to the town gardens and the Pier and the harbour, and looked at men at work there, loading and unloading as in the time of the Phoenicians'.

Along came a former college acquaintance, now a schoolteacher, Charles Stow. He was disappointed to learn that she was expected to return to the island and marry Mr. David Heddegan, but after persuasive discussion she surprisingly agreed to marry him instead, and by Tuesday morning they were back in Pen-Zephyr awaiting the island boat: 'The heat of the morning was by this time intense. They clambered up some cliffs, and while sitting there, looking around at St Michael's Mount and other objects, Charles said to her that he would run down to the beach at their feet and take just one plunge into the sea. She gazed at the still outline of St. Michaels, now beautifully toned in gray', but Charles had vanished – he had swum too far out, and drowned. Baptista decided to say nothing of this marriage, and return to St Maria's to marry Heddegan. Within a day or two they were back in a crowded Pen-Zephyr, the only hotel they could find being the one in which the drowned Charles had been placed in the next room. It is thus a heavily contrived story of how a young woman came to spend her first bridal night between two husbands, one dead and the other living, in a thinly sketched Penzance.[59]

Leslie Thomas arrived in this part of Cornwall: 'As I drove down the final stretch of road to Penzance on that winter day, the rain and the mists were left behind clothing the moors. The sky cleared miraculously and I arrived at Mount's Bay on what could only be described as a perfect spring evening. Fading light over blue water, cormorants diving in the empty seas, the last of the sun on the shingle and children running and calling on the beach.

'That night the western wind banged about the town like a drunkard, rattling at my window and whooping through the empty channels of the streets. But morning came with a great grin of sunshine and from my bed I could hear that free, salty sound of seagulls crying over the bay, a sound that can almost be smelled: I went to the window and lifted the sash and there it was again, like a vision. The wide unruffled sea, the lambent sky, the unseasonal sun and the birds like paper in the breeze. It was January the sixth.'[60]

Newlyn

Newlyn, nearby, around the bay, has long been a busy fishing harbour, and in the eighteen-nineties it was the centre for the group of artists who became the Cornish impressionists. It even has a 'Rue des Beaux Arts'. Kenneth McConkey wrote of these Impressionists: 'Stanhope Forbes who first went there at the beginning of 1884, discovered Walter Langley, E.A. Waterlow and several other painters already in residence. Within a short time the village became an 'artistic Klondike', playing host to Frank Bramley, Edwin Harris, Leghe Suthers, Ralph Todd, Albert Chevallier Tayler, Thomas Cooper Gotch and for a short time, Henry Scott Tuke. At Newlyn [according to Forbes] "every corner was a picture and more important from the point of view of the figure painter, the people seemed to fall naturally into their places, and to harmonize with their surroundings."[61]

'Stanhope Forbes's school of painting lasted until the Second World War, and only his declining health brought it to a close. After his success in 1885 with 'A Fish Sale on a Cornish Beach' at the Royal Academy, his painting continued, detailed and careful, showing a wide knowledge of the lives of the fisherfolk he lived amongst and with whom he was so popular.

'His colleague at Newlyn until 1895, Henry Scott Tuke, continued to paint in a very similar but more delicate style. Tuke exhibited at the Royal Academy from 1879. His drawings and paintings of the sea and ships were as sensitive as those he made of naked boys and youths bathing, standing on the shore or lying upon rocks, a subject historians and critics would no doubt have remarked upon far less had they been women or girls.'[62]

Stanhope Forbes wrote: 'What lodestone of artistic metal the place contains I know not, but its effects were strongly felt in the studios of Paris and Antwerp, particularly by a number of young English painters studying there who just about then, by some common impulse, seemed drawn towards this corner of their native land.'[63] Dylan Thomas spent his honeymoon here in 1937, and wrote to Pamela Hansford Johnson that he was 'a long way from everywhere, in a high huge haystack of a studio over the harbour...drinking scaly beer in the pubs near the fish market.'[64]

Jean Goodman told of another painter, Laura Knight, who came to live in Newlyn in 1907: her picture 'The Beach' was shown at the Royal Academy. She 'enraged the locals by bringing professional models down from London and posing them nude on the rocks in the sunlight.'[65]

Mousehole

Mousehole, in a tiny cove to the south of Penlee Point, is another fishing village, the harbour, partly sheltered by rocky St Clement's Isle. In 1595 the Spaniards invaded and briefly occupied this area, and this is where Dolly Pentreath, who claimed to be the last Cornish speaker, died in 1777. Mousehole was used in the 'Poldark' television series as the setting for the miners' riot.

Leo Tregenza told of his boyhood in this part of Cornwall early in the present century, and described Mousehole: 'The older cottages, whose granite has weathered to a softer brown, seem with their little windows to enclose the narrow streets, which, if they have any plan at all, run mostly inland from the harbour and are joined to each other in unexpected places by a few shorter passage ways. Wherever you are walking inside this concentration of houses you have the feeling of being hidden from the world outside. Only the gulls and jackdaws on the roofs above know exactly where you are, and the slightly ringing sound of your own footsteps reminds you of the heavier tread of sea-boots that used to move slowly up and down in the old days. Here and there a dark alley may lead you into a sequestered square of unsuspected size, where flowers in window boxes and climbing roses look out on to a central garden. If you look carefully you can still find old nail holes in some of the house walls and even the rusty nails themselves on which gutted and flattened fish, mostly ling, used to be hung and dried in the sun and open air'.

Mousehole artist

Just offshore is St Clements Isle: 'The Island, straight out from the harbour and The Cliff, is a familiar landmark in our view of the sea. It is a typical example of the hard metamorphic rock, weathered a dark brown, that still clings to the granite in different places around our shores. It is best seen at high tide and from perhaps a couple of hundred feet up on the hillsides at the back, for from that height its distance from the shore, the depth of the surrounding water, and its real shape and size are revealed. It has always seemed the ideal island-form to me, in the graceful way it sends out its little promontories to meet the rippling impact of the tides; in the level platform at mid-height where the grass and sea pinks grow; and in the off-centre peak, broad-based and narrowing to just the shapely height required, seeming from that eminence to say, "I am the lord and master of these waves".

'It has its own 'Shag Rock' too, just separate from it at its southern end, and it is the natural haunt, not of shags only, but of the more numerous gulls. Their white forms are always to be seen standing there or circling in the air above, and their calls, so strident and so plangent from the rooftops of the village, seem at that distance to merge softly into the wide sea atmosphere.'[66]

The Ship Inn was frequented by Dylan Thomas; he described Mousehole as 'the loveliest village in England', and called Raginnis Hill 'Ragginis-is-good-for-you-Hill'.

Shipwreck at Tater-du

Newlyn and Mousehole are famous for lifeboatmen who have gone out to so many ships in distress. On 19 December 1981 the dark blue door of a lifeboat house on Penlee Point opened once again and the lifeboat *Solomon Browne* was launched into the stormy waters of Mount's Bay. Nigel Calder continued the story: 'The Dutch captain of an Irish coaster, *Union Star*, had reported engine failure in the Channel some six miles offshore. A storm-force wind gusting to ninety knots was blowing from the south and driving the disabled ship towards the Cornish shore. A British naval helicopter from Culdrose, piloted by Russell Smith of the U.S. Navy, tried repeatedly to rescue the people aboard *Union Star*, but the weather made it impossible. The ship was close to the shore near Tater-du when the lifeboat reached her.

'As Coxswain Richards tried to manoeuvre alongside, a huge wave lifted the lifeboat and smashed her down on the coaster's deck. The boat slithered back into the sea. At another attempt, the same thing happened again. Still the lifeboat did not give up. She went in once more, and slammed hard against the *Union Star*'s side. This visit gave four of the coaster's people the chance to jump aboard the lifeboat. It was already a gold-medal rescue, but there were still four others aboard the coaster, and the rocky shore was only fifty metres away. When last seen, the lifeboat was turning as if for another attempt. A wave overwhelmed the coaster and pitched her on the shore. The lights of the lifeboat disappeared.

153

Victims and rescuers died together in the frenzied sea. Daylight found the *Union Star* upside down at the foot of the cliffs west of Tater-du.

'Another lifeboat was sent at once to Newlyn to provide temporary cover in Mount's Bay, while fresh volunteers from Mousehole began immediate training for the lifeboat that very soon replaced *Solomon Browne*'.

There have been many shipwrecks around the south-west coast over the past two centuries. As Nigel Calder explained: 'Coxswains command the lifeboats, but the crew are all volunteers who train and risk their lives because they choose to, not because they are bullied or bribed. For a coastal community to have a lifeboat station is a matter of privilege and pride; it is their boat, and local people man it and run it. Fund-raising, the design of boats and equipment, and certain practicalities of search and rescue procedures are coordinated at the headquarters at Poole in Dorset, but the 'National' in the Royal National Lifeboat Institution's title only means nationwide, and nothing governmental. Since 1824 the organisation has been run entirely on donations from the public, and makes no charge for its services.'[3]

The Cornish writer J.T. Blight described the coast south of Mousehole in 1861: 'The beach here is covered with great loose rocks, very fatiguing to walk over, some of them immediately at the base of the cliff being overspread with trailing weeds which creep down from the top of the precipice, hanging about in wild luxuriance. They do not at all seem timid to approach the great waves, yet in winter they must lose the ground they gain in summer and be ruthlessly swept away. I have seen growing here in great vigour, within a few yards of the surf, a not very common variety of the great bindweed, having flowers beautifully striped with pink. *Hookeria loetevirens* is also found in one or two caves along this part of the coast, indeed, it is the only known English habitat for this rare moss.'[67]

Lamorna Cove

The grey granite cliffs continue south of Mousehole to Lamorna Cove, with its granite shores and boulder-strewn slopes below quarries. A delightful lane runs down, through Lamorna Valley, to the cove where there is a small, sandy beach. S.P.B. Mais thought that: 'This is a valley that must be taken slowly and every temptation to wander casually succumbed to. Everything here seems to have been touched by a magic hand from the moment you first look down into the clear water of the cove.'[68]

The impressionist painter John Birch came to live here in 1890 and, to distinguish himself from another with the same name, became Lamorna Birch.

In the 1920s W.H. Davies wrote a poem:

> *I see at last our great Lamorna Cove,*
> *Which, danced on by ten thousand silver feet,*

Has all those waves that run like little lambs,
To draw the milk from many a rocky teat,
Spilt in white gallons all along the shore.
Who ever saw more beauty under the sun?
I look and look, and say, "No wonder here's
A light I never saw on earth before –
Two heavens are shining here instead of one."
And, like the wild gulls flashing in my sight,
Each furious thought that's driving through my brain
Screams in its fresh young wonder and delight.[69]

Lamorna Valley

Close by, Derek Tangye and his wife Jeannie lived in their cottage 'Minack' in six acres of land on the rugged coast. He has written a series of books, inspired by the local countryside, beginning with *A Gull on the Roof*: 'Lamorna, then, is a pilgrimage of the day tripper and though the narrow road on a summer afternoon is choked with cars, charabancs and dust, the evening comes and the valley is silent again. In winter it is always silent except for the wind in the trees and the echo of the surf in the cove, and it becomes a valley to cure a cynic. The air is sweet with the scent of the violet plants which climb up the hillside in neat cultivated rows, and as you walk along you will meet a picker, a basket of violets or anemones in either hand, taking them home to bunch.

'The path we walked along was only the shadow of a path, more like the trodden run of badgers. Here, because there was no sign of habitation, because the land and boulders and the rocks embraced the sea without interference, we could sense we were part of the beginning of time, the centuries of unceasing waves, the unseen pattern of the wild generations of foxes and badgers, the age-less gales that lashed the desolate land, exultant and roaring, a giant harbour of sunken ships in their wake. And we came to a point, after a steep climb, where a great Carn stood balanced on a smaller one, as if it were a sentinel waiting to hail the ghosts of lost sailors. The track, on the other side, had tired of the undergrowth which blocked its way along the head of the cliff, for it sheered seawards, tumbling in a zigzag course to the scarred grey rocks below. We stood on the pinnacle [and saw] the curve of Mount's Bay leading to the Lizard Point on the left, the Wolf Rock lighthouse a speck in the distance, a French crabber a mile off-shore, pale blue hull and small green sail aft, chugging through the white speckled sea towards Newlyn, and high above us a buzzard, with is wings spread motionless, soaring effortlessly into the sky.'[70]

A little to the west J.T. Blight described the granite buttress on a high headland: 'The rocks at Cairn Boscawen are piled up in a very extraordinary manner: at one place is a curious opening; beneath this 'pensile stone' Dr. Borlase conjectured the Arch-Druid might have sat and delivered his decisions and predictions, No one can say that it was not used for such a purpose, the Druids adopted imposing masses of rock to produce a greater effect, and they may as well have used this as any other. Then again it is pleasant to rest here in the sunshine on the beautiful green sward, above the blue sea, and look into the ages back, and fancy these awful priests gliding in a mysterious manner about the Cairns, performing some peculiar ceremony, and we cannot but feel obliged to the Doctor for his specu-lations, which have cast a halo of romance around the spot.'[67]

Penberth and Porthcurno

Leo Tregenza considered headlands on the coast between Penberth and Porthcurno were 'ideal places on which to sit and laze away the time. Here the sea is on the south side and seems to possess a softer, mistier blue as the sun shifts its sparkling wake across it throughout the long summer's day. The coloured Persian carpets of spreading gorse and heather are bright and fair to view on the coastal downs, beautifully placed somewhere between the widespread blue of sea and sky whose soft bloom seems to be surrounding them everywhere, lending an unblemished purity to the yellow of the gorse where it lies and luxuriates in the full warmth of the day. The weathered granite of the clifftops, shaggy with lichen's sober green and grey, has its own little outcrops of sea-pinks and sea-campions, and squills like miniature bluebells abound in the short grass.

'Sitting or lying back on the deeper, cushioning grass of the steep slope a few yards down, one can feel the air rising smooth and cool upon the face as one watches the birds and the sea below. One of the larger rocks, fully exposed at low tide, has a level surface on its landward side that is a favourite haunt of seals. You may watch half-a-dozen or more lying idly there for hours on end, until the rising flood starts washing in upon them from the outside and they slip one by one into the inshore water again.'[66]

The Logan Stone

Here, on a rocky promontory called Horrace, stands the Logan Stone, a perched and rocking granite block that weighs 66 tons, amid granite buttresses, a rough, noisy, and dangerous place in a high west wind. Darrell Bates related how 'William Borlase [the Cornish antiquarian] had asserted that it was "morally impossible that any lever or indeed force applied in a mechanical manner can remove it from its present position". This of course was asking for trouble, and in 1824 a young Lieutenant of the Royal Navy named Goldsmith, a nephew of Oliver Goldsmith, took up the challenge with the aid of a dozen sailors. They succeeded in dislodging the stone from its position of delicate balance'. This act provoked a letter of complaint to the Admiralty, who 'responded by ordering Goldsmith to put the stone back which he did, with the aid of a forest of derricks, poles, block and ropes.'[7] The cost of this exercise almost ruined the young Lieutenant.

Minack Theatre

The steep cliffs continue to Porthcurno, where Derek Parker described the sea 'grumbling against the bases of towers of rock far below the path. Porthcurno is one sandy beach, not the safest in the country for bathing. Above it hangs at the very edge of the cliff the little open-air Minack Theatre, built single-handedly by Rowena Cade in 1932. There is a season of plays by local and visiting companies here each summer, and on a fine evening (provided one is well supplied with creature comforts – cushions, blankets, coffee or similarly warming liquids) it is a good place to be as Ariel is set free over the Cornish coast, or Lear totters in the face of a very tangible storm, or music moves out over the face of the water.'[71]

In recent years theatrical people have been elaborating The Minack Theatre, and a large car park and associated buildings have appeared on the cliff. It will be unfortunate if this development expands and disfigures this fine coastal headland.

A Granite Coast

Wilkie Collins' ramble brought him along this coast in 1860: 'On approaching the wondrous landscapes between Treen and the Land's End, the first characteristic that strikes you is the change that has taken place in the forms of the cliffs since you left the Lizard Head. You no longer look on variously shaped and variously coloured 'serpentine' rocks; it is granite, and granite alone, that appears everywhere – granite, less lofty and less eccentric in form than the 'serpentine' cliffs and crags; but presenting an appearance of adamantine solidity and strength. In these wild districts the sea rolls and roars in fiercer agitation, and the mists fall thicker, and at the same time fade and change faster than elsewhere.

'Up on the top of the cliffs, furze and heath in brilliant clothing of purple and yellow, cluster close round great white, weird masses of rock, dotted fantastically with patches of grey-green moss.

'Suddenly, you discern a small strip of beach shut in snugly between protecting rocks. A spring bubbles down from an inland valley; while not far off, an old stone well collects the water into a calm, clear pool.

'Sturdy little cottages, built of rough granite, and thickly thatched, stand near you, with gulls' and cormorants' eggs set in their loop-holed windows for ornament. Down on the beach, where the rough old fishing-boats lie, the sand is entirely formed by countless multitudes of the tiniest, fairy-like shells, often as small as a pin's head, and all exquisitely tender in colour and wonderfully varied in form.'[4]

The granite headlands along this Penwith coastline have Cornish place-names like Pedn-men-an-mere, which are immediately understood by Bretons and have counterparts in other Celtic languages of the Atlantic seaboard. There are carns (headlands with heaped granite blocks) and zawns (coastal chasms). It is a wild coast, a coast for sea-birds, such as choughs:

> *Desolate that cry as though world were unworthy.*
> *See now, rounding the headland, a forlorn hopeless bird,*
> *trembling black wings fingering the blowy air,*
> *dainty and ghostly, careless of the scattering salt.*
>
> *This is the cave-dweller that flies like a butterfly,*
> *buffeted by daws, almost extinct, who has chosen,*
> *so gentle a bird, to live on furious coasts.*

Here where sea whistles in funnels, and slaps the back
of burly granite slabs, and hisses over holes,
in bellowing hollows that shelter the female seal
the Cornish chough wavers over the waves.

By lion rocks, rocks like the heads of queens,
sailing with ragged plumes upturned, into the wind
goes delicate indifferent the doomed bird.[72]

Porthgwarra

This little cove was the setting for Sheila Bird's story 'All for Love', which began: 'In the late 18th century, the fisherfolk of Porthgwarra lived in a world of their own, far removed from other communities by land, and unnoticed from the sea, tucked away as they were at the head of a small inlet on the western tip of Mount's Bay. Although so close to the bare and barren extremity of Land's End, the little hamlet was cosseted between the flower-strewn hills, where the humming of the bees and the sounds of the ocean blended contentedly on the summer air. But the wild Atlantic was their garden, and it governed their lives. When cruel winds howled across the eastern plateau and raging seas pounded relentlessly along the steep and rocky shoreline, the hardy fisherfolk of Porthgwarra hauled their boats up to a higher level, and maintained a seaward vigil until the storm abated. For these proud and handsome seafarers, said to be descendants of Spaniards cast upon these shores, owed a debt to humanity, and were renowned for their skill and daring when it came to preserving life from the perils of the deep. One might imagine that Porthgwarra, with its background of smuggling, fishing and adventure at sea, would be remembered for its swashbuckling, colourful exploits, but strange to tell, the memory which lingers on in legend concerns the pain of true love, which never did run smoothly, and ultimate tragedy. It was a tale of a farmer's daughter and a lowly fisherman's son; a sad story of love among the crabpots.'[73]

Land's End

Londoner Walter White arrived here in July 1854: 'Soon after passing Treves-can, the westernmost village of England, we came to the top of a slope, from which the ground falls away to the edge of the cliffs. There was the sea before us, and this was the Land's End. Those who expect to see a towering or far-stretching promontory will be disappointed. We form our ideas from ordinary maps, and imagine England's utmost cape to be a narrow tongue thrust out from the firm shore along which we may walk to meet the advancing waves. But we find the reality to be merely a protruding shoulder or buttress of the vast irregular bluff that terminates the country. Cape Cornwall, which looks so good about two miles distant, appears to extend farther to the west than the Land's End.

'Sit still and gaze: the scene grows upon you. Here the two Channels co-mingle with the ocean, and far out as eye can reach and round on either hand till it meets the remotest point of the rugged shore, stretches the watery expanse. The billows come tumbling in, and break in thunder at the base of the cliffs, dashing the impatient spray well nigh to their summit.

'You may descend by steep paths to a lower level and see the cavernous opening which their plunging assaults have worn through from one side of the buttress to the other. With what fury they rush into the recess, and make horrid whirlpools behind the mass which some day will be an isolated member of the rocky group scattered along the shore. There on the largest of the cluster nearly two miles from shore stands the Longships Lighthouse, and all between is foam and swirl; waves running together and leaping high with the shock; a dangerous channel, known as the Kettle's Bottom. See how the water chafes around the Armed Knight there on the left, and the Irish Lady on the right, and all the nameless lumps. Yonder, under the Cape, at the extremity of Whitesand Bay, are the Brisons, invested by shipwreck with a fearful interest.'[74]

In the early years of this century, W.H. Hudson enjoyed the solitariness:

'Although the vague image of an imagined Land's End fades from the mind and is perhaps lost when the reality is known, the ancient associations of the place remain, and, if a visit be rightly timed, they may invest it with a sublimity and fascination not its own. I loitered many days near that spot in mid-winter, in the worst possible weather, but even when pining for a change to blue skies and genial sunshine I blessed the daily furious winds which served to keep the pilgrims away, and to half blot out the vulgar modern buildings with rain and mist from the Atlantic. At dark I would fight my way against the wind to the cliff, and down by the sloping narrow neck of land to the masses of loosely piled rocks at its extremity. It was a very solitary place at that hour, where one feared not to be intruded on by any other night-wanderer in human shape. The raving of the wind among the rocks; the dark ocean – exceedingly dark except when the flying clouds were broken and the stars shining in the clear spaces touched the big black incoming waves with a steely-grey light; the jagged isolated rocks, on which so many ships have been shattered, rising in awful blackness from the spectral foam that appeared and vanished and appeared again; the multitudinous hoarse sounds of the sea, with throbbing and hollow booming noises in the caverns beneath – all together served to bring back something of the old vanished picture or vision of Bolerium as we first imagine it. The glare from the various lighthouses visible at this point only served to heighten the inexpressibly sombre effect, since shining from a distance they made the gloomy world appear vaster.'[75]

Leslie Thomas arrived at Land's End in winter: 'I was all at once confronted with the wide and utter magnficence of the untrammelled sea. It was spread gloriously around Cornwall, shining like new, incredibly and unjanuarably blue.

The salt breeze came directly from it, getting into the eyes and nose, enough to make your hair curl. The Longships lighthouse stood up straight, miles out. Ships crept like mice along the skyline.'[60]

The scientist, Sir Humphry Davy, turned to poetry 'On Land's End':

> *On the sea*
> *The sunbeams tremble, and the purple light*
> *Illumes the dark Bolerium, seat of storms.*
> *High are his granite rocks, his frowning brow*
> *Hangs o'er the smiling ocean. In his caves*
> *The Atlantic breezes murmur; in his caves,*
> *Where sleep the haggard spirits of the storm.*
> *Wild, dreary, are the frowning rocks around,*
> *Encircled by the wave, where to the breeze*
> *The haggard cormorant shrieks; and far beyond,*
> *Where the great ocean mingles with the sky,*
> *Are seen the cloud-like islands, grey in mist.*[76]

Land's End used to be tawdry, but was tidied up by Peter de Savary, and now belongs to an American businessman. There are neat whitewashed buildings, with a variety of tourist attractions including the lifeboat *James and Catherine MacFarlane*, formerly based at Padstow and the Lizard / Cadgwith Station. It is much like American reconstructions of English villages, alongside the Queen Mary at Long Beach in California, for example. Perhaps it is an English version of how Americans imagine Cornwall?

The castellated granite cliffs step down into the Atlantic surf, and offshore is the Longships Reef with its lighthouse, and beyond that the Isles of Scilly.

THE ISLES
OF SCILLY

Islands of Granite

The Isles of Scilly are a wild Atlantic archipelago lying about twenty-five miles from Land's End. The poet Swinburne called them 'a small, sweet world of wave-encompassed wonder'. Although there are numerous small islands, some no more than rocky crags jutting out of the sea, only five are inhabited. All of them were once the tor-crowned peaks of an undulating granite landscape, much like Penwith, Dartmoor or Bodmin Moor, which has been largely submerged by the sea.

Lyonesse

So obvious is this submergence that many have claimed that this is where the legend originated of Lyonesse, the Arthurian lost land beneath the sea. On a clear, calm day, passengers in the helicopter from Penzance may catch a glimpse, down through the waves, of lines and circles of stones that may have been roads, farm walls, and huts before the sea rose over them. Walter de la Mare put this into a poem, 'Sunk Lyonesse':

> *In sea-cold Lyonesse,*
> *When the Sabbath eve shafts down*
> *On the roofs, walls, belfries*
> *Of the foundered town,*
> *The Nereids pluck their lyres*
> *Where the green translucency beats,*
> *And with motionless eyes at gaze*
> *Make minstrelsy in the streets.*
> *And the ocean water stirs*
> *In salt-worn casement and porch.*[1]

Ruth Manning-Sanders recounted the legend: 'Under the shallow waters between the Islands and the mainland lies the lost land of Lyonesse, with its one hundred and forty churches, whose bells still sound a mournful cadence as the waves surge and swell. A rich and fruitful land, this Lyonesse, low-lying and sheltered between the Cornish moors and the peaks of Scilly; its inhabitants carefree, industrious, pious, basking in content: till came the deluge. A monstrous wall of water fell on Lyonesse drowning the fields and orchards, drowning the towns and villages, drowning the churches, drowning the people. This happened, so Florence of Worcester tells us with grave precision, on 11th November 1099. Only one man escaped riding a fleet white horse that out-galloped the flood and brought his master safe ashore where the waters fell back from Sennen cliffs. At least two Cornish families claim the honour of descent from this intrepid rider. But, legend apart, the Isles of Scilly are undoubtedly the granite peaks of a drowned country, once connected with the mainland. They have a fairy-like, "other-world" atmosphere, at once fascinating and disturbing. So much of them is underwater (for time was when they were not many islands but one, and time was when they were not even an island but a peninsula) that one would not be surprised to wake any morning and find them vanished. To return to the mainland, and watch the massive cliffs of Cornwall draw near and even nearer, is to return to a sense of strong, solid, time-defining reality out of a world of dreams.'[2]

In 1756 William Borlase, the Cornish antiquary, wrote: 'It is reckoned only six or eight hours passage (with a fair wind) from St. Michael's Mount to Scilly, but we made it a great deal more. Putting off from the Mount in the Godolphin Sloop about seven in the morning, in about ten hours we got a-breast of the Gulph midway from Penzance to the Islands, keeping at a proper distance from the large and dangerous rock; some call it the Wolf, either from its devouring so many vessels as split upon it, or more likely from the howling which the waves make continually round it.

'These Islets and Rocks edge this Sound in an extremely pretty and very different manner from anything I had seen before. The sides of these little Islands continue their greenness to the brim of the water, where they are either sur-rounded by rocks of different shapes, which start up here and there as you advance, like so many enchanted castles, or by a verge of sand of the brightest colour. The sea, having eaten away passages between these hillocks, forms several pretty pools and lakes, and the crags which kept their stations, look so broken, intercepted, and so numerous, that the whole seemed but one large grotesque piece of rock-work.'[3]

Wilkie Collins
Wilkie Collins took a trip to the Isles of Scilly in the cutter-rigged *Tomtit*; they set out from "a famous watering-place on the western coast, called Mangerton-on-Mud" [possibly Weston-super-Mare]. After an eventful voyage lasting for several days, Collins saw the islands 'low-lying, and picturesque in an artistic point of view; but treacherous-looking and full of peril to the wary nautical eye.

Horrible jagged rocks, and sinister swirlings and foamings of the sea, seem to forbid the approach to them. The Scilly Islands seem, at a rough glance, to form a great irregular circle, enclosing a kind of lagoon of sea, communicating by various channels with the main ocean all around.

Tooth Rock, St. Mary's

'The circumference of the largest of the group is, as we heard, not more than thirteen miles. [The] masses of rock [are] wonderfully varied in shape and size. Inland, in the larger islands, the earth, where it is not planted or sown, is covered with heather and with the most beautiful ferns. The views are chiefly remarkable as natural panoramas of land and sea – the two always presenting themselves intermixed in the loveliest varieties of form and colour. On the coast, the granite rocks, though not notably high, take the most wildly and magnificently picture-seque shapes. They are rent into the strangest chasms and piled up in the grand-est confusion; and they look down, every here and there, on the loveliest little sandy bays, where the sea, in calm weather, is as tenderly blue and limpid in its clearness as the Mediterranean itself. The softness and purity of the climate may be imagined, when I state that in the winter none of the freshwater pools are strongly enough frozen to bear being skated on. The balmy sea air blows over each little island as freely as it might blow over the deck of a ship.'[4]

165

The novelist John Fowles began his essay on islands by considering these Isles: 'The wise visitor to the Scillies does not drive straight to Penzance and board a helicopter or a ship, but finds time, so long as the weather is clear and visibility good, to go out first to Land's End. And there they float, an eternal stone armada of over a hundred ships, aloofly anchored off England; mute, enticing, forever just out of reach. The effect is best later in the day, when they lie in the westering sun's path, more like optical illusions, mirages, than a certain reality. I say 'they', but the appearance at this range is of one island; which has a justice in it, since in remote antiquity all the larger islands except St. Agnes very probably were conjoined.'[5]

St. Mary's

Alfred Lord Tennyson came to the Isles of Scilly in 1860 and 'never saw anything quite like them'. On the terrace of the Tregarthen Hotel in Hugh Town, St. Mary's, a plaque says: 'Lord Alfred Tennyson on his visit to these Isles stayed at Tregarthen's Hotel and spent the most of his time in these gardens where he is supposed to have written *Enoch Arden*.'

Alphonse Esquiros sailed out from the mainland in 1865 and his description is as evocative today as it was over a hundred years ago. 'After two or three hours at sea we perceived on the horizon the Scilly Isles. For some time we coasted frowning rocks, prodigious natural fortresses. The first sight of these islands is most singular; if ever our continents are swallowed up by the sea they will have this form. Scattered and torn strips of granite seem to float on the surface of a sea full of terror and grandeur. At first sight these islets appeared uninhabited; they might be called the ruins of a world. A vast ocean, on which the sunbeams were beginning to decline, roared with an imperious air around this truly wrecked land, which was, however, protected by a bristling belt of cliffs.

'The interior of St Mary's is a delicious garden, surrounded by a formidable belt of rocks and cliffs, among which ranges the haughty promontory of Penninis. You find there all the charms of a green and well-tilled country, watered by streams and rills, and forming a perpetual contrast with the gloomiest landscape and the wildest beauties.'[6]

Major Vigoureux

Sir Arthur Quiller Couch described the islands as they were in the latter part of the nineteenth century in his romance, *Major Vigoureux*.

'Saaron Island lies about due south of Brefar, which looks eastward upon Iniscaw across the narrow gut of Cromwell's Sound. There was a time (the tale goes) when these three Islands made one. At low-water springs you may cross afoot between Saaron and Brefar, and from either of them, with a little more danger, to Iniscaw, picking your way between the pools and along the sandy flats that curve about the southern end of the Sound. Also there are legends of stone walls and foundations of houses laid bare from time to time as the waters have receded after a gale, and by the next tides covered again with sand.'

'The Garrison occupied the heights of a peninsula connected with St. Lide's by a low sandy isthmus, across which it looked towards the "country side" of the island, though this country side was in fact concealed by rising ground, for the most part uncultivated, where sheets of mesembryanthemum draped the out-cropping ledges of granite. At the foot of the hill, around the pier and harbour to the north and east, clustered St. Hugh's Town, and climbed by one devious street to the Garrison gate. From where he stood the Commandant could almost look down its chimneys. Along the isthmus straggled a few houses in double line, known as New Town; and beyond, where the isthmus widened, lay the Old Town around its Parish Church. These three together made Garland Town, the capital of the Islands; and the population of St. Lide's – town, garrison, and country side - numbered a little over fourteen hundred. Garrison Hill, rising with a pretty steep acclivity, attains the height of a hundred and ten feet above sea level. It measures about three quarters of a mile in length and a quarter of a mile in breadth, and the lines of fortification extended around the whole hill (except upon the north-west side, which happened to be the most important), a circuit of one mile and a quarter'.

From this eminence, the Commandant could catch 'a glimpse of blue sky and lilac-coloured cloud, touched with gold by the newly risen sun; a perfect morning, clean and crisp, with the sea a translucent blue, and sunlight glittering on the Island beaches'. The islands changed little:

'They would be unchanged', the Commandant was told, 'were I to come back after a hundred [years]. The same rocks, the same beaches, the same hum of the tides; the same flowers; the same blue water here below us; the same outline of a spear-head there, beyond St. Anne's, where the tide forces its way through the slack water; the same streak of yellow yonder on the south cliffs of Saaron.'[7]

We think Saaron must be Samson, due south of Brefar, which is Bryher; which makes Iniscaw Tresco. St Lide's is St Mary's, St Hugh's Town Hugh Town, where indeed The Garrison stands on a smaller island linked by a low isthmus. The location of Garland Town, the capital of the islands, is a puzzle.

167

Samson

Walter Besant set his turn-of-the century melodrama, *Armorel of Lyonesse,* on Samson. The island is no longer inhabited but people visit it and seek out the cottage that Armorel Rosevean is said to have lived in.

'The hill which rises behind the house is the southern hill of the two, which, with the broad valley between them, make up the island of Samson. This hill slopes steeply seaward to south and west. It is not a lofty hill, by any means. In Scilly there are no lofty hills. When Nature addressed herself to the construction of this archipelago she brought to the task a light touch. At the moment she happened to be full of feeling for the great and artistic efforts which may be produced by small elevations, especially in those places where the material is granite. Therefore, though she raised no Alpine peak in Scilly, she provided great abundance and any variety of bold coast-line with rugged cliffs, lofty carn, and headlands piled with rocks.

'It would be strange on any evening, even after the calmest day of summer, when the sun is setting low, to see a small boat going out beyond Samson towards the Western islets. There the swell of ocean is always rolling among the rocks and round the crags and headlands of the isles. Only in calm weather and in broad daylight can the boatmen who know the place, venture in those waters. Not even the most skilled boatman would steer for the Outer Islands at sunset. For there are hidden rocks, long ridges of teeth that run out from the islands to tear and grind to powder any boat that should be caught in their devouring jaws.'[8]

Armorel left the islands and travelled the world, but eventually returned: '"There is Scilly, Miss," said the steward, pointing out to sea. Yes; low down the land lay, west by north. It looked like a cloud at first. Every moment it grew clearer; but always low down. What one sees at first are the eastern shores of St. Agnes and Gugh, St. Mary's and the Eastern Islands. They are all massed together, so that the eye cannot distinguish one from the other, but all seem to form continuous land. By degrees they separated.'[8]

Tresco

Wendy Aldridge came to the Isles of Scilly after the Second World War to make a living growing flowers: 'Archie and I spent four happy hours exploring the high downs and near-cliffs – steep rocky slopes ending in giant boulders by the shore – of the northern end of Tresco, which we had not visited before. Piper's Hole – a cave and adit fit for any tale of smugglers – eluded us; but views north, south, east and west of blue and purple sea – the sand-bottomed shallows swimming-bath green – among and around the Islands; light and shadow on fearsome rocks, where comorants dried their wings; grey-green humps of land, bordered by white beaches or heaped granite boulders; Round Island - a hassock all gadgetry on top, where the lighthouse shared the enclosure with intriguing-looking apparatus, stark against the sea; all these provided beauty and interest enough to fill a hundred, a thousand, such days.'[9]

St. Agnes

Kevin Crossley-Holland wrote: 'St. Agnes is a small place, a mile long and half a mile wide. Perhaps half the acreage is given over to the two landing places, three diminutive villages, and the fertile fields protected by high hedges of veronica, escallonia and pittosporum, where flowers and potatoes grow. The other half consists of Wingletang Downs, a place of impenetrable gorse and great weathered boulders, nothing man-made. Along the shore, there are a dozen granite fortresses, fanged and forbidding, but on Wingletang itself the rocks are mostly curved and hollowed. There are giants, slumbering lumbering shapes, whales, above all embryonic forms. That is why it is possible to enter into a relationship with them. Indeed it is impossible not to be reminded there of Henry Moore: two or three great slabs, once part of each other, still part of each other, half-buried now; natural formation irresistibly suggesting animal form, human form; everywhere the sense not only of mass but also of space; relationships.

'The granite of these rocks, and of all the rocks in Scilly, is a beautiful compound, because the felspar in it is pink or pale brown. But on Wingletang Downs there has been an invasion of lichen. It mutes the pinks and browns, the shining quartz and glittering mica, so that at any distance the boulders look mottled white and grey, a subdued colour even under the sun.

'There is nowhere else in Scilly anything like this. And there can be no more savage sight in Britain than the grim prospect from Wingletang towards that graveyard of ships, the Western Rocks. Vicious teeth, stumps, tusks, castellations, serrations stretch as far as the eye can see. When islanders sun themselves and talk of a 'flat calm', the water still churns and froths and foams in this cauldron.'[10]

Modern catastrophes have visited the islands too: 'The *Torrey Canyon* disaster will not lightly be forgotten. It was in Easter 1967 that this mammoth, carrying 100,020 tons of crude oil, slammed into the Sevenstones. The tanker's back was broken by the impact and two thirds of her cargo of oil poured into the sea. Detergents were poured on the water, troops stood by on the beaches, and finally the Government ordered that the *Torrey Canyon* should be bombed open and the remaining oil burned – an episode not without its humorous side when the RAF bombers displayed a startling inability to hit their target. Photographs of the enormous mushroom clouds of smoke that fanned out over the burning ship feature in most photograph albums in St. Agnes, and there was no day during my visit there when it was not mentioned in conversation.'[10]

Granite Landscape

Paul Ashbee looked at the rock formations: 'The Scillonian carns and rocks convey an infinite spectrum of colour, varying with sky and season. No words can properly portray the subtle shifts of texture and tint, or the myriad varieties of substance. In grey winter, with a dull leaden sky lowering with the promise of more rain, they seem nearly black. In spring and summer, when struck by sunlight, they glow as if activated by inner phosphorescence. When closely examined, each stone has its individual grain in which there is quartz varying in appearance from coarse marble to fine white lump sugar, while innumerable micas sparkle like diamonds. Luxuriant growths of grey-green lichen mantle all but the most exposed surfaces, which are sometimes stressed by vivid patches of scaly yellow. Plants such as sea-pink, hawkweed, ling and stonecrop, often thrive in their fissures. Other stones have only their furring and bearding of lichen, the tufts of which whisper and rustle in the wind. These ever-present rocks give to the Scillonian landscape a quality of timeless permanence, but everywhere they are being etched and ground by the relentless agencies of wind and weather, tide and time.' [11]

Lady Wilson

The former British Prime Minister, Lord Harold Wilson and his wife Lady Mary Wilson have, for many years, had a holiday home on St. Mary's. Here are two of her poems; the first called 'Spring':

> *Now that the dreary days have run their course*
> *We'll travel down to Scilly once again,*
> *To smell the sweet vanilla scent of gorse,*
> *The froth of garlic in the climbing lane.*
>
> *The unreaped fields are full of daffodils,*
> *We hear the cuckoo calling clear and plain;*
> *The spring tides surge and seethe across the quay,*
> *And watery sunsets glisten through the rain.*[12]

And the second the 'Isles of Scilly':

> *Nature is not more gentle here*
> *Than in the city's crowded core;*
> *For suddenly dark clouds appear,*
> *Green waves beat up along the shore,*
>
> *And on their crests black seaweed floats*
> *Adrift in rain and driving spray*
> *While all the gaily-coloured boats*
> *Rock at their moorings in the bay*
>
> *But when at last the storm is spent*
> *The sun bursts out with burning force,*

And draws towards the sky the scent
Of rain-washed earth, and rocks and gorse.

And, thrusting through the thinning haze,
Each little island gleams anew,
Its long white beaches all ablaze
With shining shells of every hue.

Now, when the starry dusk comes down,
With what a sure tranquillity
The lights glow from the little town!
And lights flash back across the sea.

From watchers round the coast, who keep
Night-long their vigil without rest,
That all of us may safely sleep
Among the Islands of the Blest.[12]

N O R T H
C O R N W A L L

Sennen Cove

Returning to the mainland at Land's End, we resume our journey along the coast past Sennen Cove, where the Atlantic surf rolls in strongly to rugged Cape Cornwall. Surfers ride the waves in Whitesand Bay, and the Sennen Cove lifeboat has been frequently launched in bad weather. A granite breakwater built by public subscription (according to a plaque on the wall) shelters a tiny harbour below the village of whitewashed cottages.

Botallack Tin Mine

Botallack, close to Cape Cornwall, was once a tin-miner's village. Wilkie Collins visited the mines during his summer holiday in Cornwall in 1851, and mentioned them and the local countryside in *Rambles Beyond Railways*: 'We left the Land's End, feeling that our homeward journey had now begun from that point; and walking northward, about five miles along the coast, arrived at Botallack. We were told to go to the counting-house to present our credentials; and on our road thither, we beheld buildings and machinery of the mine, literally stretching down the precipitous face of the cliff, from the land at the top to the sea at the bottom.

'Here, we beheld a scaffolding perched on a rock that rose out of the waves – there, a steam-pump was at work raising gallons of water from the mine every minute, on a mere ledge of land halfway down the steep cliff side. Chains, pipes, conduits, protruded in all directions from the precipice; rotten-looking wooden platforms, running over deep chasms, supported great beams of timber and heavy coils of cable; crazy little boarded houses were built, where gulls' nests might have been found in other places. There did not appear to be a foot of level space anywhere, for any part of the works of the mine to stand upon; and yet, there they were, fulfilling all the purposes for which they had been constructed, as safely and completely on rocks in the sea, and down precipices in the land, as if they had been cautiously founded on the tracts of smooth solid ground above!'[1]

He went down the mine and out beneath the sea: 'We are now four hundred yards out, and twenty fathoms below the sea level. Coast-trade vessels are sailing over our heads. Two hundred and forty feet beneath us men are at work, and there are galleries deeper yet.

'After listening for a few moments, a distant unearthly noise becomes faintly audible - a long, low, mysterious moaning, which never changes, which is felt on the ear as well as heard by it – a sound that might proceed from some incalculable distance, from some invisible height – a sound so unlike anything that is heard on the upper ground.

'At last the miner speaks, and tells us what we hear is the sound of the surf, lashing the rocks a hundred and twenty feet above us, and of the waves breaking on the beach beyond. The tide is now at the flow, and the sea is in no extraordinary state of agitation; so the sound is low and distant just at this period. But when storms are at their height, when the ocean hurls mountain after mountain of water at the cliffs, then the noise is terrific; the roaring heard down here in the mine is so inexpressibly fierce and awful that the boldest men at work are afraid to continue their labour. All ascend to the surface, to breathe the upper air and stand on the firm earth: dreading, though no such catastrophe has ever happened yet, that the sea will break in on them if they remain in the caverns below.'[1]

Botallack Mine

R.M. Ballantyne also came here in 1868 and his tale *Deep Down*, was about these Cornish miners : 'Botallack is the most celebrated mine in the great mining county of Cornwall. It stands on the sea-coast, a little more than a mile to the north of St. Just. The region around it is somewhat bleak, and almost destitute of trees. Botallack, like all the other mines, has several "shafts" or entrances to the works below, such as Boscawen Shaft; Wheal Button; Wheal Hazard; Chicornish Shaft; Davis Shaft and Wheal Cock, the most interesting of which are situated among the steep rugged cliffs that front and bid defiance to the utmost fury of the Atlantic Ocean.

'Here. amid the most savage gorges of the sea and riven rocks, - half clinging to the land, half suspended over the water – is perched the machinery of and entrance to the most singular shaft of the mine named the "Boscawen Diagonal Shaft" Starting as it does from an elevated position in the rocks that are close to the edge of the sea, and slanting down through the cape, outward or seaward, this vehicle descends only a few fathoms when it is *under the ocean's bed*, and then its further course is far out and deep down – about two thirds of a mile out, and full 245 fathoms down!

'The Prince and Princess of Wales did not shrink from descending this deep burrow under the sea in the year 1865.'[2]

Gurnard's Head

The rugged cliffs continue past Pendeen Watch on a coast explored by W.H. Hudson: 'The rocky forelands I haunted were many, but the favourite one was Gurnard's Head, situated about midway between St. Ives and Land's End. It is the grandest and one of the most marked features of that bold coast. Seen from a distance, from one point of view, the promontory suggests the figure of a Sphinx, the entire body lying out from the cliff, the waves washing over its huge black outstretched paws and bearing on its breast, its stupendous deformed face composed of piled masses of granite looking out on the Atlantic. I was often there afterwards, spending long hours sitting on the rocks of the great head and shoulders, watching the sea and the birds that live in it; and later, when April set the tiny bell of the rock pipit tinkling, and the wheatear hovering over the crags, dropped his brief delicious warble, and when the early delicate flowers touched the rocks and turf with tender, brilliant colour, I was more enamoured than ever of my lonely castle by the sea. Forced to leave it I could but chew samphire and fill my pockets with its clustered green finger-like leaves, so as to have the wild flavour of that enchanting place as long as possible in my mouth and its perfume about me.'[3]

In R.M. Ballantyne's *Deep Down* a visitor, George Clearmont, came to Gurnard's Head: 'Above him there were wild undulating slopes covered with rich green gorse; below were the cliffs of Gurnard's Cove, with rocky projections that resemble the castellated work of man's hand, and intermingled therewith, much of the *materiel* connected with the pilchard fishery, with masses of masonry so heavy and picturesque as to resemble nature's handiwork. Beyond lay the blue waves of the Atlantic, which at the time were calm almost as a mill-pond, studded with a hundred sails, and glittering in sunshine.

'The spot appeared a beautiful solitude, for no living thing was visible save the romantic gentleman and a few sea-gulls and sheep. The pilchard fishery had not yet convened, and the three or four fishermen who pitched and repaired their boats on the one little spot of sand that could be seen from below on that rugged coast, appeared like mice, and were too far distant to break the feeling of solitude.'[2]

It was perhaps this part of the coast that Bertrand Russell had in mind when he wrote: 'When I come home to die I shall not feel that I have lived in vain. I have seen the earth turn red at evening, the dew sparkling in the morning, and the snow shining under a frosty sun; I have smelt the rain after drought, and have heard the stormy Atlantic beat upon the granite shores of Cornwall.'[4]

Gerald Priestland, a BBC correspondent, wrote of this area in 1980:

'Whether granite or greenstone, the cliffs of Penwith are far from being passive and dead. I have contemplated them for hours from a point between the Gurnard's Head and Zennor Cliff and marvel at their architecture, at the great lines of force running up through them carrying the strains and stresses down to their foundations. Before you, you can *see* the curvature of the horizon, and at your feet the sudden drop down to the water leaves you with space into which your imagination - your sense of dance, even of flight – can fling itself.'[5]

Zennor

The bold, rugged coast of Penwith curves round to Zennor, a grey granite village where W.H. Hudson stayed in the winter of 1906-7 collecting material for his book *The Land's End: A Naturalist's Impressions of West Cornwall.* He called Zennor a 'lonely little village nestling among its furze thickets and stone hedges, with the rough granite hills, clothed in brown dead bracken, before it and the black granite cliffs and sea behind.'[3]

On the hill-top behind an overgrown quarry Hudson used to sit watching sea-birds and sunsets. Edwin Way Teale, an American naturalist, came here in 1970 and was taken by a local farmer, Maurice Griggs, to the summit of a high granite tor above his farm, Tremedda: 'We were 700 feet above the tide line when we ended our climb. My eyes, wandering over the maze of interconnecting stone walls that cut the landscape into a vast patchwork of small fields, could trace, almost from Land's End to Newquay, a distance of nearly 30 miles, the windings of the cliff-edged coast. As we walked among the great rocks that lay in tumbled profusion on the summit of the tor, Griggs pointed out one like a huge bench with a vertical back rising to a projecting mass that extended out like an awning of granite. A little higher than my head, cut in the upright stone, ran a line of letters about five inches high. They were dimmed by the accumulating lichens of half a century, I ran my fingers slowly down the line, making out the words. The sentence read: "W.H. HUDSON OFTEN CAME HERE". To commemorate his association with the spot, the painter Arnold Forster, living at nearby Eagle's Nest, had had the words cut in granite.'[6]

John Seymour went into Zennor church to see 'the Mermaid of Zennor carved on a bench end in the small south chapel. She is very beautiful. Her original swam to the little stream that runs into Pendour Cove to listen to the singing of a chorister called Michael Trewhella. She enticed him into the sea and he was never seen again, but for many years afterwards the sound of his singing could be heard coming up from under the waves.'[7]

D.H. Lawrence and his German wife Frieda came to Zennor in 1916, staying first at the Tinner's Arms, then renting a small farm cottage, Higher Tregerthen, in a lane to the north of the village. They hoped to establish a literary settlement, and persuaded Katherine Mansfield and John Middleton Murry to come and live in an adoining cottage, but they soon left and went to Mylor. Lawrence was writing *Women in Love*, but his reputation as a bearded pacifist and his German wife aroused the suspicions of the village people, and in October 1917 their cottage was searched by the police, and they were told to leave.

In 1922 Lawrence and his wife went to spend a few months in Australia, briefly visiting Sydney, then living in a bungalow in Thirroul, on the coast thirty miles to the south. While there, he wrote very quickly his novel *Kangaroo*, based on some real, but mostly imaginary happenings in Australia. The hero, Richard Lovat Somers, and his German wife Harriet, bear a strong resemblance to the Lawrences, and the twelfth chapter, 'The Nightmare', is a vivid recollection of their time in Cornwall, again a mixture of real and imaginary:

'Somers tiresomely belonged to no group. He would not enter the army, because his profoundest instinct was against it. Yet he had no conscientious objection to war. It was the whole spirit of the war, the vast mob-spirit, which he could never acquiesce in. The terrible, terrible war, made so fearful because in every country practically every man lost his head, and lost his own centrality, his own manly isolation in his own integrity, which alone keeps life real.'[8]

In this frame of mind in the winter of 1915 Somers and Harriet went down to Cornwall. 'Away in the west Richard and Harriet lived alone in their cottage by the savage Atlantic. He hardly wrote at all, and never any propaganda. But he hated the war, and said so to the few Cornish people around. He laughed at the palpable lies of the press, bitterly. And because of his isolation and his absolute separateness, he was marked out as a spy.

'The war-wave had broken right over England now: right over Cornwall. Probably throughout the ages Cornwall had not been finally swept, submerged by any English spirit. Now it happened – the accursed later war spirit. Now the tales began to go round full-tilt against Somers. A chimney of his house was tarred to keep out the damp: that was a signal to the Germans. He and his wife carried food to supply German submarines. They had secret stores of petrol on the cliff. They were watched and listened to, spied on, by men lying behind the low stone fences. Harriet could not hang out a towel on a bush, or carry out the slops, in the empty landscape of moors and sea, without her every movement being followed by invisible eyes.

'Day followed day in this tension of suspense. Submarines were off the coast: Harriet saw a ship sunk, away to sea. Horrible excitement, and the postman asking sly questions to try to cach Somers out. Increased rigour of coast watching, and *no* light must be shown. Then a Spanish coal vessel, three thousand tons, ran on the rocks in a fog, straight under the cottage. She was completely wrecked. Somers watched the waves break over her. Her coal washed ashore, and the farmers carried it up the cliffs in sacks.

'Autumn drew on, corn-harvest was over, it was October. John Thomas drove every Thursday over the moors to market – a two hours' drive.

'To-day Somers would go with him. It was a lovely October morning. They passed the stony little huddle of the church town, and on up the hill, where the great granite boulders shoved out of the land, and the barrenness was ancient and inviolable. They could see the gulls under the big cliffs beyond – and there was a buzzard circling over the marshy place below church town.'[8]

When he returned his house had been ransacked, and soon afterwards came the order for them to leave the county of Cornwall within the space of three days. It was a chilling experience, but perhaps we should remember that Cornishmen were being killed and wounded while Lawrence grappled with his spiritual problems, and that he was in any case a sick man, a consumptive who had been summarily exempted from military service.

Melbourne actor Barry Humphries, perhaps better known as Dame Edna Everage, came on a script-writing holiday in the 1960s, staying with his wife in Loosemoore Cottage: 'In the evenings we would put on our coats and mufflers and walk the windswept mile to the Tinners Arms for a drink before dinner. I was getting on quite well with my script until one morning in late February, my wife and I decided to go for a walk along the cliffs. Patches of snow still lay on some of the fields like scattered laundry and as I crossed a small fast-flowing stream of melted snow, I put the heel of my Wellington boot very carefully on a central stone before swinging my right leg across to the opposite bank. But the stone was icy, my boot slipped and I sat rather absurdly, but with a freezing shock, in the shallow rushing water. Rosalind was close behind me and in reaching out to help, tripped and also fell. It was ridiculous, but there for an instant we sat. It was only when I tried to get up and slipped again that I realized how close to the precipice we were and how steeply inclined the stream. Unable to clutch at any vegetation on the bank, we had started to move, first slowly and comically, and then very fast, as the stream became a stone chute that abruptly turned a corner and jettisoned us over the cliff's edge.

'I came to, sitting on a narrow rock ledge, my legs dangling over an abyss of some two hundred feet. Below were jagged black rocks around which the sea frothed and crashed. Over my left knee splashed the icy cataract which had deposited me on this precarious shelf'. His wife managed to scramble up the cliff and go for help, but Barry had dislocated his shoulder and broken his arm.

'I was alone on the face of the cliff for many hours. I watched the light on the rocks below change, the sea grow calmer; I saw the shadow of my own cliff fall across the water and still no help came. It was a very unfrequented coastline and I began to entertain the idea of jumping. If I missed the rocks and landed on my feet perhaps I could walk to safety. The pebbles, two hundred feet below, began to look soft and inviting. I desperately tried to make my past life flash before my eyes, but nothing happened. Was this an omen? It had become bitterly cold on the cliff face and I was trembling; moreover my water-logged jeans began to slip, centimetre by centimetre, and with a minute squeaking noise, on the glassy rock. I must have dozed off, for I awoke suddenly to the sound of calling voices and there was a great wind ruffling my hair.'[9] A helicopter had come to rescue Dame Edna, Sandy Stone, Sir Les Patterson, and the author of Barry McKenzie from a Cornish cliff.

Porthmeor Beach

Denys Val Baker came to live here with his wife: 'When we were settled permanently in a house whose back door opened on to the Atlantic beach of Porthmeor at St. Ives, I think I can truthfully say that we came to know the sea in most of its moods, and yet it never failed to turn up with a surprise. It was a little like living with a tiger or a lion in your back garden - much of the time the creature would probably be sleeping peacefully, but there would always be the odd times when he prowled around balefully, and perhaps now and then actually tried to attack you.

'It was very much like this with Porthmeor. Our house was part of a rather graceful sweep of buildings which formed a semicircle curve around the beach, reaching from the cliffs at Clodgy round to the foot of the Island. Many of the buildings are artists' studios from which, in the summer, the occupants lower long ladders to enable them to have quick access to the sea. Otherwise most of the houses are high up from the sands, and ours was the only one with direct steps on to the beach, a luxury which we much enjoyed in the evenings when we sat on the wooden steps and watched the sun sinking behind the sea beyond Clodgy Point. This had all been very fine on a summer evening, but needless to say there were times when it would have been virtual suicide to sit on those steps – *i.e.* the half a dozen times year when the tides were exceptionally high.

'Once a year, with almost monotonous regularity, our steps used to be washed away by angry seas. In particular was this so in the winter when high seas appeared to take away more and more sand. One winter we were amazed to see parts of the sea wall exposed that had probably not been uncovered for twenty or thirty years. We measured the drop and found it was thirteen feet!'[10]

St. Ives – The Artists

St Ives nestles across a rocky headland beside a wide sandy bay, a fishing village that is also a seaside resort and artists' colony. James McNeill Whistler was at St. Ives in 1883-4 with Mortimer Menpes and Walter Sickert, and it was here that he probably painted the 'Angry Sea'. Hilary Taylor in her biography confirmed that: 'The sea is, indeed, a winter one, the strong creamy strokes of the waves playing over heavy slate tones in the sea. A ship is tossed on the horizon.'[11] In a letter to Ernest Brown, Whistler wrote: 'The sea to me, is, and always was, most fascinating. Perhaps you will think that there is a novelty about the little things I bring back....I am doing things quite new down here.' He also painted 'Cliffs and Breakers with Open Sea.'

Denys Val Baker suggested that the local concentration of art was because of the 'Atmosphere! Yes, that is the important ingredient of St. Ives as an art colony: an atmosphere that gives as well as takes, to and from the artists. Did St. Ives have an atmosphere before the artists came and settled? Of course. But is that atmosphere stronger because of their presence? Again, of course. We are on subtle ground here, but then the atmosphere of an art colony is a subtle thing. The fishermen drying their nets on the green slopes of the Island, with the white-capped waves of the Atlantic breaking on Porthmeor Beach below - that is a view, an image or a series of images, which might inspire any artist. John Park might have made of it a richly-coloured oil painting showing the scene as it was; Sven Berlin might have resolved it into a carving of an heroic bent figure merging into granite; John Barclay might have translated it into black and white figurines of an etching; Ben Nicholson might have seen it in geometrical patterns, or Barbara Hepworth in elongated curving shapes pierced with hollow spaces and holes; while one of the younger painters might have seen the whole thing in a series of impressionistic daubs and splashes. Thus, that one scene, perhaps one moment, of local life, might be translated into a series of other moments, many of which would later be sent out into the world, to be hung in galleries, reproduced in books, and so on. And because of seeing those results, all kinds of people might be tempted to visit the place first hand - the cobbled streets, the fairy-like harbour, the Mediterranean-blue sea, the artists at work before their easels, pictures hanging everywhere, studios tucked away down almost every little by-way'.

'The rugged coastline, the turbulent seas, the weather-beaten faces of the fishing-folk – these have always inspired painters. Whether it be a moonlit sea or simpy a quiet study of old St. Ives, the material is all there, waiting to be transformed on canvas into a living picture.'[12]

In 1993 The Tate Gallery at St. Ives opened in a new building overlooking Porthmeor Beach.

St. Ives Bay

'The town of St. Ives', wrote Alphonse Esquiros in the nineteenth century, 'is admirably situated at the end of a bay, round which it forms a crescent, and is surrounded by sand-hills bordered by cliffs. It has been compared to a Greek village. It is quite certain that the blue sky, the green sea, the hills with their white sides, and the black rocks with their vigorous lines, compose, with the town seared in a hollow, a delicious picture. On the quay stand the old buildings of an abandoned mine; farther on, a church, protected from the sea by a stout wall, and surrounded by a cemetery, bravely offers to the waves its old stained glass windows, which have many times been beaten by the storm.'[13]

Arthur Norway was another nineteenth century visitor: 'When we climb the hill above the station the whole of the noble bay lies spread out at our feet. Here is no huddled heap of houses tumbling one over another in a cleft of precipices, but a wide bay forming an almost perfect arc, and having on its left a sheltered tongue of land, rising to a height at its extremity, thus forming a natural break-water against west and south-west winds, a bay within a bay, a safe anchorage in heavy weather. The ancient church stands there, close to the water's edge, right in the centre of her work, surrounded by a labyrinth of fisher houses, which break away at last into a beach where the fishing boats are hauled up in safety. It is a sweet and sunny place, a harbour full of clear green water, the sandy shores of the wide back curving round past Phillack and Gwithian, past Godrevy Island, where the lighthouse gleams tall and white against a background of blue sea. Here is nothing grand, but soft and sunny and exquisite; and always some little fishing boats are slipping in and out of the harbour or scudding to and fro on the blue bay.'[14]

Towards the end of the nineteenth century Virginia Woolf, then Virginia Stephen, used to come here on family summer holidays, staying in Talland House on the slope above the harbour. Many years later she recalled that 'The town was then much as it must have been in the sixteenth century: a scramble, a pyramid of whitewashed granite houses, crusting the slope made in the hollow under the Island. It was built there for shelter – built for a few fishermen, when Cornwall was a county more remote from England than Spain is now. It was a steep little town. Many houses had stairs running up from the pavement to the door. The walls were thick blocks of granite, to stand the sea and gale, I suppose. They were splashed with a wash the colour of Cornish cream. There was nothing mellow about them. There was no red brick: there was no thatch; the eighteenth century had left no mark, as it has in the south. St. Ives might have been built yesterday; or in the time of the Conqueror. It had no architecture; no conscious arrangement. The market place was a jagged cobbled open place; the Church was a granite church – of what age, I do not know. It was a windy, noisy, fishy, vociferous, narrow streeted town; the colour of a mussel or a limpet; like a bunch of rough shells, oysters or mussels, all crowded together.'[15]

On these holidays there were days on the beach and days out in boats, and games of cricket in the garden. Her biographer Quentin Bell, recorded her sporting prowess and: 'the cricket pitch, where "small cricket" was played all through the afternoon and so late into the evening that the ball had to be covered with luminous paint that they might continue.'[16] Virginia was called the demon bowler by her brothers in the nursery.

In *To the Lighthouse*, Mrs Ramsay was surely looking across St. Ives Bay: 'For the great plateful of blue water was before her; the hoary lighthouse, distant, austere in the midst; and on the right, as far as the eye could see, fading and falling in soft low pleats, the green sand dunes with the wild flowing grasses on them, which always seemed to be running away into some country, uninhabited of men'. At night she watched the beam of the lighthouse cross her bedroom floor, 'watching it with fascination, hypnotised, as if it were stroking with its silver fingers some sealed vessel in her brain, whose bursting would flood her with delight'[17]

The novel hints at a location on the Scottish coast, but the descriptions fit St. Ives Bay and Godrevy (see below).

Hayle

East from St. Ives the coast declines to Hayle, where Denys Val Baker recalled: 'After school we often took the children there and wandered out to the mouth of the estuary, a part which holiday-makers usually miss. Sometimes, it is possible to obtain the most extraordinary effect; standing on the white sands and looking up to see the enormous hull of an oil tanker apparently gliding along beside as the ship comes steaming in on the evening tide. The experience can be even more striking on the Hayle side of the estuary where from certain positions it is possible to look across the sands and see the clustering houses of St. Ives rising up out of the water, like some medieval city of old.

'Hayle itself, too, laid its almost perverse charm upon us: a most misleading town, outwardly rather drab and ugly and symbolized by its ghastly yellow street lighting - yet in fact full of relics of gracious living, lovely old Georgian manor houses now turned into flats or scrap yards, quiet and rather beautiful backwaters, and not forgetting the bird watcher's paradise, the inland lake of the estuary, bordering the A30 road from Hayle towards St. Erth. Sometimes I used to stand where the Hayle docks merged into the sands of the Towans or over by the Lelant ferry boat, and it would seem as if I was enclosed in a curious forlorn world all of its own.'[10]

Godrevy Lighthouse
Across the bay is Godrevy Lighthouse, prominent by day on its rocky islet off the headland, Godrevy Point. In *Literary Britain*, Frank Morley said: 'Virginia Woolf returned to St. Ives in 1926 - at least, friends have reported that she wrote *To the Lighthouse* at St. Ives, and that the lighthouse to which "they should have gone already – they had to catch the tide or something", is the lighthouse on Godrevy Island.'[18]

Dorothy Richardson came to stay with the Beresfords in St. Ives in 1912, and had the use of the adjacent chapel to write her novel, *Pointed Roofs* (1915) in the intervals of coastal walks with Hugh Walpole.

The Towans
W.H. Hudson looked at: 'The Towans, as the sandhills or dunes on the north-east side of St. Ives Bay are called – is a curiously attractive bit of country. It is plainly visible from St. Ives, looking east over the water – a stretch of yellow sands where the Hayle River empties itself in the bay, and behind it, a grey-green desert of hummocky or hilly earth, where the hills are like huge broken waves in "fluctuation fixed". And in a sense they are waves, formed of sand which the ocean brings out of its depths and exposes at low water, to be swept up by the everlasting winds and heaped in hills along the sea-front; and no sooner are the hills built than the wind unbuilds them again, carrying the yellow dust further inland to build other hills and yet others, burying the green farm-lands and houses and entire villages in their desolating progress. As you walk there, when the wind blows from the sea, the fine, dry, invisible particles rain on your face and sting your eyes; but all this travelling sand comes from the beach and can do no harm, for where it falls it must lie and serve as food for the conquering sea rush. If you examine the earth you will find it bound down with a matting of tough roots and rootlets and that in the spaces between the tussock the decaying rush had formed a thin mould and is covered with mosses and lichen, and in many places with a turf as on the chalk downs.'[3]

Perranporth
W.H. Hudson also went to Perranporth 'one of the loveliest bays in Cornwall, providing once again, you are here in winter when enormous seas build up the entire length of the sand, coming in like moving fortresses upon the distressing holiday town in front. Here, above all, one can stand and be mesmerised by this vast extent of water which is held back – by what ? One wonders why it does not crash in and devour the town, so that the gentle stream flowing off the land across the bay, to be absorbed into the sea, seems only the trickle of tap water compared. Here, the full length of the sand, groups of black-headed gulls stand amongst herring gulls; the cormorant dives into the winter sea and the rubbish of the summer is drawn out and split into fragments. Shells are banging together

and being reduced to powder and the shape of the sands altered immeasureably. The rollers ride in unceasingly.'[3]

Fine cliffs face the Atlantic along the coast that runs from Perranporth to Newquay.

Newquay

Newquay appeared as Buddlecombe (which, as we have seen, was also Henry Handel Richardson's name for Lyme Regis in Dorset) in James Payn's humorous story *A Cornish Harbour* set in the 1870s, before the railway came. 'The Lookout was the one private house upon the cliff-top that had already excited my envy; and we were very glad to get it. It really was a pleasant residence, with a verandah over the sitting-room, and a small garden, full of myrtles and fuchsias. Steep winding steps led down from this last to the very heart of the little harbour, about which whatever had life and motion in Buddlecombe lived and moved. Two piers of rough masonry held in their curved arms a fleet of fishing-smacks, and sheltered them from the pitiless sea in its most wrathful hour. The great seine boats, with their vast nets piled in front, were always moored in such positions as to be out at work in a few minutes, in case of a shoal of pilchards being signalled.

'Not an hour passed but either a coasting-vessel, laden with some mineral produce, stone, or plastic clay, moved slowly out with stir and strain, and much melodious clamour. If the winds blew strong from seaward, unwilling guests, whom we could watch for hours battling against their power, and striving in vain to round the stretching headland, would seek refuge with us for the night and either in the early morning would have flown, or would remain day after day imprisoned, their crews by no means chafing at the delay, but cheerfully adding to the local stock of human idleness. For all the sailor-folk who were not watching in the little towers upon the steep for pilchards, stood leaning against the sea-wall, or, if wet, beneath the projecting roof of the fish-cellars, watching also with folded arms and slow-consuming pipes. The whole attitude of nautical Buddlecombe was, in short, one of expectation for pilchards.'[19]

A century ago Arthur Norway was at Newquay, standing on Towan Head: 'On Newquay Head a strong breeze is blowing off the land, and all the sea in that wide bay which lies between the great headland of Trevose far away to eastward and Pentire, on the west, is ruffled over with white splashes, which come and go and change perpetually upon a bed of that glorious dark colour which is neither green nor blue. The coastline is half veiled by a little haze, shadowy, faint, and opalescent, so that one can hardly say where cliff meets sea till some sudden flash of white surges up from a breaking wave and goes again in haze as the swells come back and the broken water passes. Far away the dim line stretches, past Porth Island, with its blowhole spouting high as each wave rushes up the gulley, past Watergate, where huge dark caverns open upon golden sands, past Mawgan Porth, that loveliest of coves, where towering headlands enclose a beach as fine and even as a ball-room floor, past Bedruthan Steps, its strange rock forms all mingled and lost in the fine dim shadow, till, at Trevose, the land ends suddenly and nothing further east is visible.

'In the opposite direction great rollers are curling in across the mile-wide Bay of Fistral, torn into clouds of flying spray as they curve and break and scatter into whirlpools of lashing foam. Often when the afternoon sets towards evening there are seals diving and plunging in quiet spots around this headland: and I recollect climbing down to the caverns which, from old tales of smuggling, derive the name of the 'Tea-Caverns', and hearing in the dark recesses a long-drawn bellowing, which rose and fell and sometimes was like the sobbing of a child frightened by the darkness, and the slimy rock and the rattling of the pebbles dragged down by the waves on the little beach outside.'[14]

Surfing in Cornwall

The riding of waves on a surfboard is a sport that originated in Hawaii and became popular in California, Australia and eventually around the oceanic coasts of the world, wherever large waves move in smoothly to break upon a sandy shore. In recent decades it has become popular in Cornwall, partly through promotion by visiting Australians, despite the fact that the swell is rarely as high, and never as consistent, as it is around the larger and wider Pacific Ocean. Surfing began in Watergate Bay, near Newquay, and has spread to many beaches, from Sennen Cove and Porthmeor in the south to Widemouth and Bude (where the first Surf Life Saving Club was set up in 1953 by an Australian, Alan Kennedy) in the north. However, there seem to have been no literary surfers as yet, although there are several manuals explaining where and how surfboard riding should be done. A gentleman from Bondi, interviewed in Newquay, commented that surfing literature had not yet progressed far beyond the pithy comments scrawled on the walls of Life Saving Clubs.

Watergate Bay

G.T. Roberts explained that Watergate Bay 'is ideally suited to board riding, and was the first beach on which board riding was practised in this country. On Watergate break the largest waves in the area, and to sit on the adjacent cliff and watch surfers riding these waves provides a never-to-be-forgotten memory.'[20] At the southern end, is Black Humphrey's Rock, named for a notorious wrecker whose philosophy is recorded in a rhyme known locally:

> *When the Wind is in the East*
> *I'll go to church as soon as Priest,*
> *But when the Wind is in the West*
> *Do pray for me among the Rest.*

Trevose Head

The high cliffs of Watergate Bay run north past Bedruthan Steps, where you can descend to sandy beaches among gnarled rock stacks, one of which is called Queen Bess Rock because its profile recalls that of Queen Elizabeth the First. The high cliffs then curve out to rugged Trevose Head, where the Lifeboat Station is tucked in a cove on the eastern side, bordering Mother Ivey's Bay. It seems that Mother Ivey was a beachcomber. This is a wild coast, with jagged rocky islands and reefs offshore, and great Atlantic rollers moving in to the beaches. In Trevone a straggling village which runs down to the shore, Dorothy Richardson lived between 1917 and 1938 while writing her sequence of autobiographical novels entitled *Pilgrimage*. It is a landscape of narrow lanes between high banks on which grow tamarisk trees.

Padstow

Just over a mile to the east is Padstow, an ancient port on the Camel estuary, which is wide and sandy with waves breaking over the Doom Bar. On May Day the famous 'Obby Oss Festival takes place in the town. D.H. Lawrence (and his wife Frieda) stayed here in 1915-16: 'The wind blows very hard, the sea all comes up the cliffs in smoke. The sea rages under the black rocks, and the western sky is iridescent at evening, so that the water stretches far back into the distance, into the unknown. I lie looking down at a cove where the waves come white under a low, black headland which slopes up in bare green-brown, bare and sad under a level sky. It is a cove like Tristan sailed into from Lyonesse – just the same. It belongs to 2000 years back – that pre-Arthurian Celtic flicker of being which disappeared so entirely. The landscape is bare, yellow-green and brown, dropping always down to black rocks and a torn sea. All is desolate and forsaken.'[21]

The Lawrences were planning to head for Florida and establish a literary colony, but as we have seen they went instead to Zennor.

A plaque on a building beside the harbour is dedicated to Claude Berry (1895-1976) 'writer, broadcaster and devoted son of Padstow'. He wrote that 'Padstow was probably in Elizabethan times a boisterous rough-and-tumble little port, with its own shipyards and ropewalks. Here was a harbour spacious enough for a great fleet to ride at anchor in it; [but] it was so choked with sand that the entrance was difficult and perilous and, as Sir Martin Frobisher found in 1577 "riding there, a very dangerous Road" was a worse evil than putting to sea again. Countless billions of shells, ground to tiny particles and whirled in by the Atlantic seas, have obstructed trade here almost as effectively as skyscrapers or tariff barriers.

'You might cite Padstow as an example or a victim of geographical determinism. But we Cornish look at realities rather more obliquely. We have, in fact, invented a fable of a mermaid, who was mortally stricken by the longbow of a greedy and obtuse Padstow man. Whereupon she cursed the harbour and foretold its doom from sand which, even as she spoke, began to drift inexorably in from [the] sea.'[22]

A traveller on the Atlantic Coast Express, which ran from Waterloo to Padstow, from 1899 to 1964, and which was a favourite journey for Sir John Betjeman, would 'pass the original Bodmin & Wadebridge sheds and quay, and emerge from the town alongside the broadening Camel estuary. Grey river mud gives way to golden sea sand, seen to best advantage at this time of day with autumn sunlight painting up the fields and farmhouses on the far bank. The firemen checks his fire, trickles a few in across the back and takes his seat to watch the road and the scenery. A man painting a boat at Oldtown Cove turns and waves as the train passes on the causeway behind him. Speed is reduced to 15 mph for Little Petherick Creek bridge, which consists of three 150ft trusses set on a curve, the train passes through a last rock cutting and we coast into Padstow station.[23]

The Camel at Padstow

E.P. Leigh-Bennett arrived here on the Atlantic Coast Express in the 1930s: 'The Padstow scene opened out suddenly at Wadebridge; for thence the river Camel really begins to assert itself and become maritime in manner. Pale fawn sand and clumps of green glistening seaweed on its widening banks – that arch glance of the sea. Besides, a tang of salt came in at the dropped window. Presently the bay opened its graceful arms in a welcoming gesture as if to say "I am yours". And a heart seeking a holiday missed a beat or two. The train wriggled round a bend and its engine shrieked joyfully, as well it might, for the evening sun was kissing the grey roof tops of Padstow which sits deep set in a corner of the hills ahead, and the sight of it was very lovely.[24]

The railway to Padstow was closed in 1967, but you can still walk or cycle along the Camel Trail, which has taken its place. Leigh-Bennett wrote effusively on seaside resorts served by the Atlantic Coast Express, but only one or two can still be reached by train.

Another traveller who came to the Padstow terminus of the Atlantic Coast Express was S.P.B. Mais, who found it 'an ancient place of narrow, crooked alleys and palm trees and fuchsias growing in every garden, the landing-place of St. Petroc, who sailed to Rome in a silver bowl and lived for seven years on the miraculous diet of one fish which he ate every day. He came back to Padstow to find a wolf guarding the robe he left on the beach'. The estuary opens to 'white waves breaking over the Doom Bar, raised by a mermaid who threw a handful of sand into the water with a curse, as a vengeance on a young man who tried to shoot her with an arrow.'[25]

Trevorrick Sea-Mills

In *The Stone Peninsula*, James Turner remarked that 'A taste for ruins need not necessarily mean that one has always to be looking at monasteries, churches or convents. In Cornwall are other ruins such as sea-mills like those at Trevorrick, near St. Issey. The mills, or what is left of them, are on the creek shore. In use until 1880, these sea-mills were used for milling wheat brought before the railway was built, by ship from Padstow. They were driven by tidal water caught by a sea wall with sluices. Power came from a waterwheel driven by freeing the water at low tide. Now little remains but the grey water of the Camel sluicing in over the brown-green ruins, the vivid seaweed and the red-seeded dock standing straight in the marshes.'[26]

Trebetherick

Low cliffs border the estuary at Trebetherick, in a countryside enhanced by the writings of John Betjeman, who spent much time here, and often walked the footpath along the cliffs:

> *Those moments, tasted once and never done,*
> *Of long surf breaking in the mid-day sun,*
> *A far-off blowhole booming like a gun –*
>
> *The seagulls plane and circle out of sight*
> *Below this thirsty, thrift-encrusted height,*
> *The veined sea-campion buds burst into white.*
>
> *And gorse turns tawny orange, seen beside*
> *Pale drifts of primroses cascading wide*
> *To where the slate falls sheer into the tide....*

Nut-smell of gorse and honey-smell of ling
Waft out to sea the freshness of the spring
On sunny shallows, green and whispering.

The wideness which the lark-song gives the sky
Shrinks at the clang of sea-birds sailing by
Whose notes are tuned to days when seas are high.[27]

St. Enodoc Church

A little to the east of Trebetherick, in a valley behind the high Bray Hill, nestles St Enodoc church, which was once so buried in the sands that the parson had to climb through the skylight to take his services, but it is now completely excavated. John Betjeman loved this church, even if he daydreamed during Sunday Afternoon Service, his mind out on the nearby coast:

Where deep cliffs loom enormous, where cascade
Mesembryanthemum and stone-crop down,
Where the gull looks no larger than a lark
Hung midway twixt the cliff-top and the sand,
Forced by the backwash, see the nearest wave
Rise to a wall of huge, translucent green
And crumble into spray along the top
Blown seaward by the land-breeze. Now she breaks
And in an arch of thunder plunges down
To burst and tumble, foam on top of foam,
Criss-crossing, baffled, sucked and shot again,
A waterfall of whiteness, down a rock,
Without a source but roller's furthest reach:
And tufts of sea-pink, high and dry for years,
Are flooded out of ledges, boulders seem
No bigger than a pebble, washed about
In this tremendous tide.[27]

Polzeath

In 1934 James Turner came to Cornwall: ' One afternoon I went from St. Minver across the sands at Polzeath and walked up the deep ravine to the farmhouse on Pentire Head where I had so often spent holidays from London. I spent the afternoon about the farm and was given an enormous tea of saffron buns and cream. I decided to return the same way, but across the rocks at the head of the beach from Pentireglaze to Polzeath. I was strong enough now to face anything.

'Or so I thought when I saw that the tide had come in while I was at tea and was fairly raging into the rock ravines I had to cross. So that when I came to the really deep cleft in the rocks, wide and black, with the full sea now tearing in over covered sand, I slipped down the north face, waited a moment as the sea receded for a second, and flung myself on to the south face, tearing the skin off one hand.

'Now that the tide was in, this was my only way home. In short, I was cut off unless I wanted to go back to the farm and walk some ten miles along the road back to St. Minver. I flung myself against the black rock and began to climb away from the sea, not realising that I was still weak.

'No one was within miles of me, that January evening. I was completely alone on the rock face which, in truth, was hardly very high. To me, then, it was like the last few feet of Everest as I lay panting against the cold, wet, hardness unable to move. The last rays of the sun were beginning to touch the horizon and the sea to make more fearful noise. If anyone had been walking on the headland they could not have seen me in this dusk light and hidden in this ravine.

'I do not know to this day how I managed those last few feet, except that the noise of the sea below, licking its lips for me, was so frightening that it gave me strength. I believe, actually, that the strength came from anger at the thought of being trapped by my own self-confidence. I was alone here merely because my body was weak. As the sun set I managed it. I fell on the headland grass and lay gasping for breath and thought of the peace of my burial ground and refused, with the sea birds still hovering, to die.'[26] Others have scrambled on these cliffs and not lived to write their tale.

Port Isaac

To the north of St Endellion is the fishing village of Port Isaac, and the cliffs rise high along the rugged coast to Tregardock. Betjeman disliked the damage done to the Cornish landscape by the motor car and the road widening, the poles and wires that brought electricity; the proliferating petrol stations, the hoardings, the caravans and chalets: 'Several stretches of the coast have been rescued by the National Trust or saved, at any rate for their lifetime, by those landowners who can still afford to hold out against the blandishment of "developers". The old and beautiful Cornwall is now mostly to be found on foot or in a small car by those skilled in using the one-inch ordnance survey map. It is a consolation that no one yet has discovered how to build houses on the sea.'[28]

Snowstorm

Many people have walked the North Cornwall coastal footpath. Among the more determined was John Merrill, marathon walker, who in 1978 made a 6,824 mile journey around England, Wales and Scotland, raising more than £40,000 for the Royal Commonwealth Society for the Blind. On this coast in mid-February he encountered rather difficult conditions: 'This Saturday was a day I shall never forget. The weather had taken a decided turn for the worse, and it was exceedingly cold with galeforce winds. The prospect of walking in these conditions was daunting, but as I liked the idea of sitting around even less, I set off from Port Gaverne to cross the steep cliffs to Tintagel, six miles away. The wind grew stronger and stronger and in no time I was fighting for my life. I had experienced equally strong winds near Lulworth in Dorset, but there the winds had come off the sea, keeping me on the cliffs and enabling me to make progress. Near Tintagel the wind changed direction and came off the land. I could not stand upright and the only way to safeguard myself from being blown over the edge was to hold onto the barbed wire fence. Bent almost double, and being blown off my footing almost constantly, I struggled on. It began to snow, and then almost immediately to hail; both snow and hail were blown horizontally into my face, stinging it badly. In no time I was drenched and very cold. I called at a friend's house at Tintagel and had a bowl of soup. He pressed me to stay, but I declined and fought my way northwards to Boscastle. Even the birds seemed stunned by the raging storm. Since leaving Port Gaverne I had seen many that just stood still as I passed; several had lost their tail feathers. At Boscastle I stopped and in my log wrote: 'Foolish to go on – some of the worst conditions experienced anywhere. Stopped at 3 pm.'[29]

He was forced to abandon walking for a day, but on Monday morning he continued from Boscastle: 'The snow had stopped, so I resumed the walk. The wind was still strong and as the weather became milder it began to rain. Low cloud. Poor visibility. Soaked to the skin. Walked over stiles submerged in snow. Kicked steps in snow up the cliffs. Dead birds. Blocked roads.'[29]

Wreckers

Until the eighteenth century, Cornwall was notorious for its "wreckers", men who lured ships on to a rocky shore in order to plunder them, murdering any survivors who might have been able to give evidence of their crime. Daphne du Maurier's heroine, Mary Yellan, came from the Helford River after the death of her widowed mother to live with her Aunt Patience, who had married Joss Merlyn, landlord of Jamaica Inn, a remote hostelry high upon Bodmin Moor. The landlord proved to be a wild and dangerous man, and the sinister mystery of Jamaica Inn was finally revealed to Mary one night when, drunk, he told her that his gang of wreckers brought plundered cargo to the Inn before dispersing it around the country. After she had tried to inform on him, he forced her to go with him and his companions on 'a nightmare journey of two hours or more to the coast' in a captured carriage. The site is not named, but could have been close to Tregardock on the shores of Port Isaac Bay. When their nocturnal journey ended, they left her locked in the carriage in a gully that led down the cliffs to the sea, but she escaped and, following the gully, found herself on the shore:

'The mist began to lift very slowly, disclosing the narrow outline of the bay. Rocks became more prominent, and the cliffs took on solidity. The expanse of water widened, opening from a gulf to a bare line of shore that stretched away interminably. To the right, in the distance, where the highest part of the cliff sloped to the sea, Mary made out a faint pin-prick of light. At first she thought it a star, piercing the last curtain of dissolving mist, but reason told her that no star was white, nor ever swayed with the wind on the surface of a cliff. She watched it intently, and it moved again; it was like a small white eye in the darkness. It danced and curtseyed, storm-tossed, as though kindled and carried by the wind itself, a living flare that would not be blown. The group of men on the shingle below heeded it not; their eyes were turned to the dark sea beyond the breakers.'[30]

Suddenly Mary Yellan realised the reason for their indifference, and the real purpose of the light up on the cliff: 'The small white eye that seemed at first a thing of friendliness and comfort, winking bravely alone in the wild night, became a symbol of horror. The star was a false light, placed there for her uncle and his companions. The pin-prick gleam was evil now, and the curtsey to the wind became a mockery. Someone watched by the light so that it should not be extinguished. She saw a dark figure pass in front of it, obscuring the gleam for a moment, and then it burnt clear again. The figure became a blot against the grey face of the cliff, moving quickly in the direction of the shore. Whoever it was climbed down the slope to his companions on the shingle.

'Out of the mist and the darkness came another pin-prick of light in answer to the first. This new light did not dance and waver as the one on the cliff had done; it dipped low and was hidden, like a traveller weary of his burden, and then it would rise again, pointing high to the sky. The new light drew nearer to the first. The one compelled the other. The second light dipped again; and now Mary could see the shadowed outline of a hull, the black spars like fingers spreading above it, while a white surging sea combed beneath the hull, and hissed, and withdrew again. Closer drew the mast-light to the flare upon the cliff, fascinated and held, like a moth coming to a candle.'[30]

Horrified, Mary realised that she was about to witness the deliberate wrecking of a ship on the rugged shore.

Wrecking was by no means confined to Cornwall, but the wild, rugged and largely empty coastline, the frequency of Atlantic storms, and the arrival inshore of more and more ships laden with cargo intended for Bristol or up-Channel provided opportunities which greedy men of a backward province found hard to resist. Vicious and murderous, the wreckers made smuggling seem an amiable naughtiness by comparison.

Tintagel

Farther north is Tintagel, standing high above the rocky Atlantic coast. Tintagel Head, a bold promontory attached by a narrow ridge of land, bears the ruins of a medieval castle, the fortress of successive Earls of Cornwall from the twelfth to the fifteenth century. It was built over an earlier earthwork which includes relics of a sixth century monastery. This is one of the West Country sites claimed as the birthplace and castle of King Arthur in the fifth or sixth century A.D. a notion developed by Alfred Lord Tennyson:

> *... and on the night*
> *When Uther in Tintagil past away*
> *Moaning and wailing for an heir, the two [Merlin and Bleys]*
> *Left the still King, and passing forth to breathe,*
> *Then from the castle gateway by the chasm*
> *Descending thro' the dismal night – a night*
> *In which the hounds of heaven and earth were lost –*
> *Beheld, so high upon the dreary deeps*
> *It seemed in heaven, a ship, the shape thereof*
> *A dragon wing'd, and all from stem to stern*
> *Bright with a shining people on the decks,*
> *And gone as soon as seen. And then the two*
> *Dropt to the cove, and watch'd the great sea fall,*
> *Wave after wave, each mightier than the last,*
> *Till last, a ninth one, gathering half the deep*
> *And full of voices, slowly rose and plunged*
> *Roaring, and all the wave was in a flame:*
> *And down the wave and in the flame was borne*
> *A naked babe, and rode to Merlin's feet,*
> *Who stoopt and caught the babe, and cried 'The King!'.*"[31]

Algernon Swinburne stayed in Tintagel in the autumn of 1864, completing 'Atalanta in Calydon'. His 'Autumn in Cornwall' is set hereabouts:

> *The year lies fallen and faded*
> *On cliffs by clouds invaded.*
> *With tongues of storms upbraided,*
>   *With wrath of waves bedinned:*
> *And inland, wild with warning,*
> *As in deaf ears or scorning,*
> *The clarion even and morning*
>   *Rings of the south-west wind.*
>
> *The wild bents wane and wither*
> *In blasts whose breath bows hither*
> *Their grey-grown heads and thither,*
>   *Unblest of rain or sun:*
> *The pale fierce heavens are crowded*

With shapes like dreams beclouded,
As though the old year enshrouded
Lay, long ere life were done.

A shrill-winged sound comes flying
North, as of wild souls crying
The cry of things undying,
   That knows what life must be;
Or as the old year's heart, stricken
Too sore for hope to quicken
By thoughts like thorns that thicken,
   Broke, breaking with the sea.[32]

Swinburne also referred to it in his 'Tristram of Lyonesse':

About the middle music of the spring
Came from the castled shore of Ireland's king
A fair ship stoutly sailing, eastward bound
And south by Wales and all its wonders round
To the loud rocks and ringing reaches home
That take the wild wrath of the Cornish foam,
Past Lyonesse unswallowed of the tides
And high Carlion that now the steep sea hides
To the wind-hollowed heights and gusty bays
Of sheer Tintagel, fair with famous days.[32]

A cliff path descends to a gravelly beach in a cove bordered by a cave, which of course must be the wizard Merlin's Cave. In Christopher Fry's play, 'Thor, With Angels', Merlin could have spoken from this very spot:

But I can hear
Faintly on the twittering sea a sail
Moving greatly where the waves, like harvest-home,
Come hugely on our coast: the men of Rome
Returning, bringing God, winter over, a breath
Of green exhaled from the hedges, the wall of sky
Breached by larksong. Primrose and violet
And all frail privileges of the early ground
Gather like pilgrims in the aisles of the sun.
A ship in full foliage rides in
Over the February foam, and rests
Upon Britain.[33]

Tintagel Castle

Arthur Norway came here in the eighteen-nineties: 'The approach is through a long and winding village into a ravine which falls steep and narrow towards the sea. Looking upwards when the shore is close at hand, one sees that the spur of high ground on the left has been cleft by a vast wedge-shaped chasm, leaving its extremity connected by a tongue of rocks so narrow that it will some day surely be an island. On both sides of this ravine are the remains of old grey walls, and towers approaching the edge of the cliff so closely that one can hardly doubt both to have been integral parts of the defences. But what has become of the intervening space? Did solid rock once stretch between the mainland and the island, and was the fortress continuous between the two? Tradition tells us of a drawbridge which spanned the gorge: but the width and depth are far too sheer and awful in these days for any such expedient. Probably many yards of the rock have slipped and slid away in modern times, making the chasm much wider than it was of old; for there is now no access to the island save for a climb so steep and difficult as forbids the supposition that there was no other road by which supplies could be brought in. It is a strange eyrie which one finds at the top, a rough waste of grass slopes and low walls, amid which one may yet make out the enclosure of a chapel, a strange wild place in which to plant a human dwelling, at the mercy of every storm that blows.'[14]

One can clamber the 300 steps to The Island where there are the remains of a Celtic monastery and wonderful views along the rugged coast. In the village, much given over to gift shops abounding with Arthurian knick-knacks, is a fourteenth century building, the Old Post Office, owned by the National Trust.

It is a rare example of a medieval manor house but was used as a Post Office from 1844 to 1892.

Rocky Valley

Off the B3263 a wooded path runs down Rocky Valley to the sea. Wilkie Collins was here in the 1850s: 'A walk of little more than half a mile brings us to the entrance of a valley, bounded on either side by the waterfall of which we were in search. We now follow a footpath a few hundred yards, pass by a mill, and looking up the valley, see one compact mass of vegetation entirely filling it to its remotest corners, and not leaving the slightest vestige of a path, the merest patch of clear ground, visible in any direction, far or near.

'It seems as if all the foliage which ought to have grown on the Cornish moorlands, had been mischievously crammed into this place, within the narrow limits of one Cornish valley. Weeds, ferns, brambles, bushes and young trees, are flourishing together here, thickly intertwined in every possible position, in triumphant security from any invasion of bill-hook or axe.'[1]

Daphne du Maurier also visited Rocky Valley: 'The road from Boscastle to Tintagel cuts the valley, bridging the stream, and today, in summer, with Tintagel a high spot for tourist traffic rivalling Land's End in popularity, the hermit would find his solitude disturbed. Not so in winter. Both Rocky Valley and St. Nectan's glen have all the loneliness that the most passionate of pilgrims could desire.

'The first, despite its name suggesting a tortuous climb, has a path that winds with comparative ease towards the sea, and can be followed without strain on heart or limb; yet the steepness of descent, the rugged nature of the cliffs on either side towering above the head, the dark and slippery surface of the rocks themselves, still spell disaster to the more venturesome who crane forward and downwards to glimpse the rushing stream. The narrowness of the gorge impels the water, swollen with winter rains, to course the faster, and white with foam it twists and tumbles over its stony bed to a sudden flat surface where, smooth for an instant, it plunges from the canyon to the open sea. There is no cove here to receive the fall, no spit of shore, no shingle bay as at Marsland Mouth. The full surge of the Atlantic sweeps against the cliffs, forever turbulent, forever grey, like the rocks encompassing the gully, awaiting at flood tide or ebb the torrent from the Rocky Valley.

'If this was where the hermit walked in centuries gone by, then nothing has changed. The ceaseless sound of water is the same, the tumble of foam into the sea, the slippery surface of the rocks that winter or summer will never dry. The place has the impersonality of somewhere superbly dissociated from humankind, even from life itself. There are no gulls perching upon the ledges or the clefts, no sheep grazing on the headlands beyond. The force of matter is pre-eminent, hard rock challenging the elemental thrust of water.'[34]

Boscastle

Boscastle is strung along a deep valley that zigzags to the sea through a deep inlet, where stone breakwaters shelter boats In 1864 Swinburne, in a letter to his cousin, Mary Gordon, described how he came on horseback over the cliffs to Boscastle: 'This important and flourishing seaport does not exactly boast of a highway to the sea, but it has a path cut or worn in the slopes of the down, along which we let our horses (being surefooted Cornish ones who know the nature of their sea and their down) feel their way till we came out one after another on a narrow standing place of rocks, breaking sharply down to the sea on both sides. This ridge of rocks shuts in the harbour, and the sea having incautiously poured in through a strait between the ridge and the cliff opposite turns twice at right-angles upon itself and makes a sort of double harbour; one parallel with the outer sea, blocked out by the rocks to which we had ridden; the other running straight up the valley to the houses of the little town and as there is no beach or shore of any kind, you can imagine how the sea swings to and fro between the cliffs, foams and swells, beats and baffles itself against the steep faces of rock. Seen from above and on horseback it was very queer, dark grey swollen water, caught as it were in a trap, and heaving with rage against both sides at once, edged with long panting lines of incessant foam that swung and lapped along the deep steep cliffs without breaking, and had not room to roll at ease.'[35]

Boscastle

'Boscastle', wrote S.H. Burton, 'was once a Cornish harbour (there is record as far back as 1584 of the inhabitants repairing the quay after damage by storm) but nothing puts in now except an occasional yacht seeking shelter. A few boats are kept in the picturesque harbour for a little fishing, and for the pleasure of visitors, but trade has stopped. Vessels [used to be] 'hobbled' in and out of the harbour which, with its narrow entrance between frowning cliffs, and its double bend, was not easy to navigate even in fair weather.

'For most visitors the pleasures of Boscastle are scenic rather than historic. Certainly, the twisted harbour and the steep street, the splendour of the cliffs with their extensive views and interesting objects – the celebrated 'blowing-hole' for example, which snorts and spumes out the sea when the tide is right - the seals that haunt the coast and which may occasionally be seen inside the harbour itself, the lovely Valency Valley coming down from the windy uplands, all constitute a spell of potent might.'[36]

Valency Valley

Up the Valency Valley from Boscastle, St Juliot gained literary fame after the young architect Thomas Hardy came here in March 1870. He had been sent by his employer, Crickmay of Weymouth, to draw the plans and survey the work for the restoration of the fifteenth century church at St Juliot. At the Old Rectory, nearby, a young woman opened the door to him, and later wrote: 'I was immediately arrested by his familiar appearance, as if I had seen him in a dream – his slightly different accent, his soft voice. He was quite unlike any other person who came to see us'. This was Emma Lavinia Gifford, sister of the rector's second wife. Emma was born in Plymouth, the daughter of a solicitor, and had been convalescing at Tintagel when her visiting sister met the St. Juliot rector, the Reverend Caddell Holder. After their marriage Emma went to live with them in the rectory. The encounter with Thomas Hardy was to lead to their courtship, when on successive visits he walked the coast and countryside, usually beside Emma riding her mare.

Emma later wrote: 'Scarcely any author and his wife could have had a much more romantic meeting. A beautiful sea-coast, and the wild Atlantic ocean rolling in with its magnificent waves and spray, its white gulls and black choughs and grey puffins, its cliffs and rocks and gorgeous sun-settings. I showed him more of the neighbourhood – the cliffs, along the roads and through the scattered hamlets, sometimes gazing down at the solemn small shores below, where the seals lived, coming out of great deep caverns occasionally.

'Often we walked to Boscastle Harbour down the beautiful Valency Valley where we had to jump over stones and climb over a low wall by rough steps, or get through a narrow pathway, to come out on great wide spaces suddenly, with a sparkling little brook going the same way.'[37]

Thomas Hardy and Emma Gifford

Emma had become Hardy's "West of Wessex Girl", and in 1874 they married. By then, Hardy had set a novel, *A Pair of Blue Eyes*, in this region, and as usual invented his own local place names. St Juliot's church became St Agnes's, and was moved closer to the sea, and St Juliot's village West Endelstow, with nearby Lesnewth as East Endelstow. Endelstow House, Lord Luxellian's mansion, had some features borrowed from Lanhydrock House near Bodmin, although others were from Athelhampton near Puddletown in Dorset. Boscastle became Castle Boterel, St Launce's was Launceston, Stratleigh stood for Bude, Barwith Strand was Trebarwith Strand, and Rou'tor Town disguised Camelford.

The story was about a triangular courtship between Elfride Swancourt, Stephen Smith and Henry Knight: 'The next morning chancing to break fine after a week of cloudy weather, it was proposed and decided that they should all drive to Barwith Strand. The journey was along a road by neutral green hills, upon which hedgerows lay trailing like ropes on a quay. Gaps in these uplands revealed the blue sea, flecked with a few dashes of white and a solitary white sail, the whole brimming up to a keen horizon which lay like a line ruled from hillside to hillside.

'They mounted the last crest, and the bay which was to be the end of their pilgrimage burst upon them. The ocean blueness deepened its colour as it stretched to the foot of the crags, where it terminated in a fringe of white – silent at this distance, though moving and heaving like a counterpane upon a restless sleeper. The shadowed hollows of the purple and brown rocks would have been called blue had not that tint been so entirely appropriated by the water beside them.'[38]

Subsequently, Elfride and Henry were walking along the high hill leading to the coast west of St Juliot: 'The composition of the huge hill was revealed to its backbone and marrow at its rent extremity. It consisted of a vast stratification of blackish-grey slate, unvaried in its whole height by a single change of shade. It is with cliffs and mountains as with persons; they have what is called a presence, which is not necessarily proportional to their actual bulk.

"I cannot bear to look at that cliff", said Elfride, "It has a horrid personality, and makes me shudder".

'The crest of this terrible natural facade passed among the neighbouring inhabitants as being seven hundred feet above the water it overhung. It has been proved by actual measurement to be not less than six hundred and fifty. That is to say, it is nearly three times the height of Flamborough, half as high again as the South Foreland, a hundred feet higher than Beachy Head – the loftiest promontory on the east or south side of this island* – twice the height of St Aldhelm's, thrice as high as the Lizard, and just double the height of St Bee's. One seaboard point on the western coast is known to surpass it in altitude, but

---

* Hardy should have remembered that Golden Cap in Dorset (see page 54) is higher than Beachy Head.

only by a few feet. This is Great Orme's Head, in Caernarvonshire. And it must be remembered that the cliff exhibits an intensifying feature which some of those are without – sheer perpendicularity from the half-tide level. Yet this remarkable rampart forms no headland: it rather walls in an inlet - the promontory on each side being much lower. Thus, far from being salient, its horizontal section is concave. The sea, rolling direct from the shores of North America, has in fact eaten a chasm into the middle of a hill, and the giant, embayed and unobtrusive, stands in the rear of pigmy supporters. Not least singularly, neither hill, chasm, nor precipice has a name. On this account the precipice may be called the Cliff without a Name.'[38]

In the Preface to *A Pair of Blue Eyes* this 'enormous sea-board cliff' is again mentioned. It is almost certainly Beeny Cliff, nearly 800 feet high, and a mile or so north-east of Boscastle. Henry Knight lost his hat, and slipped over the edge of this cliff in pursuit of it. Stranded, he found that 'He could see the vertical face curving round on each side of him. He looked far down the facade and realized more thoroughly how it threatened him. Grimness was in every feature, and to its very bowels the inimical shape was desolation'. Clinging to the cliff he saw 'an imbedded fossil, standing forth in low relief from the rock. It was a creature with eyes. The eyes, dead and turned to stone, were even now regarding him. It was one of the early crustaceans called Trilobites. Separated by millions of years in their lives, Knight and this underling seemed to have met in their place of death. It was the single instance within reach of his vision of anything that had ever been alive, and had had a body to save, as he himself now had'. Fortunately, Elfride was tearing her voluminous underclothing into strips, and knotting it to form the rope which Henry could use to haul himself up to safety.[38]

Hardy wrote much more about the district in a series of retrospective poems written when he returned to Cornwall after Emma had died. He recollected his first visit ['rising at four in the morning, and starting by starlight'], arriving in Launceston at four in the afternoon, then driving the additional 16 miles along the moorland road towards Boscastle:

> *When I set out for Lyonnesse,*
> *A hundred miles away,*
> *The rime was on the spray,*
> *And starlight lit my lonesomeness*
> *When I set out for Lyonnesse*
> *A hundred miles away....*
>
> *When I came back from Lyonnesse*
> *With magic in my eyes,*
> *All marked with mute surmise*
> *My radiance rare and fathomless.*[39]

In 1913 he was to recall Beeny Cliff:

> *O the opal and the sapphire of that wandering western sea,*
> *And the woman riding high above with bright hair flapping free -*
> *The woman whom I loved so, and who loyally loved me.*
> *A little cloud then cloaked us, and there flew an irised rain,*
> *And the Atlantic dyed its levels with a dull misfeatured stain,*
> *And then the sun burst out again, and purples prinked the main.*[39]

Later it seemed like a dream:

> *Does there even a place like Saint-Juliot exist?*
> *Or a Valency Valley*
> *With stream and leafed alley*
> *Or Beeny, or Bos with its flounce flinging mist?*
>
> *'...........But was there ever*
> *A time of such quality, since or before,*
> *In that hill's story? To one mind never,*
> *Though it has been climbed, foot-swift, foot-sore*
> *By thousands more.*[39]

'The Famous Tragedy of the Queen of Cornwall', his last work, was a play started in 1914, abandoned, and eventually completed in 1923. Merlin's Iseult of Brittany had 'corn-brown hair' like Emma Hardy's, and the story was of unhappy mating.

Bude

The cliffs run on north from Beeny, past the sharp promontory of Cambeak, the deep valley at Crackington Haven, and the lofty bluffs at Dizzard Point to the straight sandy and rocky beach of Widemouth, pronounced Widmouth. Next comes Bude, a resort that appealed to S.P.B. Mais: 'About three miles beyond Widemouth the cliffs lead us to Bude, a seaside resort of fine sands and bare cliffs. The place has been much abused by countless writers as lacking beauty, which only proves how rich the rest of Cornwall must be. The truth is that Bude's special charm lies in the invigorating air and surf-riding over the Atlantic breakers, on sands that are as open to the winds as the treeless cliffs are. The most fascinating feature of the town is a canal, constructed over a hundred years ago at a cost of more than a hundred thousand pounds, which is only navigable for a mile.'[39]

In the 1860s Alphonse Esquiros found Bude: 'A humble village composed of a group of cottages, but which, for some years past, has been aspiring to become a watering-place. [The] sand, pure and golden, composed in great measure of fragments of pulverized shells, has been driven and heaped up on to the coast by the stormy south-west winds. The rocks belong to the Carboniferous formation, and run at right angles to the beach with Titanic contortions. Stern promontories – Compass Point and Beacon Hill – spread out wide shadows over the stern waves of the Atlantic. In calm weather this bay is delicious: the sea at high tide advances describing foaming semicircles, which enlarge and become appeased as they invade the beach; but let a west wind begin to blow, and the spectacle at once changes. Just as wild horses take to flight before a prairie fire, the impetuous coursers of the ocean, so the sailors say, escape from the presence of these terrible winds with a loud snorting, and rush towards the barrier of cliffs at the risk of being broken on them.'[13]

Bude Canal

The octagonal tower on the headland above the strongly folded rocks of Compass Point was built by Sir Thomas Dyke Acland in the 1830s on the lines of the Temple of the Winds in Athens. The south-west window looks back to Tintagel Head and Pentire Point, the north window on to the Sharpnose Points and Lundy Island.

Ships that traded far and wide from Bude Haven included the Ketch *Ceres*, commemorated in a poem by C. Fox Smith:

> *She loaded nuts and oranges, she carried coal and props*
> *And bricks and hay and china clay and barley-malt and hops,*
> *She traded north to Derby and she traded south to Spain,*
> *And east about to Wells and Lynn and back to Bude again.*
> *She knew the rips and overfalls from London to the Lizard*
> *And once she nearly left her bones off Padstow in a blizzard*
> *And when the winter fogs were thickest she mostly smelt her way*
> *By the old familiar sea marks into Bude and Watchet Bay.*[41]

Ebbingford Manor, a medieval house built of local stone, stands in the lee of the coastal ridge. According to its present owner, Bryan Dudley Stamp, 'It was in 1953 that my father, the late Sir Dudley Stamp, C.B.E., who is perhaps best known for his Geographical text-books, agreed after a splendid Christmas dinner with the then Vicar, Canon Walter Prest, to switch over their Bude houses. The operation was started on the following Boxing Day. Thus Ebbingford has changed hands for the eighth time in 800 years.'[42]

Sir Dudley Stamp, Professor of Geography in the University of London, wrote many of his later works on land use, food supply and medical geography in the library of Ebbingford Manor, but he referred only incidentally to the coast. His many students have travelled far and wide as geographers; among them is one of the compilers of this book.

The Bude Mermaid

In the 1820s the eccentric Robert Stephen Hawker, who was to become the Vicar of Morwenstow [north of Bude] rented Ivy Cottage nearby. Here he had formed for himself a perch on the edge of the cliff, where he could be alone with his books, his thoughts, and, as he would say with solemnity, "with God." Baring-Gould related the following: 'At full moon in the July of 1825 or 1826, he swam or rowed out to a rock at some little distance from the shore, plaited seaweed into a wig, which he threw over his head, so that it hung in lank streamers half-way down his back, enveloped his legs in an oilskin wrap, and, otherwise naked, sat on the rock, flashing the moonbeams about from a hand-mirror, and sang and screamed till attention was arrested. Some people passing along the cliff heard and saw him, and ran onto Bude, saying that a mermaid with a fish's tail was sitting on a rock, combing her hair, and singing.

'A number of people ran out on the rocks and along the beach, and listened awestruck to the singing and disconsolate wailing of the mermaid. Presently she dived off the rock, and disappeared.

'Next night crowds of people assembled to look out for the mermaid; and in due time she reappeared, and sent the moon flashing in their faces from her glass. Telescopes were brought to bear on her; but she sang on unmoved, braiding her tresses, and uttering remarkable sounds, unlike the singing of mortal throats which have been practised in do-re-mi.

'This went on for several nights; the crowd growing greater, people arriving from Stratton, Kilkhampton, and all the villages round, till Robert Hawker got very hoarse with his nightly singing, and rather tired of sitting so long in the cold. He therefore wound up the performance one night with an unmistakable "God Save the King," then plunged into the waves, and the mermaid never again revisited the "sounding shores of Bude".'[43]

North from Bude the cliffs ascend gradually, interrupted by the deep wooded Coombe Valley opening into a cove at Duckpool, and on to Lower Sharpnose Point with the huge satellite dishes of the Composite Signals Organisation Station. Several short valleys run down towards the coast, one of them containing the little church of Morwenstow.

Morwenstow and Stephen Hawker

The Reverend Robert Stephen Hawker (whom we have just met as the Mermaid of Bude) was vicar of Morwenstow from 1834 to 1875, restoring the church and building the vicarage. On an early visit he wrote:

> *Welcome, wild rock and lonely shore !*
> *Where round my days dark seas shall roar,*
> *And thy grey fane, Morwenna, stand*
> *The beacon of the Eternal Land.*

He was an eccentric poet, and the originator of the Harvest Festival. He was usually dressed in a clerical coat, seaman's jersey and high boots. He sat in a wooden hut built of driftwood hauled up from the wreckage of ships on the rocky shore to a spot over 400 feet above the sea, now known as Vicarage Cliff, and preserved by the National Trust. Here he is said to have written the poem 'The Quest of the Sangraal' (1863). Much earlier, as an undergraduate staying in Whitstone, near Bude, he had written 'The Song of the Western Men' (1825). Published anonymously in *The Royal Devonport Telegraph and Plymouth Chronicle*, it was noticed by Davies Gilbert, President of the Royal Society, and reprinted in *The Gentleman's Magazine* as an "ancient traditional ballad". Scott referred to it in one of his prefaces to a later edition of the *Border Minstrelsy*, as a "remarkable example of the lingering of the true ballad spirit in a remote district". Macaulay admitted that, until undeceived by the writer, he had always supposed the whole song to be genuinely ancient. But the ballad that deceived Scott and Macaulay was composed by Hawker:

> *And have they fixed the where and when*
> *And shall Trelawny die?*
> *Here's twenty thousand Cornish men*
> *Will know the reason why!*[44]

Rev. Hawker's Hut, Morwenstow

The approach to Morwenstow is bleak, as Baring Gould noted: 'the road passes between narrow hedges, every bush on which is bent from the sea. Not a tree is visible. The glorious blue Atlantic is before one, with only Lundy Isle breaking the continuity of the horizon line. In very clear weather, and before a storm, far away in faintest blue, the Welsh coast can be seen to the north-west.

'Suddenly the road dips down a combe; and Morwenstow tower, grey-stoned, pinnacled, stands up against the blue ocean, with a grove of stunted sycamores on the north of the church. Some way below, deep down in the glen, are seen the roofs and fantastic chimneys of the vicarage. The quaint lyche-gate and ruined cottage beside it, the venerable church, the steep slopes of the hills blazing with gorse or red with heather, and the background of sparkling blue sea half-way up the sky – from such a height above the shore it is looked upon – form a picture, once seen, never to be forgotten.

'The beach is inaccessible save at one point, where a path has been cut down the side of a steep gorse-covered slope, and through slides of ruined slate rock, to a bay, into which the Tonacombe Brook precipitates itself in a broken fall of foam.

'The little coves with blue-grey floors wreathed with sea-foam; the splintered and contorted rock; the curved strata, which here bend over like exposed ribs of a mighty mammoth; the sharp skerries that run out into the sea to torment it into eddies of froth and spray – are of rare wildness and beauty.'[43]

The Rescuer

The Reverend Hawker vigorously condemned the Cornish wreckers and did his utmost to rescue those sailors who were shipwrecked along his stretch of the coast.

The church and churchyard at Morwenstow seem to belong to an earlier age; when one of the writers of this book visited the church on a gloomy April afternoon, as the shadows were thickening, she almost expected to see the Reverend step out from a corner of the church. Indeed it is said that he has been seen standing by his first wife's grave, where he too had hoped to be buried. Sadly he died in Plymouth, whilst on a visit there.

The cliff footpath to the north goes over Cornakey Cliff and down into the deep Marsland Valley. It was at Marsland Mouth that Rose Salterne took her midnight bathe in Charles Kingsley's *Westward Ho!* : 'Rose went faltering down the strip of sand, some twenty yards farther, and there slipping off her clothes, stood shivering and trembling for a moment before she entered the sea.

'She was between two walls of rock: that on her left hand, some twenty feet high, hid her in deepest shade; that on her right, though much lower, took the whole blaze of the midnight moon. Great festoons of live and purple seaweed hung from it, shading dark cracks and crevices, fit haunts for all the goblins of the sea. On her left hand, the peaks of the rock frowned down ghastly black; on her right hand, far aloft, the downs slept bright and cold.

'The breeze had died away; not even a roller broke the perfect stillness of the cove. The gulls were all asleep upon the ledges. Over all was a true autumn silence – a silence which may be heard. She stood awed, and listened in hope of a sound which might tell her that any living thing beside herself existed.'[45] She peered into her mirror in the hope of seeing her future husband, but at that moment was disturbed by the arrival of two Jesuits.

The county boundary runs along the little stream in the Marsland Valley, and as you cross the footbridge you step out of Cornwall and into North Devon.

NORTH DEVON

Welcombe and Cruel Coppinger

Just north of the boundary between Cornwall and Devon a high cliff separates Marsland from Welcombe, a deep valley that comes down to the rugged Atlantic coast. It is still, as J.L.W. Page wrote in 1895: 'A wild spot fit for the doings of one of the greatest scoundrels that ever cheated the Revenue, or lured sailors to a cruel death on the rocks of this pitiless shore. For this district was the haunt of 'Cruel Coppinger'.

'Mr Hawker tells us that he was a Danish sea captain, that his ship was wrecked off Hartland, and that he was the only survivor. The manner of his appearance was singular. While the crowd had gathered at the wreck, like eagles to the carcass, more intent, it is to be feared, on plunder than on saving the lives of their fellow creatures, Coppinger rushed naked into their midst. Snatching her red cloak from an old woman he threw it round him, and, springing on the horse of a girl who sat looking on, he seized the reins and rode off with her at full speed.

'Coppinger probably knew that if he once got into the hands of these lawless characters his life would not be worth many minutes purchase, and so he chose this desperate method of escape.'[1]

The horse delivered Coppinger and the girl to the home of a friendly farmer, and here they stayed. He eventually married the girl, but was soon organising wreckers, smugglers and ruffians in this rural region far from towns and magistrates. Page continued:

'His coming had been romantic – his going was hardly less so. Such crimes as his could not for ever remain unpunished, and the toils of the exasperated Revenue officers began to draw closer and closer. Cutters haunted the coast from Hartland Point to Bude, and Coppinger saw that he must fly. He said not a word to any, but one evening a watcher saw him on the Gull Rock, waving his sword to a vessel in the offing. No one knew whence she came or whither she was bound, but she responded to his signals; a boat was lowered, and Coppinger was seen to descend the crag and embark. The boat reached the vessel, and she disappeared in a moment, vanishing like a ghost at cockcrow. Then arose a frightful storm, and neither man nor vessel was ever seen more. The general opinion was that she foundered with all on board:

> *Will you hear of Cruel Coppinger?*
> *He came from a foreign land;*
> *He was brought to us by the salt water,*
> *He was carried away by the wind*[1]

To the north the high cliffs continue to Speke's Mill Mouth, where the stream falls over a fifty foot cascade, white water and spray down a black glistening wall of rock on to the shore.

Hartland Quay

A mile beyond is Hartland Quay, where the grey rocks in the cliffs show sharp angular folds, sawn across by the flat coastal plateau. A small harbour was built here in Elizabethan times. A century ago J.L.W. Page wrote: 'The Quay is a massive arm of masonry thrust out among the rocks for the protection of the occasional coaster that in fair weather ventures to tempt Providence and the reefs of Hartland. The bottom is none of the best, for, with the exception of a few yards of sand or shingle, which may alter with the first raking sea, it is of solid rock.'[1] The harbour has not been used since the breakwater was smashed by gales at the end of the nineteenth century.

Hartland Quay

Hartland Point

Undulating cliffs run on northward to Hartland Point, which may have been the Ancient Romans' Promontory of Hercules. According to R. Pearse Chope: 'The name *Hercules Promontorium* dates back just eighteen hundred years, for about

AD120 a famous geographer, Ptolemy of Alexandria, gave the latitude and longitude (both incorrect) of what he calls in Greek *Heracleous Acron*, the Promontory of Heracles or Hercules.'[2]

Lundy Island, which seems to have grown larger as we travelled north, is only eleven miles out from Hartland Point, but the coast now swings eastward to Bideford Bay. It consists of steep cliffs and wooded bluffs, with several dells that descend to the bouldery shore.

Gallantry Bower

One of the precipitous cliffs, nearly 400 feet high, is known as Gallantry Bower, a name that, as S.H. Burton commented 'is not fully understood. The old legend that it arose from the leap of a broken-hearted lover into the sea seems to get little support nowadays. The Cornish *Col-an-Veor* (the 'great ridge') sounds less improbable. It fits the physical features of the cliff with its sheer drop on one side and gradual slope on the other; and greater corruptions in place-names have been known than the twisting of Col-an-Veor into Gallantry Bower.'[3]

Clovelly

In the next dell is the pretty village of Clovelly. W.G. Hoskins in his *The Making of the English Landscape* told how in the late sixteenth century the 'Devon village of Clovelly was given a breakwater or quay by the squire, George Cary. Clovelly had been an obscure agricultural parish until this time, turning its back on the sea in which it had no interest. But all was changed by the building of the massive stone pier, which created the only safe harbour on this merciless coast between Appledore in Devon and Boscastle in Cornwall. Until this, Clovelly had merely been a parish of scattered farms and cottages on the plateau. The squire built cottages up the narrow valley on either side of a tumbling stream – the only practicable way down to the seashore – and fish-cellars and warehouses below the cliffs. The watercourse was later diverted into a cascade to fall into the sea elsewhere, and its dry bed converted into a series of terraces or broad steps paved with cobbles. The village scene as we know it was then complete.'[4]

In 1860 Charles Dickens collaborated with Wilkie Collins to write of Clovelly (which they called Steepway) in *A Message from the Sea*: 'There was no road in it, there was no wheeled vehicle in it, there was not a level yard in it. From the sea-beach to the cliff top two irregular rows of white houses, placed opposite to one another, and twisting here and there, and there and here, rose, like the sides of a long succession of stages of crooked ladders, and you climbed up the village, or climbed down the village by the staves between, some six feet wide or so, and made of sharp irregular stones. No two houses in the village were alike, in chimney, size, shape, door, window, gable, roof-tree, anything. The sides of the ladders were musical with water, running clear and bright. The staves were musical with the clattering feet of the pack-horses and pack-donkeys, and the voices of the fishermen urging them up, mingled with the voices of the fishermen's wives and their many children. The pier was musical with the wash of the sea, the creaking of capstans, and windlasses, and the airy fluttering of little vanes and sails. The rough, sea-bleached boulders of which the pier was made, and the whiter boulders of the shore, were brown with drying nets. The red-brown cliffs, richly wooded to their extremest verge, had their softened and beautiful forms reflected in the bluest water, under the clear North Devonshire sky of a November day without a cloud.'[5]

Daniel Farson in *A Window on the Sea*, wrote of 'The harbour and the jutting ferry, with bollards reputed to be Spanish cannon salvaged after the Armada, The houses leaning in a row over the pebbled beach have changed slightly in their usefulness over the years: the limekiln, which supplied the houses with their white-wash, is dormant; the old lifeboat station built in 1870 has been replaced by a modern lifeboat moored permanently outside the harbour in case of emergency. But the limekiln and the old lifeboat slipway are still there, if retired.

'Then there is the richness of the surrounding woods, of birch and oak. A three-mile road guides you through the surrounding denseness, with sudden panoramic views of the coastline and Clovelly itself. It is known as Hobby Drive, because this was the personal hobby of Sir James Hamlyn Williams, who supervised the construction from 1811 until his death eighteen years later. When part of it subsided at the turn of the century, a new stretch was substituted and called the Sailor's Cut because so many fishermen were involved in its building.'[6]

Clovelly owes its architectural preservation largely to Christine Hamlyn, who owned the estate between 1884 and 1936.

Westward Ho!

The steep bluffs run inland at Westward Ho!, which was founded in 1863, and has the literary distinction of being named after a book – Charles Kingsley's adventure story, set in Elizabethan times and written in 1855.

> *Westward Ho! With a rumbelow*
> *And hurra for the Spanish Main, O!*[7]

It has become a seaside resort, with hotels, caravans, and holiday camps. Rudyard Kipling was at school (the United Services College) here from 1878 until 1882. The College is now a terrace of twelve houses tucked away behind an iron gate and known as Kipling Terrace. He used the setting in *Stalky & Co.* (1899), especially in the first story 'In Ambush': 'In summer all right-minded boys built huts in the furze-hill behind the College – little lairs whittled out of the heart of the prickly bushes, full of stumps, odd root-ends, and spikes, but, since they were strictly forbidden, palaces of delight. And for the fifth summer in succession, Stalky, M'Turk and Beetle (this was before they had reached the dignity of a study) had built, like beavers, a place of retreat and meditation, where they smoked.

'They were walking through a combe half full of old high furze in gay bloom that ran up to a fringe of brambles and dense wood of mixed timber and hollies. It was as though one half of the combe were filled with golden fire to the cliff's edge. The tough stems parted before them and it was a window opened on a far view of Lundy, and the deep sea sluggishly nosing the pebbles a couple of hunded feet below. They could hear young jackdaws squawking on the ledges, the hiss and jabber of a nest of hawks somewhere out of sight; great grey and black gulls screamed against the jackdaws, the heavy scented acres of bloom were alive with low-nesting birds, singing or silent as the shadow of the wheeling hawks passed and returned, and on the naked turf the combe rabbits thumped and frolicked.'[8] This walk is now part of the South West Coast Path. The area now known as Kipling Tors was donated to the National Trust by the Rudyard Kipling Memorial Fund in 1938.

Stalky was the boyhood nickname of Major-General L.C. Dunsterville; M'Turk was G.C. Beresford, and Gigger was Kipling, from Giglamps, the large glasses he wore for his acute short-sightedness. In *Stalky's Reminiscences* Dunsterville described how he came to the United Services College in 1875 at the age of ten: 'The locality was perfect, with wild scenery and glorious air, at a distance from any large town and out of reach of parents. Bideford was the nearest town, and was of course "out of bounds", which added to its attraction.

'Kipling did not join till several years later. During those troublous years I had to develop my character, without his shrewd guidance, from artless simplicity to artful guile, and by the time that he and Beresford united with me in the occupancy of a study I was in the passive condition of a bundle of Chinese fire-crackers to which his fertile brain eagerly applied the torch.

'I made a little money almost honestly by collecting copper nails, and bits of copper sheeting from pools on the beach, and selling them in Bideford where I got quite a good price for them.

'Wrecks were not uncommon in Bideford Bay, and my copper came from sailing ships that had gone to pieces on the bar.'[9]

The Pebble Ridge

Beresford also wrote of those days in *Schooldays with Kipling*: 'The sea, the shore and the sands were the great attraction at Westward Ho! There were no quick-sands on that great expanse of beach at low tide that we could find; but there was an old wreck of a schooner that had gone ashore in a gale and remained embedded in the sands, its black skeleton ribs six feet thick in the air. This looked fairly poetic. There were rocks standing up made of a curious kind of tough, greasy, grey clay, which the sea did not erode very quickly, though it cut lanes through the mass. The incoming tide used to surround the rocks, and at high tide was over them. Anyone on the rocks could be cut off; but as the rocks were only two or three feet high there was no real danger.

Of the Pebble Ridge he wrote: 'It was perhaps fifteen feet high and fifty yards broad, and seemed of human construction; as if some industrious navvies had placed it there but forgotten the cement. The summit was a sharp ridge: the whole, the work of old Oceans and placed at the highest limit of the tides.

'Neptune had quarried his materials for the Ridge out of the [cliffs] and, in the course of ages, had slowly rolled the broken masses across the sea floor, rounding them in the journey and piling them up as a wall two or three miles long that protected the low-lying sandy flats of the Northam Burrows at the river's mouth.

'Amongst the beauties and wonders that lay about us was that floating amethyst, Lundy Island, with its ever-changing colour and depth of tone, its rocks and precipices now clean and distinct, now one with the mass of the island. How fair to see were the breakers curving into the bay, the yellow sweep of the sands at low tide, the brown rocks to the west, their colours deepening as the onrushing waves swept over them and receded. In the summer a cloudland hung over the ocean and the land – a realm of gigantic snowy billows, more awesome than the foaming waves.'[10]

Clive Gunnell also described the Pebble Ridge: 'It is about three kilometres long, 15 metres wide and 6 metres high. It protects from the sea not only Northam Burrows [an area of grassy sand dunes] but the Royal North Devon Golf Club, formed in 1863 and one of the oldest links in Great Britain. Often during periods of high tides and fierce gales the ridge is breached and sometimes flattened, and a great deal of it has been enclosed in wire mesh to try and hold the pebbles in position.

'For many centuries repairing breaches in the ridge has been the responsibility of the 'Potwallopers' of Northam, who undertook the task in exchange for certain rights dating back to feudal times. These rights were made available to all who 'boiled their pots in their own hearths' within the Northam area (hence their name), and allowed them to graze their stock on the Burrows. Every August the Potwallopers assemble on the ridge and work throughout the day restoring and repairing it, refreshed by having food and cider brought to them.'[11]

Tarka the Otter

The estuaries of the Taw and Torridge meet just north of the Pebble Ridge, where a vast expanse of sand is exposed at low tide, and ocean swell rolls in from the Atlantic. A little lighthouse stands on Crow Spit, which has grown out at the mouth of the Taw.

Taw and Torridge were the home of *Tarka the Otter* in Henry Williamson's story: 'One evening, when the ebb-tide was leaning the channel buoys to the west, and the gulls were flying silent and low over the sea to the darkening cliffs of the headland, the otters set out on a journey. The bright eye of the lighthouse, a bleached bone at the edge of the sandhills, blinked in the clear air. They were carried down amidst swirls and topplings of waves in the wake of a ketch, while the mumble of the bar grew in their ears. Beyond the ragged horizon of grey breakers the day had gone, clouded and dull, leaving a purplish pallor on the cold sea.

'The waves slid and rose under the masted ship, pushing the white surge of the bar from her bows. A crest rolled under her keel and she pitched into a trough. On the left a mist arose off a bank of grey boulders, on which a destroyer lay broken and sea-scattered. It had lain there for years, in bits like beetle fragments in a gorse-spider's grey web-tunnel. One of the great seas that drive the flying spume over the pot-wallopers' grazing marsh had thrown it up on the Pebble Ridge. During the day Tarka and Greymuzzle had slept under the rusty plates, curled warm on the wave-worn boulders.'[12]

Appledore

On the shore of the Torridge estuary is Appledore, which in 1977 Daniel Farson found to be: 'too down-to-earth, or down-to-sea, to be a tourist attraction like Clovelly. With Westward Ho! as the invaluable buffer nearby, it is isolated, on the way to nowhere.

'The alleys behind the quay are too narrow for cars, which should be banned, and it is a village to explore on foot, discovering old cottages decorated with small figureheads or plates above the doorways, and the peeling façade of the former Gaiety Cinema with a mermaid announcing 'Continuous Performances'. On the shore, opposite, where the old lighthouse used to stand, the salmon fishermen pull their nets, and ships outside wait patiently to ride the Bideford Bar when the tide is full, on their way to Bideford and Barnstaple.'[6]

Christopher Somerville wrote of 'Appledore's long waterfront, curving for well over a mile in a semi-circle round the nose of land formed by the scouring waters of the Torridge. Tiny cobbled courtyards, deep in shadow yet bright with flower baskets, run off between thick cottage-walls as they do along the other narrow, unevenly curving streets just behind the waterfront road.

'The view over the estuary changes hour by hour, according to the state of the tide. At high water the whole channel is filled from bank to bank, a broad highway of water lying almost motionless between the dunes of Braunton Burrows and Northam Burrows. As the sea ebbs back into Bideford Bay, the mingled waters of Taw and Torridge chase it out with a far-off roaring over the bar, the flow speeding up and shrinking inwards until the Torridge under Appledore has dwindled away to a winding stream of contrary tides between vast mud and sandbanks gleaming with drying pools of water. These contrasts and shifts of speed, depth and direction where three opposing water forces meet, a constant challenge to the skills of sailors and fishermen, glue onlookers to the waterfront railings in fascination for hours at a time. An added fillip to their enjoyment of the scene comes once or twice a year, when one of Appledore's two shipyards waves goodbye to another brand-new offspring.'[13]

Charles Kingsley convalesced here in 1854, and wrote: 'The rich, hot, balmy air, which comes in now through the open window, off Braunton Burrows, and the beautiful tide river, a mile wide, is like an elixir of life to me. No night frosts here. It is as warm as day. I expect a charming sail tomorrow, and to catch mackerel on the way. The coast down here looks more lovely than ever; the green fern and purple heather have enriched the colouring since the spring; showers succeeded by gleams of sun, giving a wonderful freshness and delicacy to all the tints.'[14]

Bideford

Early in the eighteenth century Daniel Defoe was one of several people commissioned to report on the state of the country to the Speaker of the House of Commons. 'Bideford,' he wrote, 'is a pleasant, clean, well built town; the more ancient street which lies next the river, where is the bridge, a very noble quay, and the custom house.' He mentioned 'considerable and wealthy merchants' and commented on 'the trade of this town being very much in fish. I observed here that several ships were employed to go to Liverpool, and up the River Mersey to Warrington, to fetch rock salt, which is found in that county, which they bring to Bideford to cure herrings. There is indeed a very fine bridge over the river here, but the passage is so narrow, and they are so chary of it, that few carriages go over it; but as the water ebbs quite out of the river every low water, the carts and waggons go over the sand with great ease and safety.'[15]

Charles Kingley's statue, unveiled in 1906, with a manuscript of *Westward Ho!* in his left hand, looks along the tree-lined quay towards the bridge. The book, published in 1855, begins thus: 'All who have travelled through the delicious scenery of North Devon must needs know the little white town of Bideford, which slopes upwards from its broad tide river paved with golden sands and many-arched bridge where the salmon wait for autumn floods, toward the pleasant upland on the west. Above the town the hills close in, cushioned with deep oak woods, through which juts here and there a crag of fern-fringed slate; below they lower, and open more and more in softly-rounded knolls, and fertile squares of red and green.'[7]

Instow

Instow, across the estuary from Appledore, has a diminutive quay, some seaside villas, and a cricket ground with a thatched pavilion. At high tide, sixes are hit occasionally into the sea. At low tide the Instow Sands are half a mile wide, out to where the Torridge meets the Taw. J.L.W. Page commented that 'the quay, a small affair of sea-weed hung masonry, projects half the day into the mud of the foreshore, for Torridge when the tide leaves it is but a narrow-streak, and the water only laps the quay wall for a couple of hours at most. It is not a bad place, though, for a quiet half-hour and a yarn with the ancient mariner.'[1]

Barnstaple

A few miles up the Taw estuary is Barnstaple, a town similar to, and rivalling Bideford. The Ordnance Survey map diplomatically names the bay off the combined mouth of the Torridge and Taw estuaries 'Barnstaple or Bideford Bay'. Lady Rosalind Northcote thought Barnstaple 'very prettily placed. The river sweeps round a bend of a green and pleasant valley, and along the Strand is a wall shaded with trees. Seagulls flutter among the sand banks from which the sea retires itself at low tide, leaving only a small shining stream which seems to creep between shelves and sands.'[16]

Barnstaple also has a long bridge, and was prominent in trading with the American colonies, Canada and Newfoundland. Shipbuilding was important as Lois Lamplugh recorded: 'The summer of 1852 saw the launching of the *Lady Ebrington* of over 400 tons; in October of the same year she sailed for Australia with 129 emigrants. Throughout Victoria's reign shipping companies were competing to offer passage to tens of thousands eager to emigrate to more spacious countries, and by the time Westacott's larger yard was in operation [1846] advertisements were appearing in the *North Devon Journal*, seeking to entice the adventurous with hints of fortunes to be gained in the goldfields, or on the sheep ranges of Australia.'[17]

Tom Faggus, the highwayman in R.D. Blackmore's *Lorna Doone*, was 'caught upon Barnstaple Bridge, with soldiers at either end of it (yet doubtful about approaching him). He set his strawberry mare, sweet Winnie, at the left hand parapet, with a whisper into her dove-coloured ear. Without a moment's doubt she leaped it, into the foaming tide, and swam, and landed according to orders.'[18]

Torridge Estuary

Downstream from Barnstaple the Torridge estuary widens rapidly, with the Chivenor air base and Braunton marshes on its northern shore. Tarka the Otter played in the meadows beside the little River Caen which flows out from the hills through the large village of Braunton and into the Torridge: 'With the ebb he floated by ketches and gravel barges, white ring-plover and little stints running at the line of lapse cried their sweet cries of comradeship. The mooring keg bobbed and turned in the ebb, the perches, tattered with seaweed, leaned out of the trickling mud of the fairway, where curlew walked, sucking up worms in their long curved bills. Tarka rode on with the tide. It took him into the estuary where the real sea was fretting the sandbanks.

'Suddenly he heard the mumbling roar of surf and saw the lighthouse across the Burrows. He galloped joyfully down a field of arrish, or stubble. He travelled so swiftly that soon he stood on the edge of sandy cliffs, where spray blew as wind. He found a way down to the pools by a ledge where grew plants of great sea-stock, whose leaves were crumbling in the autumn sleep.

'The trail led over sandhills with their thin stabbing marram grasses, and to the mossy pans behind them, where grew privet bushes and blunt-head club-rushes. Tarka crossed the marsh to Horsey Island– where grew Russian thistles, sprung from a single seed blown from the estuary off a Baltic timber ship years before - until he came to the sea-wall, and below the wall, to the mouth of Branton pill. The tide took him slowly in a patch of froth, which the meeting waters had beaten up, the gossip of the Two Rivers.'[12]

Crow Point: Taw and Torridge Estuary

Victor Canning's thriller *The Mask of Memory* was set in this area: 'The tide was half in, sweeping rapidly over the last sand banks in mid-stream. Where the two rivers met and the tide fronted their outflowing waters a cloud of gulls wheeled noisily in the air.' His heroine, Margaret Tucker, '..climbed the dune above the beach and dropped down to the summer-filthy stretch of sand that awaited the winter gales to cleanse it. The beach stretched westwards three miles to the estuary mouth, the far waters lost in a low, russet haze. A few people, some with dogs, studded the wet hard sand at the tide's edge in pygmy perspective. They would mostly be residents like herself, glad to have the long vistas and lonely sweeps of dune, marsh and burrows restored to them. A flock of sanderlings, little white and grey ghosts of birds, worked the water's edge, running and feeding ceaselessly as the returning sea brought life to the beach fringe, stirring shrimp and sandhoppers to activity. Now and again the birds took to the air, wheeling and curving low over the water on a remarkable precision of black and white-barred wing beats. They were here for the winter now, to join the moorland curlews and the oyster catchers working the tide flows. Other migrants were beginning to pass through. There had been dozens of golden plover on the marsh pasture this morning with the lapwings and she had seen knots, dunlin and whimbrels each day for two weeks.'[19]

Saunton Sands

Daniel Farson looked across 'the sweeping expanse of Saunton Sands. The view is so amazing, so bizarre, that people stop their cars to get out and stare.

'It is a mixture of Egypt and Paradise – or so the film companies would have us believe. The sands were used as desert in Alexander Korda's 'Caesar and Cleopatra', and when the airman in 'A Matter of Life and Death' recovered consciousness on the dunes, he thought he was in heaven.

'Saunton Sands stretch for several miles, bending into the estuary where the rivers Taw and Torridge pour out to sea and clash whitely and often wildly at Bideford Bar. Behind the beach lie interminable sand-dunes.'[6] These are known as Braunton Burrows.

Baggy Point

Daniel Farson went for a swim at Baggy Point with a friend – a swim that almost ended in disaster: 'The cliffs at the end are tremendous and sheer, and the cave known as Baggy Hole goes so far back that when a dog was taken inside and ran away, it was "next seen in Barnstaple". The idea of entering Baggy Hole from the sea, with the hope of seeing the grey seals basking at the entrance, seemed like a mild adventure when the sea was calm. But the sea can turn in an instant. The jagged rocks may look more harmful, but it is the water that demands a constant respect. When the tide flows, the current is so strong that it is impossible to row against - the best procedure is to drift out and start again when the tide slackens. Of course you only realise the treachery of the water when you are on it. To add to the deception, small coasters pass unnervingly close – a few feet away from the rocks – with the easy strength of their engines. The water here is deep, and if the captains skirted further out – where it *looks* safe – they would be in danger of striking the isolated rock that rises from the surf on certain days with an explosion of spray, like a polaris missile. The day was so still that the possibility of a sudden sea-change did not occur to us, but as we rounded the point the swell rose with a vengeance. It surged up the rocks for ten or fifteen feet and fell violently back. We watched without too much dismay at first, näive enough to imagine that it might die down. The cliffs defied contemplation. In quick succession, the air grew colder, the swell became more ferocious, and the sun disappeared over the horizon. The darkness fell as if we were in the

Mediterranean. Almost before we were aware of what had happened, we were shivering on a rock with the sea advancing every moment.'[6] Fortunately they were eventually rescued by the Clovelly lifeboat.

Baggy Point

Woolacombe

Woolacombe Sands stretch for just over two miles between Baggy Point and Morte Point, behind Morte Bay. The seaward view frames the length of Lundy Island. Woolacombe, once a tiny fishing village with a single remote farmhouse, now has lines of hotels, villas and holiday flats on the south-facing slopes overlooking the surf-washed sands. A granite memorial on the lawns records that: 'In the autum of 1943 the United States Army Assault Training Centre was established at Woolacombe, with headquarters in the village, and encompassed Woolacombe and Saunton Sands, their adjacent hinterlands and sea approaches'. The story is told in a recent book by Richard T. Bass: 'If Waterloo was won on the playing-fields of Eton, surely the sands of the North Devon beaches contributed importantly to the success of the assault on the Normandy beaches.'

On arriving here, one of the American officers, Major Finn, said "When I first saw the beach I thought I was in California or Florida. It seemed an ideal vacation site'.[20]

E.P. Leigh-Bennett came on the Atlantic Coast Express in the 1930s to holiday a little breathlessly at Woolacombe: 'Taking it all round, the afternoon is the best time. Dash it, we've got three miles of dead flat sand here for every sort of game. There's a lot of riding goes on here, by the way, ponies by the dozen for the children (don't think I'm putting on side, will you?) but they seem largely to dispose of that pastime in the morning – which gives us a clear pitch as 'twere. And very nice too.

'Do you know, honestly, there was a Rugger match in progress yesterday afternoon – full size ground all marked out – North v South. Tries only, of course. I played stand-off but was too heavily marked by one of their disgusting wing forwards to do any good. A cricket match – mixed, and I hear some girl knocked up 43 l.b.w, which is pretty priceless. And a very hot game of rounders – the semi-final of the Woolacombe Wassail Bowl. Solid silver; given by some old bird, I've forgotten his name. The trouble about rounders here is that if you swipe a tennis ball good and hearty with a sawn-off cricket bat, the infernal thing goes meandering on for a quarter of a mile or more – that is unless your out-fielding is frightfully reliable: meanwhile the striker is piling up a sickening score. Oh, there was a tremendous "touch last" tourney in progress too – but I'm afraid I'm a a bit past that.'[22]

Barricane Beach

Philip and Emily Gosse came to Barricane Beach in 1853: 'A steep footpath leads down to an area of what you would suppose to be minute pebbles; but which, when you come down to them, you find to be almost entirely composed of shells. A group of women and girls may always be seen raking with their fingers among the fragments for such specimens. They usually lie at length upon the beach, to work with greater ease; but when a visitor comes down, they throng round him like bees, and he must be a skilful tactician if he be not at least sixpence the poorer when he leaves the cove.'[22]

Charles Kingsley travelled the North Devon coast in the 1870s with his friend Claude Mellot and also visited Barricane Beach: "Look at that sheet of yellow sand below us now, banked to the inland with sand-hills and sunny downs, and ending abruptly at the foot of that sombre wall of slate hill, which runs out like a huge pier into the sea some two miles off. That is Woolacombe: but here on our right is a sight worth seeing. Every gully and creek there among the rocks is yellow but not with sand. Those are shells; the sweepings of the ocean bed for miles around, piled there, millions upon millions, yards deep, in every stage of destruction. There they lie grinding to dust; and every gale brings in fresh pyramids from the inexhaustible sea-world, as if Death could be never tired of devouring, or God of making. The brain grows dizzy and tired, as one's feet crunch over the endless variety of their form".'[23]

Lundy Island

Lundy Island means Puffin Island in Norse. As well as many species of birds, grey seals, sika deer, wild goats and sheep inhabit the island, which belongs to the National Trust. Michael Drayton wrote of it in *Polyolbion* in 1613 as

A lusty black-brow'd girle,
With forehead broad and high,
That often hath bewitched
The sea gods with her eye....[24]

Charles Kingsley in *Westward Ho!* described *Vengeance* chasing a ship of the Spanish Armada: "Land right ahead ! Port your helm, sir! For the love of God, port your helm !"

'Amyas, with the strength of a bull, jammed the helm down, while Yeo shouted to the men below. She swung round. The masts bent like whips; crack went the foresail like a cannon. What matter? Within two hundred yards of them was the Spaniard; in front of her, and above her, a huge dark bank rose through the dense hail, and mingled with the clouds; and at its foot, plainer every moment, pillars and spouts of leaping foam.

' "Lundy !" said Yeo. "The south end ! I see the head of the Shutter in the breakers ! Hard a-port yet, and get her close-hauled as you can, and the Lord may have mercy on us still! Look at the Spaniard !"

'On their left hand, as they broached-to, the wall of granite sloped down from the clouds toward an isolated peak of rock, some two hundred feet in height. Then a hundred yards of roaring breaker upon a sunken shelf, across which the race of the tide poured like a cataract; then amid a column of salt smoke, the Shutter, like a huge black fang, rose waiting for its prey; and between the Shutter and the land, the great galleon loomed dimly through the storm.

'He too, had seen his danger, and tried to broach-to. But his clumsy mass refused to obey the helm. He struggled a moment, half hid in foam, fell away again, and rushed upon his doom.'[7]

J.L.W. Page wrote about the dramatic western coast of the island: 'Close to the Half Way Wall the rock scenery is again very fine. Here are the tall pinnacles of the Cheeses, so named from the round, cheese-shaped layers of rock which, piled one upon another, rise high above the slopes. Resting for a moment in the sunny corner beneath the wall, we look back. What a glorious sweep it is! In the foreground, rising from a declivity almost unscalable, lofty pillars of granite seamed and weathered stand forth against the blue. Between them you look down a gorge to the sea spouting over the reefs four hundred feet below. To the south, full in view, the Devil's Chimney stands like a sentinel over against a great cleft in the precipice, while off the next headland the ever-restless surf breaks against the Needle Rock. Inland, almost over the tops of the Cheeses, the white column of the lighthouse looks down over an undulating steppe of purple and gold.'[1]

'Lundy granite,' wrote Kevin Crossley-Holland 'is altogether less welcoming than the pinkish granite of Cornwall and Scilly. It is more grey than white; the colour of unripe Danish blue seen at a distance. The Charing Cross Hotel and the Victoria Embankment are built out of it. The Lundy Granite Company lasted only 7 years and defeated by east winds which all too often prevented shipment, went into liquidation in 1870.'[25]

Morte Point

North-west of Woolacombe, Morte Point is a rocky headland owned by the National Trust. Many ships have been wrecked on the outlying Morte Stone, a reef where the sea is angry even on calm days. Henry Williamson's *Tarka the Otter* came this way too: 'Day was beginning. The tide, moving northwards across Morte Bay, was ripped and whitened by rocks which stood out of the hollows of the grey sea. One rock was tall above the reef – the Morte Stone – and on the top pinnacle stood a big black bird, with the tails of fish sticking out of its gullet. Its dripping wings were held out to ease its tight crop.

'Tired and buffeted by the long Atlantic rollers, Tarka turned back under the Morte Stone, and swam to land. He climbed a slope strewn with broken thrift roots and grey shards of rock, to a path set on its seaward verge by a fence of iron posts and cables. Salt winds had gnawed the iron to rusty splinters. The heather above the path was tougher than the iron, but its sprigs were barer than its own roots.

'Over the crest of the Morte, heather grew in low bushes, out of the wind's way. There were green places where, among grass cropped by sheep, grew mushrooms mottled like owl's plumage. The sky above the crest was reddening, and he found a sleeping place under a broken cromlech, the burial place of an ancient man, whose bones were grass and heather and dust in the sun.'[12]

Philip and Emily Gosse were at Rockham Bay: 'It is a little cove, wild and silent, no trace of the vicinity of man being perceptible. Cliffs of hard blue slate surround it on three sides, and the ground itself, the floor of the enclosure, is formed of the same slate, which, though uneven has been rubbed smooth by the action of the waves. A coating of sand and shingle fills the hollows, but every where the slate crops out, and runs in bristling ridges far away into the sea, where it is covered with a rude drapery of yellow seaweed.

'I strolled down to the water's edge. In one place I found a large bed of minute pebbles, most of them of white quartz, beautifully smooth, regular and pure, looking exactly as if a cart-load of comfits and sugar-plums had been shovelled out there, or as if all the humming-birds' eggs in South America had been collected into one spot.'[22]

Lee Bay

Beyond the lighthouse on Bull Point the coast becomes higher and steeper, swinging eastward to Lee Bay, which J.L.W. Page described as: 'a rocky cove, bounded by shattered cliffs, the light tints of which are all the more noticeable because contrasted with the bright green and dark brown seaweed that covers the floor of the cove. At the head of the bay stands an old cottage, once a mill.

But the wheel has been removed and the millstream falls to the beach uninter-rupted. Round the shore sweeps the road, separated only from the beach by a low wall, against which the waves break when the tide is high.'[1]

Ilfracombe

Ilfracombe has developed along an east-west valley behind a high coastal ridge that is breached at Wildersmouth and again at the harbour. Tunnels cut by Welsh miners in 1863 lead through to sandy beaches and a walled tidal swimming pool west of Wildersmouth.

The American writer Henry James came to North Devon in 1872 to admire 'the bosky flanks of Devonshire Combes. The little watering-place of Ilfracombe is seated at the lower verge of one of these seaward-plunging valleys, between a couple of magnificent headlands which hold it in a hollow slope and offer it securely to the caress of the Bristol Channel. It is a very finished specimen of its genus. On the left of the town one of the great cliffs I have mentioned rises in a couple of massive peaks and presents to the sea an almost vertical face, all muffled in tufts of golden broom and mighty fern. You have not walked fifty yards away from the hotel before you encounter half a dozen little sign-boards, directing your steps to a path up the cliff. You follow their indications and you arrive at a little gatehouse, with photographs and various local gimcracks exposed for sale. A most respectable person appears, demands a penny and, on receiving it, admits you with great civility to commune with nature. The cliffs are superb, the play of light and shade upon them is a perpetual study, and the air a particular mixture of the breath of the hills and moors and the breath of the sea. I was very glad, at the end of my climb, to have a good bench to sit upon – as one must think twice in England before measuring one's length on the grassy earth.'[26]

Philip and Emily Gosse enjoyed sea-side pleasures here too: 'The coast, in common with nearly the whole of this side of the county, is rocky and presents abundance of bold and magnificent scenery. The shore consists of bluff headlands and rugged points, alternating with little coves and beaches of sand or shingle (more generally the latter) and the recess of the tide exposes a multitude of black bristling ledges and points of rock.'[22]

Above the promenade Capstone Hill rises high above the town. Gosse described: 'A narrow cove, with a beach of small pebbles, fringed on all sides with masses of rock projecting in strong angles, bears the name of Wildersmouth, from the rivulet that spreads over, and oozes through its shingles. The boundary hill-range, which on the left of the cove atttains no great elevation, rises on the right into a large, somewhat conical hill, known as the Capstone. It is an enormous mass of shale; in some parts very friable and rotten, in others more compact, with occasional narrow veins of white quartz running through.'[22]

In the museum can be seen a red flannel petticoat. There is an interesting story attached to this exhibit as Clive Gunnell related: 'On 22 February 1797, fourFrench ships were sighted off Ilfracombe, where the French commander sank several English coasting vessels by forcing them to scuttle. At that time most of Ilfracombe's 200 full-time sailors were away serving with the Royal Navy. The women of the town, realising the danger of possible invasion, removed their traditional red petticoats and draped them around their shoulders like scarlet cloaks, then took up prominent positions on the high ground around the town. The sight of the red petticoats convinced the French that Ilfracombe was garrisoned with a strong military force and they hurriedly sailed away.[11]

The historian R.N. Worth in 1895 found Ilfracombe 'a little port of great antiquity [which] has developed within the past century into a watering-place so thriving that it seems to have no history and to be all bran-new. But the town is old enough to have some dozen names, varying from Aelfringcombe through Ilfordcombe to the modern title; and to have been a harbour of some repute in the twelfth century, for the Welsh and Irish traffic. Perhaps the best evidence of its standing in the early Middle Ages is the quaint little chapel of St. Nicholas on the peaked hill [Lantern Hill] overlooking the quays, still, as it probably has always been, the harbour lighthouse.'[27]

Beatrix Potter spent childhood holidays in Ilfracombe and her description of the 'long flight of steps to the harbour basin' was used in *The Tale of Little Pig Robinson.*

An early visitor was Daniel Benham, whose handwritten diary in the Ilfracombe Museum, has been transcribed by Mervyn G. Palmer. On Saturday 25 August 1849 he 'Walked to the point of Hillsborough Hill, the prospect from which is very fine, commencing on the east with the bold craggy cliffs of Combe Martin, Smallmouth and Rillage Point, the hills form an amphitheatre of great beauty – the white line of road between Ilfracombe and Combe Martin is seen passing in the deep vale below the village of Hele after which it winds along the hillsides by the sea on the edges of the cliff.'[28]

Watermouth

At Watermouth the Sterridge valley runs parallel to the coast and opens into a cove which Newell Arber considered 'the best example of a drowned river mouth in North Devon', while J.L.W. Page compared it with a sea loch in Scotland: 'The simile is a happy one, and it may be added that there are few Scotch sea lochs that are prettier. The low range of cliffs, nearly eaten through at Smallmouth, have here given ingress to the sea, forming a cove so perfectly land-locked, that when a storm is thundering without, the water within is smooth enough for a cockleshell. This natural breakwater is broken up into peaks and knolls and undulations. In spring the place is covered with primroses and wild hyacinth. Later, the brake fern uncurls its velvety fronds, and the little valleys of the peninsula are a mass of tender green.'[1]

The neo-Gothic castle, built in 1825 in spacious grounds, is now a Theme Park, mainly for children, with a dungeon labyrinth, Gnomeland and Merrygoland. There is also an Arts and Crafts display.

Watermouth and The Great Hangman

Combe Martin

Combe Martin Bay is succeeded by rising headlands, Little Hangman then Great Hangman, the latter rising more than 1000 feet above sea level. Silver was mined here for many centuries, the last mine closing in 1848. Gorsey hummocks indicate the remains of shafts and adits, and there is still a ruined engine-house on Knap Down.

The village originated inland, and has grown more than a mile down the valley of the River Umber on either side of a long street to the sandy cove overlooked by the Fo'c'sle Inn. Southey came here in 1799: 'We passed through Coombmartin, an old, and dirty, and poor place; one house, once a good one, bears the date 1584: another is built in a most ridiculous castle style, and called the Pack of Cards'.[30] This is an odd-looking hotel, so-called because a seventeenth century gambler, George Ley, won a large sum of money playing cards, and built the house to commemorate the event.

Little Hangman

J.L.W. Page reported on Little Hangman: 'The strange name of the hill is due, say the inhabitants of Combe Martin, to a still more strange accident. A sheep stealer passing over the hill, with his prey slung round his shoulders, paused to rest on a rock, when the sheep, in its struggles, tightened the cord, which, slipping round the man's neck, strangled him. The etymologist, however, says that hangman is simply a corruption of the Celtic *An maen*, the stone, and treats the legend with scorn.'[1]

A Steep Coast

The huge cliffs of the North Devon coast have long been a challenge to geologists keen to study Devonian rock formations. Between Combe Martin and Lynmouth they are very steep and high. Newell Arber offered his fellow geologists some advice in 1911: 'The visitor to these coasts should not be content to see the coast sections and the waterfalls from the cliff top, but should insist, wherever it is possible, on inspecting them from the beach also. With a little determination at hand, it is but rarely impracticable to reach the beach and the foot of a fall. Geology from a cliff-top is, like geology from an arm-chair, a thing to be avoided.'[30]

Heddon's Mouth

The deep, steep sided V-shaped valley of the Heddon River runs northward to interrupt the steep coast at Heddon's Mouth. Here the cliffs are, as Newell Arber called them 'of hog's back type', and in the words of S.H. Burton they 'begin their rapid fall to the sea a considerable distance inland, thus commencing a long steep slope, only the lowest portion of which is sea-eroded. The highest of the hog's backs have fine escarpments below the belt of turf, gorse and bracken with which the upper slopes are covered, but on the lower cliffs vegetation creeps down almost to sea level.'[31]

J.L.W. Page wrote that 'Heddon's Mouth was thought, by more than one, to be the finest of the combes of North Devon. We look down upon the trout stream flashing seaward towards the bar of shingle which the sea has piled across its mouth, and through which it must filter, save when a storm on the moors sends down a flood, when, for a brief space, the barrier gives way. An abandoned limekiln perched on the rocky bank overlooks the struggles between stream and sea, and, worn by age and the weather to picturesqueness, is like some old castle guarding the pass inland.

'The valley is shut in by lofty hills. On the western side the stone-strewn slopes give to the scene an air of grand desolation. In the glare of mid-day the effect is not so imposing, but it is difficult to do justice to it at sunset. With the light at their back, the hills turn a deep blue purple, while the screes become a pinkish grey, and over all spreads a pale mist, so transparent as scarce to be mist at all. Up from the depths below come glints of light where, here and there, the Heddon curls back against a boulder, and the air is full of his voice, rising to this height in soft undertone.'[1]

In Henry Williamson's story, 'Stumberleap', an old stag was being pursued by the Exmoor Hunt: 'He staggered over the skyline, a long file of silent hounds pursuing him. Down the stony bed of the shallow river ran Stumberleap, past an inn, before which a group of people stood, watching the dark of the travelling storm, and the hard grey precipice-edges of the thunder clouds.

'The sea was less than a mile away. The river flowed below a towering cleave, tameless and unclimbable, its sides grey and smooth with loose flakes of shale. All things in the cleave were hidden as the hounds of the storm bayed across the sky. The wind's thong whirled, the lash of the lightning cracked, the hills resounded with the hoofs of the thunder. Far behind on the moor the horsemen rode in a bluish mist of ground lightning which flicked and swished about the huntsman's horn; icy thorns of driven rain pricked necks and ears; horses swung and swirled as though in a flood.

'Fed by a hundred torrents, the river rose many feet, and when the storm ceased an hour later a muddy stain was spread in the sea at its mouth. Beyond the stain, swimming in the rolling waves, was Stumberleap, and after him, fifteen and a half couples of stag-hounds.' The deer escaped across the Bristol Channel to the shores of Wales.[32]

Woody Bay

A mile to the east the steep bluffs recede slightly behind Woody Bay. In 1883 R.N. Worth wrote: 'The trees grow thick and tall almost from the very verge of the water and tower in slopes and terraces up the enclosing hills to the height of nearly 900 feet. Like every true Devonshire combe, Woody Bay has its stream-let here dashing and plashing over its rocky bed far down in the foliaged depths. A zigzag road on the bare hill-side of the Bay leads up to a bald, bleak common'.[33]

S.H. Burton found the coastal bluffs 'With so steep a seaward slope that it is impossible to walk along them. The roads out of Woody Bay, up from the shore and through the woods, are remarkable examples of engineering. The hairpin bends would do credit to a Swiss mountain road. Inkerman Bridge carries one of the lanes over Hanging Water. The rapid little river is typical of the hog's back streams. It rises on a moorish upland, near Greenwell Corner on the lonely road running across Mortishoe Common to the old Woody Bay station. In its short course it falls 900 feet in less than half a mile, and cascades down the Woody Bay slopes to reach the shore in a thirty-foot fall over the sea-cut escarpment.'[3]

This fall attracted the interest of a local writer, Harriet Bridle:

'Perhaps the feature which is the crowning glory of Woody Bay is the Hanging Water Fall. Such falls, which help to make the North Devon coast so special, are a feature rarely to be seen in Great Britain. The Hanging Water dashes downward making tier upon tier of cascading waterfalls of clear fresh water, falling precipitously on to the main beach where it rushes to join the salty sea. It can vary, however, from a torrent to a trickle depending on the rainfall, and though never warm, in the coldest weather it can become almost ice-bound, encrusted with huge icicles on either side. In the winter storms of 1900 a landslip occurred on the east side of the Hanging Water Fall taking away the face of the cliff there and exposing a sheet of bare pink rock.' [34]

Valley of Rocks

Beyond another Lee Bay is the Valley of Rocks, bordered by rugged pinnacles with fanciful names: Devil's Cheesewring, Ragged Jack and Castle Rock. A flock of wild goats roams amongst the boulders. Coleridge used the landscape setting of the Valley of Rocks in his prose composition *The Wanderings of Cain*: 'The pointed and shattered summits of the ridges of the rocks made a rude mimicry of human concerns, and seemed to prophesy mutely of things that then were not; steeples and battlements, and ships with naked masts. As far from the wood as a boy might sling a pebble of the brook, there was one rock by itself at a small distance from the main ridge. It had been precipitated there perhaps by the groan which the Earth uttered when our first father fell. Before you approached, it appeared to lie flat on the ground, but its base slanted from its point, and between its point and the sands a tall man might stand upright.'[35]

Mother Meldrum's Cave was named after an old lady who lived in the valley. She appeared as the witch in R.D. Blackmore's *Lorna Doone*, published in 1869. She spent each winter in this valley and here John Ridd came to visit her: 'At the fall of the leaf, when the woods grew damp and irksome, the wise woman always set her face to the warmer cliffs of the Channel; where shelter was, and dry fern bedding, and folk to be seen in the distance, from a bank upon which the sun shone. And there anyone who chose might find her, towards the close of a winter day, gathering sticks and brown fern for fuel, and talking to herself the while, in a hollow stretch behind the cliffs; which foreigners, who come and go without seeing much of Exmoor, have called the "Valley of the Rocks".

'It is a green rough-sided hollow, bending at the middle, touched with stone at either crest, and dotted here and there with slabs, in and out the brambles. On the right hand is an upward crag, called by some the "Castle", easy enough to scale, and giving great views of the Channel.

'Now Mother Meldrum kept her winter in this vale of rocks, sheltering from the wind and rain within the Devil's Cheese-ring; which added greatly to her fame, because all else, for miles around, were afraid to go near it after dark, or even on a gloomy day. Under eaves of lichened rock, she had a winding passage, which none that ever I knew of durst enter but herself.

'And to this place I went to seek her, in spite of all msigivings, upon a Sunday in Lent.

'The sun was low on the edge of the hills, by the time I entered the valley, for I could not leave home till the cattle were tended, and the distance was seven miles or more. The shadows of rocks fell far and deep, and the brown dead fern was fluttering, and brambles with their sere leaves hanging, swayed their tatters to and fro, with a red look on them. In patches underneath the crags, a few wild goats were browsing; then they tossed their horns, and fled, and leaped on ledges, and stared at me. Moreover, the sound of the sea came up, and went the length of the valley, and there it lapped on a butt of rocks, and murmured like a shell.'[18] She advised John Ridd to have nothing to do with the Doones; advice he did not take.

Lynton and Lynmouth

At the head of the Valley of Rocks is the little town of Lynton. The publisher, George Newnes, was a great benefactor to the town and built a house on Hollerday Hill in 1892. He financed the building of the Town Hall and the cliff railway, which links Lynton to Lynmouth, and came into operation in 1890. He also paid for the building of the Lynton and Barnstaple Railway at the turn of the century. It ran until 1935, and must have been a wonderful journey - the train often going no more than 15 miles an hour.

Coleridge and Wordsworth walked from the Quantocks to Lynmouth in 1797-98, and according to Dorothy Wordsworth the idea of *The Ancient Mariner* was conceived here. Others say it arose from an encounter with an old sailor, who told Coleridge seafaring yarns, perhaps along the coast at Watchet.

In 1812 Shelley was here, aged nineteen, honeymooning with his sixteen-year-old bride, Harriet Westbrook and writing 'Queen Mab.' He stayed in a cottage which is now part of the Rising Sun Inn. Harriet Bridle quoted from a letter in which his wife described it: 'We have taken the only cottage there was, which is most beautifully situated, commanding a fine view of the sea, with mountains at the side and behind us. Vegetation is more luxurious here than in any part of England. We have roses and myrtle creeping up the sides of the house, which is thatched at the top. It is such a little place that it seems more like a fairy scene than anything in reality. All the houses are built in the cottage style, and I suppose there are not more than thirty in all. We send to Barnstaple for everything and our letters come but twice a week...It seems as if Nature had intended this place should be so romantic and shut out from all other intercourse with the neighbouring villages and towns.[31]

Shelley continued to write his political pamphlets here and would row out to sea, placing the pamphlets in bottles or home-made boats. Some he launched from the top of a hill in a balloon and he was inspired to write:

> Bright ball of flame that through the gloom of even
> Silently takest thine aethereal way,
> And with surpassing glory dimm'st each ray
> Twinkling amid the dark blue depths of Heaven...

Henry James, exploring North Devon in the summer of 1872, came to 'that place of pleasantness which is locally known as Lynton. The little village is perched on the side of one of the great mountain cliffs with which this whole coast is adorned, and on the edge of a lovely gorge through which a broad hill-torrent foams and tumbles from the great moors whose heather-crested waves rise purple along the inland sky. Below it, close beside the beach where the little torrent meets the sea, is the sister village of Lynmouth. Here – as I stood on the bridge that spans the stream and looked at the stony backs and foundations and overclambering garden verdure of certain little gray old houses which plunge their feet into it, and then up at the tender green of scrub-oak and fern, at the colour of gorse and broom and bracken climbing the sides of the hills and leaving them bare-crowned to the sun like miniature mountains – I read an unnatural blueness into the northern sea, and the village below put on the grace of one of the hundred hamlets of the Riviera.'[26]

Paul Theroux, on his journey around the coast in 1982, arrived to find 'The light was strange in these sister-villages above and below the pinnacles of cliff; facing north and tucked into a cove, they lost the sun in the afternoon, so they were lit by the gleaming Channel and the near-mirage of Wales. But Lynmouth remained a cool glade, rather damp and sheltered on the banks of the two rivers that rose in Exmoor and converged among a battered and rather scoured-looking watercourse.

'I liked the liquid evening light in Lynmouth, but the village was clammy and full of shadows. Lynton had a whiter light, more sky, and a breeze, and even deserted it looked rather dignified and old-fashioned on its cliff-top.'[36]

A Victorian poet, Arthur L. Salmon, wrote 'The Mouth of the Lyn':

> *Forth from the fastness of its moorland home*
> *With ceaseless din*
> *Cometh the leaping Lyn,*
> *Seeking the coast with constant fret and foam –*
> *Bringing a wildness of the moors to wed*
> *The wildness of the sea – from ferny bed*
> *And mossy boulders breaking, till it meet*
> *The haven where its fleet*
> *Disordered pulse shall stay its fitful beat,*
> *And find a rest*
> *In the more mighty swell of ocean's breast.* [37]

As Southey wrote in 1799: 'Two rivers, each coming down a different coombe, and each descending so rapidly among huge stones to foam like a long waterfall, join at Lynmouth, and enter the sea immediately at their junction; and the roar of the sea forms with them but one sound. Of these coombes one is richly wooded, the other runs up between bare and stony hills; a fine eminence, Line Cliff, rises between them. Even without the sea this would be one of the finest scenes I ever beheld; it is one of those delightful and impressive places from which the eye turns to rest upon the minutest home object – a flower, a bank of moss, a stone covered with lichens'.[29]

The story of the Lynmouth flood disaster, in which 34 people lost their lives, was told by Eric R. Delderfield in a book first published in 1953 and now in its tenth edition. It began: 'The night of Friday, August 15th, 1952, will ever be remembered in North Devon, for within a matter of hours one of the most charming and romantic villages in Britain was visited by a major calamity which became world news.

'The two gentle streams which have given Lynmouth much of its character,[the East and West Lyn] were indirectly the cause of it all – the streams and nature in its most awful ferocious and uncontrollable mood. High up on the hills and Exmoor Forest it had rained incessantly for hours, causing the streams to become torrents. Ninety million tons of water cascaded down on to the village, sweeping all before it.

'The scene that met the eye next morning defies description. It was awe inspiring and spectacular. Except for the surrounding hills the whole landscape had changed, and it is little wonder that those who knew Lynmouth well, failed to recognise it from the pictures which appeared in the newspapers.

'At the bottom of Lynmouth Hill, the Lyndale Bridge had entirely disappeared, and where the remains of the bridge stood, there was a wide gap measuring some seventy-five feet. The trickle of a stream a few feet wide had changed to a rushing torrent that had risen by twenty feet. A chapel, shops and houses had entirely disappeared; others were so badly damaged that they were likely to fall down at any moment. Over the whole area were great boulders, trees, timber, telegraph poles, crushed and mangled motor-cars, iron girders, the remnants of household furniture and bedding, a crumpled bicycle and a thousand and one other reminders of the homes that were complete, until the day before.

'The area where the East and West Lyn rivers made junction, had been completely submerged, it is estimated, by 100,000 tons of boulders, which had cascaded down with the flood like corks.

'Round the harbour the scene was just as unfamiliar. The Rhenish Tower, which must have figured in millions of holiday snapshots, had disappeared. The mouth of the river seemed ten times its normal width, and half-a mile out to sea were hundreds of trees just standing upright, supported by their enormous roots, just as they had been carried down in the flood, when they had been snatched from the banks of the river. For a mile out to sea the water was a dirty mud colour. As the tide receded, motor-cars, pounded and crushed to compact parcels of twisted scrap, were brought to view all over the estuary.'[38] The town has been restored to its former beauty; the river was bulldozed clear of debris and the channel widened to cope with any similar flood in the future.

In R.D. Blackmore's *Lorna Doone*, John Ridd came to an earlier Lynmouth flood:

'Knowing how fiercely the floods were out, I resolved to travel the higher road, by Cosgate and through Countisbury; therefore I swam my horse through the Lynn, at the ford below our house (where sometimes you may step across), and thence galloped up and along the hills. I could see all the inland valleys ribbon'd with broad waters; and in every winding crook, the banks of snow that fed them; while on my right the turbid sea was flaked with April showers. But when I descended the hill towards Lynmouth, I feared that my journey was all in vain.

'For the East Lynn was ramping and roaring frightfully, lashing whole trunks of trees on the rocks, and rending them, and grinding them. And into it rushed, from the opposite side, a torrent even madder; upsetting what it came to aid; shattering wave with boiling billow, and scattering wrath with fury. It was certain death to attempt the passage; and the little wooden footbridge had been carried away long ago. And the men I was seeking must have their dwelling on the other side of this deluge, for on my side there was not a single house.'[18]

Foreland Point

East from Lynmouth, as the cliffs rise 991 feet above the sea, is the secluded beach of Sillery Sand. Charles Kingsley was here with Claude Mellot: "Look at the colours of that Foreland!" cried Claude. "The simple monotone of pearly green, broken only at intervals by blood-red stains where the turf has slipped and left the fresh rock bare, and all glimmering softly through a delicate blue haze, like the bloom on a half-ripened plum! And look, too how the grey pebble beach is already dancing and quivering in the mirage which steams up, like the hot breath of a limekiln, from the drying stones."[23]

The Foreland, Lynton

J.L.W. Page drew attention to 'the caves beneath the Foreland. There are four of them, and they are known as the Gun Caverns, owing to the booming sound made by the waves driven into them by a storm. With the exception of the one farthest east, they penetrate the cliffs for a hundred feet or so, and are about fifteen feet high. But the eastern cave is double the length of the others. The strata in and about these caves is interesting, the lines being nearly vertical, tilted at a sharp angle, or contorted into serpentine curves. The rocks are best seen from the sea, but the caves must be visited from the land, and then only by a very rough scramble by way of Sillery Sands and at dead low water.'[1]

Steep forested coastal slopes continue from Foreland Point eastwards across the boundary into Somerset.

SOMERSET and BRISTOL CHANNEL

Culbone and Ashley Combe

The boundary between Devon and Somerset runs down the Doone Valley, the setting of R.D. Blackmore's *Lorna Doone*, and cuts across the coastal ridge at County Gate to descend a wooded cleft to the sea. Bold wooded bluffs continue into Somerset, with deep combes, one of which contains diminutive Culbone church, the smallest (34 feet by 12 feet) complete church in regular use in England. It is mentioned both in the Domesday Book and the Guinness Book of Records.

Culbone Church.

Ashley Combe, to the east, has been described by a local writer, Barbara Milne: 'The small combe which winds its way up through Worthy Woods is enclosed by trees, the sun flickers through occasionally, catching the white waters of the stream rollicking over its stony bed by the side of the track but the place is always covered with dark shadows, secretive and remote. Were it not for the presence of Culbone Church nearby and the fact that many drivers use this steep and bumpy toll road to avoid the more fearful hazards of Porlock Hill, it is doubtful if anyone would disturb the peace and calm of this hidden combe. Indeed the road would never have been built at all were it not for one woman, Ada, the poet Byron's only child. For her a romantic house was designed and a splendid Italianate garden constructed when she married Lord King. All that now remains are a few steps and some terraced walls, the whole overgrown with bramble and weeds, hidden away in the woods to the north of the road. The once picturesque view across Porlock Bay to Hurlestone Point is now obscured by encroaching sycamores and trees which have become too large since they were planted nearly two hundred years ago, planted by Lord King in order "to make this hermitage worthy of your presence", as he assured his young bride.'[1]

Porlock Bay

Next comes Porlock Bay, a two and a half mile crescent stretching eastward to Hurlestone Point. Coleridge's unfinished poem, 'Kubla Khan', was written on the hilltop overlooking this bay. Richard Holmes in his biography of Coleridge wrote: 'The coastal path, which runs for fifteen miles above the cliffs and woods between Porlock Bay and Lynton, is very remote at this point. On the many occasions Coleridge made this journey in 1797-8 (with the Wordsworths, with Hazlitt, and alone), he must frequently have sought food and shelter at one of the two solitary farms along the way: Ash Farm, immediately at the head of Culbone Combe; and Broomstreet Farm, some two miles west by Yenworthy Common. Either would be a natural place to break a walk from Quantock, being about thirty miles across the hills from Stowey, and it is possible he sometimes spent the night at one or other of the farms.

'But Ash Farm seems the most likely setting for the composition of 'Kubla Khan' since it is the closest to Culbone Church (a field path runs directly down from the farmyard into the combe) and the view from its seaward windows is perfectly described at the opening of Act V of 'Osorio', which he was working on until the middle of October. In a speech given to his heroine, Alhadra, he evokes a wooded countryside near the seashore, "on the coast of Granada". But the original setting is clearly that of the Quantock Hills, and the woods running down to the Bristol Channel at Culbone, as he observed them that autumn at sunset, just as the moon began to rise above the lonely farmhouse:

> *The hanging woods, that touch'd by autumn seem'd*
> *As they were blossoming hues of fire and gold,*
> *The hanging woods, most lovely in decay,*
> *The many clouds, the sea, the rock, the sands,*

> *Lay in the silent moonshine; and the owl,*
> *(Strange! very strange!) the scritch owl only wak'd*
> *Sole voice, sole eye of all that world of beauty!'*[2]

Holmes went on to say in a footnote 'But any footwalker can still discover the most striking topographical "source" for themselves: it lies in what might be called the erotic, magical geography of Culbone Combe seen from Ash Farm. Between the smooth curved flanks of the coastal hills, a thickly wooded gulley runs down to the sea, enclosing a hidden stream which gushes beneath the tiny medieval chapel of Culbone, a plague-church and "sacred site" since Anglo-Saxon and possibly pre-Christian times. The place is as remote and mysterious as ever.'[2]

'Kubla Khan' was written in 1797, and in 1816 Coleridge attached to the poem, this account of its composition: 'In the summer of the year 1797, the Author, then in ill health, had retired to a lonely farm-house between Porlock and Linton, on the Exmoor confines of Somerset and Devonshire. In consequence of a slight indisposition [dysentry], an anodyne [two grains of opium] had been prescribed, from the effects of which he fell asleep in his chair at the moment that he was reading the following sentence, or words of the same substance, in 'Purchas's Pilgrimage': "Here the Khan Kubla commanded a palace to be built, and a stately garden thereunto. And thus ten miles of fertile ground were inclosed with a wall."

'The Author continued for about three hours in a profound sleep, at least of the external senses, during which time he has the most vivid confidence, that he could not have composed less than from two to three hundred lines. On awaking he appeared to himself to have a distinct recollection of the whole, and taking his pen, ink, and paper, instantly and eagerly wrote down the lines that are here preserved. At this moment he was unfortunately called out by a person on business from Porlock, and detained by him above an hour, and on his return to his room, found, to his no small surprise and mortification, that though he still retained some vague and dim recollection of the general purport of the vision, yet with the exception of some eight or ten scattered lines and images, all the rest had passed away like the images on the surface of a stream into which a stone has been cast, but, alas! without the after restoration of the latter!

So the poem which begins

> *'In Xanadu did Kubla Khan*
> *A stately pleasure dome decree........'*

Came to a premature end with

> *'For he on honey-dew hath fed,*
> *And drunk the milk of paradise'*[3]

A Victorian, G.J. Whyte Melville came here at 'High-water in Porlock Bay. The tide upon the turn – sand-pipers, great and small, dipping, nodding, stalking to and fro, or flitting along its margin waiting for the ebb; a gull riding smoothly outside on an untroubled surface, calm as the soft sky overhead, that smiled lovingly down on the Severn Sea.'[4]

Porlock Weir

'Porlock Weir,' wrote Bel Mooney 'has huddles of whitewashed cottages and a strange, wild pebbly beach that stretches along the coast to Bossington and Hurlstone Point. In places this beach looks as if a giant child wilfully smashed a vast stone tea service and flung it about, for huge thin pieces of rock lie scattered layer upon layer, sinister when storm clouds are above and yellow-grey light gleams on water sheeted on the flat surfaces.'[5]

The Weir lies at the foot of a steep wooded hillside. The beach is cobbled and the tiny harbour functional rather than picturesque.

Porlock

About a mile to the east is the colourful village of Porlock. In 1791, the historian J. Collinson wrote: 'The situation of the town is finely romantick being nearly surrounded, on all sides, except towards the sea, by steep and lofty hills intersected by deep vales and hollow glens. The vallies between these hills are very picturesque, the sides being steep, scarred with wild rocks and patched with woods. Most of the roads and fields are so steep that no carriages of any kind can be used: all the crops are, therefore carried with crooks on horse.'[6]

In 1799 Robert Southey wrote a sonnet about Porlock when he sought refuge there at the Ship Inn during a storm. A chimney corner of the Inn is devoted to his memory and a copy of the poem hangs on the wall:

Porlock thy verdant vale so fair to sight,
Thy lofty hills which fern and furze embrown,
The waters that roll musically down
Thy woody glens, the traveller with delight
Recalls to memory, and the channel grey
Circling its surges in thy level bay.
Porlock, I also shall forget thee not,
Here by the unwelcome summer rain confined;
But often shall hereafter call to mind
How here, a patient prisoner, 'twas my lot
To wear the lonely, lingering close of day,
Making my Sonnet by the alehouse fire,
Whilst idleness and Solitude inspire
Dull rhymes to pass the duller hours away.[7]

Richard Warner walked here at about this time: 'A long descent introduced me into the little sea-port town of Porlock [in] a recess of a bay, about one league from one extremity to another. Of these points the eastern one rises with prodigious magnificence from the ocean, whose maddened waves have torn its front into misshapen crags, and scooped its sides into stupendous caverns; the western extremity is of a softer character, and slopes gradually to the shore, sheltering from the prevalent south-westerly storms, the quay and a small pier (one mile and a half from Porlock), where the little commerce of the place is transacted, and its fleet (consisting of two sloops, which trade to Bristol and Wales) is freighted and unladen.'[8]

Henry James took 'the long drive along the beautiful remnant of coast and through the rich pastoral scenery of Somerset. I beheld on this admirable drive – breezy highlands clad in the warm blue-brown of heather-tufts as if in mantles of rusty velvet, little bays and coves curving gently to the doors of clustered fishing-huts, deep pastures and broad forests, villages thatched and trellised as if to take a prize for improbability, manor-tops peeping over rook-haunted avenues. I ought to make especial note of an hour I spent at midday at the village of Porlock in Somerset. Here the thatch seemed steeper and heavier, the yellow roses on the cottage walls more cunningly mated with the crumbling stucco, the dark interiors within the open doors more quaintly pictorial, than elsewhere'.[9]

Ralph Whitlock remarked that 'Porlock had its share of excitement in the centuries when England was being moulded. Its inhabitants beat off a vigorous attack by Danish pirates in the year 918, and in 1052 it was raided and set on fire by Saxon Harold, who was subsequently king but who was then in exile in Ireland. Apparently, however, here it is the sea which has retreated, leaving an expanse of silty meadow where once the tides rolled.

'Porlock is best known to travellers for the tremendous hill which leads out of it up to Exmoor – a hill notorious for its engine-testing gradients. Under its shelter Porlock enjoys an almost Mediterranean climate, seldom depreciated by frost or snow. Plans to make Porlock an important port were formulated in the mid-nineteenth century. A railway to bring down iron ore from Exmoor for shipment to South Wales was begun, but nothing came of it.'[10]

Minehead

On his tour through England, Daniel Defoe observed: ' Minehead is the best port, and safest harbour, and they told me that in the great storm anno 1703, when in all the harbours and rivers in the county the ships were blown on shore, wrecked, and lost, they suffered little or no damage in this harbour.'[11]

Southey came this way in 1799 : 'The quay is ugly, but the view very striking along the indented coast towards Stowey. From a hill on our way here we had one glorious burst of prospect. The sun fell on the sea through a mist, and on the crags of the shore they looked like a glittering faery fabric; the very muddiness of the water mellowed the splendour and made it more rich and beautiful. For almost in every part it would be practicable to walk to the beach. The descent is all furze and fern. In a clear day the houses on the opposite shore are distinct; but in hazy weather the view is finer, like the prospects of human life, because its termination is concealed.'[12]

Bel Mooney came here for the first time 'on a late summer afternoon in August, and was puzzled by the crowds. The place could not be *this* popular: everyone on the promenade, sitting in packed rows, and all staring seaward, as if they had expected some miraculous visitation from the deep. Somewhere a voice was booming through a loudspeaker system, the words indistinct. Necks craned; one or two men lifted binoculars to the horizon. I felt that I had stumbled on an alien ritual, the meaning of which would never be made plain – until I picked up a piece of paper which told me that this was the annual Minehead Raft Race. That explained the carnival atmosphere. When the first rafts hove into sight, their crews pulling for all they were worth, partisan groups roared: local villages, and clubs and pubs each put up a team, and so the competition is fierce but good-natured.'[5]

Dunster and Blue Anchor

The village is dominated by Dunster Castle, dating from Norman times, and is the scene of a painting by Turner in 1795. Thomas Hardy called Dunster 'Markton' and the castle 'Stancy Castle' in his novel *A Laodicean*, but the coast was not mentioned. Southey described the sea view from Dunster Castle: 'very striking; Minehead stands under a headland, which projects boldly. This seat is said to command one of the finest views in England; if the water were clear and boundless, I should think so.'[12]

Down on the coast to the north of Dunster is the hamlet of Blue Anchor. There have been several suggestions for the origin of the name of this old landing place.

It may commemorate a ship, or it may refer to the blue mud offshore, which is hauled up on ships' anchors.

Watchet

Hakluyt spoke of 'mariners attird in Watchet or skie-coloured cloth', and Gerard of Trent, wandering through the country in 1633, mentioned 'Watchet.... which ye Saxons called Waced port and which ye Danes in ye yeare of our Lord 888 robbed and burned. A little Harbour it hath in ye mouth of a Riverett which here falleth into ye sea, wence divers take shipping to Ireland.'[13]

According to a notice on the Tourist Information Board: 'In 1797 the poet Coleridge visited Watchet, and as a result the idea for his famous poem took shape. The following lines from 'The Ancient Mariner' seem to describe the town:

> *The ship was cheered, the harbour cleared*
> *Merrily did she drop*
> *Below the kirk, below the hill,*
> *Below the lighthouse top.*[3]

Ralph Whitlock told that Watchet was 'The terminus of the West Somerset Mineral Railway, which brought down iron ore from Brendon Hill. A new pier was built for the traffic, enabling the ore to be tipped straight into the holds of ships anchored by the jetty. Unfortunately, the decline of the iron-ore trade coincided with two tremendous gales, one in December 1900, and the other in September 1903, which smashed the harbour and destroyed a number of ships anchored there. The harbour has since been rebuilt and improved, and a new trade is developing.'[10]

Quantock Hills
The Quantock Hills reach the sea as a steep slope descending to St Audrie's Bay. On their eastern flank is the village of Nether Stowey, to which Coleridge brought his family to live in a cottage in 1796-98. The area was described in two of his poems. In 'This Lime-Tree Bower My Prison':

> *Now, my friends emerge*
> *Beneath the wide wide Heaven – and view again*
> *The many-steepled tract magnificent*
> *Of hilly fields and meadows, and the sea,*
> *With some fair bark, perhaps, whose sails light up*
> *The slip of smooth clear blue betwixt two Isles*
> *Of purple shadow!*[3]

and in 'Frost at Midnight':

> *Sea, hill, and wood,*
> *This populous village! Sea, and hill, and wood,*
> *With all the numberless goings-on of life,*
> *Inaudible as dreams!*[3]

Southey and the Wordsworths were also at Nether Stowey, and a poem by Wordsworth mentioned "Kilve's delightful shore and Quantoxhead". Locals thought they were French spies, and because of their nocturnal walks, interest in the landscape and eccentric appearance, Dorothy, William and Coleridge were thought, by a Home Office agent sent to investigate them, to be fifth columnists.

East Quantoxhead and Kilve
Bel Mooney described the beaches along this stretch of coast: 'The flat grey and pinkish-blue stones are scattered or piled on top of each other, smaller ones littering the spaces between larger 'steps'. Some of the shards of shale and Lias stone are sharp and dangerous as you walk between the pools. Everywhere there are ammonites, or "St. Keyna's serpents", according to an old legend which says that the saint turned all the snakes on the shore into stone. It makes the ordinary pebble beach look soft and inviting, although if you choose carefully it is possible, though hardly comfortable, to sunbathe on the larger flat plateaus of rock.

'My favourite approach to this weird, sculptural landscape is by the footpath from East Quantoxhead, because the short journey from that picturesque, untouched hamlet to the coast is like passing from time to timelessness, from history into eternity.

'A footpath past the pond and mill at East Quantoxhead leads to Kilve. You can walk across fields or, better still, take the cliff path. I walked on the cliffs here on a golden evening one August, with a breeze gently stroking yellow corn in the fields, and the low sun gleaming on the muddy Channel, and thought that there was nowhere else on earth I would rather be.'[5]

Maxwell Fraser came here in 1947: ' The great attraction of Kilve, for those "in the know" is the glatting - hunting for conger eels with "fish-dogs", and very exciting sport it is. All the coast from Watchet to the Parrett abounds in rock pools where conger eels can be found at low tide, and every child spends many happy hours with a long stick and a bucket, searching the seaweed covered rocks for congers, but at Kilve the neap tides bring out men and boys and the specially trained dogs - usually a terrier or spaniel. "Glatts" or congers of from two to five pounds are found, and sometimes larger ones up to twenty pounds weight are captured.'[14]

The Wordsworths at Alfoxton

In 1797-8 William Wordsworth and his sister Dorothy rented Alfoxton Park in the Quantocks, about two miles from the coast. In her journals Dorothy wrote of her walks on the hills and views of the sea: 'January 23rd 1798:'The sea perfectly calm blue, streaked with deeper colour by the clouds, and tongues or points of sand.

'3rd February:'Walked with Coleridge over the hills. The sea at first obscured by vapour; that vapour afterwards slid in one mighty mass along the sea-shore; the islands and one point of land clear beyond it. The distant country (which was purple in the clear dull air), overhung by straggling clouds that sailed over it, appeared like the darker clouds, which are often seen at a great distance apparently motionless, while the nearer ones pass quickly over them, driven by the lower winds. I never saw such a union of earth, sky, and sea.'[15]

William was entranced by the local countryside, and wrote to Coleridge:

> *That summer, under whose indulgent skies*
> *Upon smooth Quantocks airy ridge we roved*
> *Unchecked, or loitered 'mid her sylvan courts;*
> *Thou, in bewitching words with happy heart,*
> *Didst chaunt the vision of the Ancient Man,*
> *The bright-eyed Mariner.*[16]

Shurton

Berta Lawrence in her *Coleridge and Wordsworth in Somerset* found that the scenery which Coleridge saw when he wrote 'Lines Written at Shurton Bars near Bridgwater, September 1795', is little changed: 'His poem makes clear that he found his way down to the coast by a road that is still almost as remote and unfrequented. In the tiny twin hamlet called Burton a lane by the post office runs between hedges thick with elder-trees to end on a corner by the stone farmhouse of Knighton farm that stood there in Coleridge's time like the primitive, thick-walled, stone-floored empty cottage situated on the opposite side of the road and recently occupied by an old hermit. To the left of the farm a rough cart-track runs towards the sea, and for a while a stream flagged with yellow iris and shallowing to make a little ford runs alongside it before branching through a field. Meanwhile the cart-track runs on to loop over three large humps and climb to high, windy fields full of sheep and looking out to sea. In spring it is shrill with the songs of skylarks and Coleridge's poem refers in one place to skylarks settling in nests amid the summer corn and nodding poppies. He was here early in September. The sheep-field is bounded by a wire fence where its side falls steeply to the shore. If Coleridge stood here today he would see westward, on the left, the familiar cliff-side displaying strata of yellow sandstone and blue lias with intervening thin green strips of grass. The cliffs curve away towards the headland jutting out from Minehead. Nearer to view, the tamarisks used for dyeing by the Quantock weavers make a hedge level with the Lilstock shore. Eastward, a farm, brown ploughland – and the great towers of Hinkley Point nuclear power station rising near the place where Coleridge saw a ruined house.

'From the field edge he looked down on piles of brown and grey shinglestones planed smooth by the sea; on a strip of grey-brown sand strewn with black seaweeds; on a shining silver-grey tide sweeping 'with mimic thunders' over the rolling shingle under a cloudless sky. Looking straight out across the sea he saw the two islands, Flat Holm like a floating raft and Steep Holm rising abruptly from the water, while far to the right Brean Down plunged into the sea at the end of Mendip and Crook's Peak drew its faint, hooked outline. It was 'the channelled Isle' of Flat Holm that drew his eye. Today anyone looking towards it sees the white column of its lighthouse, Coleridge saw the stone pillar, erected in 1737, crowned by the redly blazing watchfire or beacon that warned sailors of the reefs.'[17] Here are some stanzas from the poem:

> And hark, my Love! The sea-breeze moans
> Through yon reft house! O'er rolling stones
>   In bold ambitious sweep
> On onward-surging tides supply
> The silence of the cloudless sky
>   With mimic thunders deep.
>
> Dark reddening from the channell'd Isle
> (Where stands one solitary pile
>   Unslated by the blast)
> The Watchfire, like a sullen star
> Twinkles to many a dozing Tar
>   Rude cradled on th' mast.

> *Even there – beneath that light-house tower –*
> *In the tumultuous evil hour*
> > *Ere peace with SARA came,*
> *Time was, I should have thought it sweet*
> *To count the echoings of my feet,*
> > *And watch the storm-vex'd flame.*[3]

Hinkley Point

Ralph Whitlock wrote: 'And so, through a group of tiny, undistinguished but quietly attractive villages, including Kilve, Lilstock, Otterhampton and Stolford, we follow a coast that lies ever flatter to the mouth of the Parrett. Here, on a coast which long remained as desolate and unvisited as any corner of England, claimed only by sea-birds, fishermen and cattle, the great nuclear power station of Hinkley Point appears to grow up abruptly from the sea-bed. A better site could hardly have been found, for, apart from the consideration that the Parrett estuary provides an unlimited supply of water for cooling, the massive squareness of the towering rectangular buildings seems somehow to match the austere horizontal lines of an otherwise featureless landscape.'[10]

Stert Flats

The coast declines past the Hinkley Point Power Station to the broad Somerset Levels, where the Parrett estuary winds out to the marshes and mudflats of Bridgwater Bay. Ralph Whitlock considered that 'the effect of the Bristol Channel's huge tides here on this flat coast is to create a vast amphibious no-man's-land of silt and sand. Over the Stert Flats the sea at low tide recedes for three or four miles and then comes galloping back at an alarming pace. The Parrett cuts a winding, deep-water channel between the Flats and the similar Gore Sands which swerve northwards towards Brean Down.'[10]

The Reverend William Gresswell, historian of the Quantocks, wrote: 'At low water the estuary is wide and glittering, reflecting the light in marvellous fashion when the sunlight plays flickering upon the smooth ridges, which, like an opaque cloud, seem to give back as much light as they receive. An amphibious region where, nevertheless, man at certain times can neither creep, crawl, walk or swim, and the catastrophe of death follows the fisherman or shrimper who ventures carelessly on it in the half-lights of a winter's afternoon.'[18]

'The river Parrett runs through Bridgwater,' wrote Bel Mooney, 'then eases itself in a great slow snaky curve out into the Bristol Channel, shedding mud like skin. This is Stert Flats. The estuary is bleak and lonely; curlews wheel and cry over the vast tracts of thick, oozing mud, like plaintive ghosts calling through dank mist. It is easy to believe the old legend – that mingled with the sound of birds and wind are the anguished cries of two of the murderers of Thomas à Becket. All four knights were from the West Country and two were Somerset men: Reginald Fitzurse from Williton and Simon de Brett from Sampford Brett. Legend has it that these two are buried on Flat Holm.

'There is nothing romantic or legendary about the local mud. So thick and treacherous is it that fishermen from Stolford and Steart still have to use the traditional Mud Horse, leaning on the wooden contraption which is rather like a surf board or sledge-with-a-superstructure, and skimming the surface of the mudflats to the water's edge. It is a dirty business.'[5] 'A mile or so out from Stert Point', wrote Ralph Whitlock, 'opposite Burnham, lies the ephemeral Stert Island. It came into existence through a shifting of tide and current probably in the eighteenth century and in recent years has been eroded at a rapid rate. Elsewhere along this unstable shore, however, the land is winning in the eternal war. In 1928 some experimental consignments of Spartina grass were brought from Poole Harbour, to see how effectively plantings of it could trap the silt and prevent the incessant scouring by the tides. The experiment proved so successful that more plantings were made, and the grass now extends for more than two miles along the shore and a quarter of a mile or so seawards. As the grass takes root and stabilizes the soil so other plants are enabled to establish themselves, and in places the level of the foreshore has been raised by more than six feet.

'More than 6,000 acres of the foreshore and flats are now the Bridgwater Bay Nature Reserve, established in 1954 and frequented by hordes of waterfowl.'[10]

Combwich

Combwich, pronounced 'Cummidge', is an ancient port on the tidal estuary of the River Parrett. Richard Warner crossed from Combwich at the beginning of September 1799: 'As I had been informed that the Parrett was remarkable for the impetuosity with which the tide enters its mouth, I waited about an hour and a half, till the commencement of the flood, in order to observe the phenomenon. Its approach is announced by a distant roaring sound, which gradually increases upon the ear, until the cause itself appears: a volume of water, like one vast wave, sometimes rising to the height of four feet (though when I saw it, not more than two) rushing on with irresistible violence, and covering instantaneously the steep banks, which had been left dry by the recess of the tide. It is called Boar, in allusion, I presume, to the formidable sounds which this indomitable animal emits. It has been known, when strengthened by spring tide, to have overturned large boats in its furious course.'[8]

Highbridge

The waters from the Somerset Levels, according to Ralph Whitlock are 'hastened on their way by many artificial cuts and drains [and] find their way to the sea just beyond Highbridge. The high bridge originally served the dual purpose of bridge and dam, for it had sluice gates which were shut when the tide came in. Quite large boats could therefore come in with their cargo and berth almost alongside the road. From Highbridge in the 1830s a canal was dug to Glastonbury, giving the old town a new water link with the sea. It lasted for only 20 years, however, and was closed when the railways took over.'[10]

Burnham-on-Sea

The story of the origin of the lighthouse here is that a fisherman's wife, who lived in a cottage on the shore, kept a light in the window; when the old lady died, people realised the value of the light and a permanent lighthouse was built in 1764. There is also a low wooden lighthouse, on stilts, on the shore nearby. Both lighthouses have broad red lines down their fronts, intended to show the fairway of the Parrett; the shifting sandbanks had made this navigational aid unreliable but in 1994 the wooden lighthouse was renovated and made operational again.

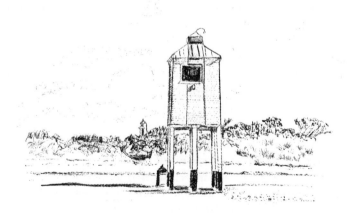

The Lighhouse: Burnham-on-Sea

Burnham is a pleasant seaside resort with a famous golf course set admist the sand dunes, which in autumn are covered with the orange-berried sea-buckthorn.

Grahame Farr wrote: 'In the 1830s a humorous effort was made to create a spa to be called Daviesville, after the Reverend David Davies, the local rector, discoverer of the mineral springs. Accounts differ radically and of the following the reader can take his pick: "The spring...proved to be a mineral water possessing active medicinal properties, but fortunately contained in a vehicle not repugnant to the most fastidious palate." "The water was turbid and slightly yellow. The smell was very offensive, resembling that of a cess-pool, mixed with an odour not unlike bad horseradish."[19]

Brean Down

A sandy beach runs north along the low-lying coast – Berrow Flats – until the limestone ridge of Brean Down suddenly protrudes. 'Brean Down,' said Ralph Whitlock, 'looms like a mountain and thrusts a mile or so out into the Channel like the Rock of Gibraltar. [It is] an outcrop of the Mendips [and] provides an exhilarating clifftop walk of a mile or so, at an altitude of about 200 feet. The springy turf on the summit is still close-cropped by rabbits, and in May carpets of bluebells bloom among the unfolding bracken. National Trust property and a Nature Reserve, it used to harbour a nesting pair of peregrine falcons and still has two or three pairs of ravens, as well as innumerable sea-birds. It is also almost the only British site of the white rock-rose, though here it is far from rare'.[10]

'Until the draining of Bleadon Level during the dark Ages', wrote Christopher Somerville, 'Brean Down was virtually an island, cut off from mainland influences. The Romans had built a temple on the Down in about 340, but it was soon abandoned – perhaps in favour of more local gods as the invaders' culture began to disappear while they themselves melted away south to the last defence of their Empire. The flatness of the surrounding fields and sea emphasises the island character of the Down, a place of refuge for present-day wildlife and walkers alike.

'On top of the knoll'. he wrote, 'is one of the most impressive sea and land views anywhere around the coasts of Britain. The enormous sweep all round the horizon that the Iron Age farmers saw has changed considerably in detail since they rested on their spades up here, but very little in outline. To the north across Weston Bay stand the two piers of Weston-super-Mare, running back into the long ranks of hotels and houses under Worlebury Hill. The slender bill of Sand Point sticks out beyond, the waters of the Severn Estuary connecting it with the great 70 mile line of the southern underbelly of Wales. The coast prospect runs west from Newport to Cardiff – with binoculars you can pick out the ships and cranes in the docks – and on around the curve to a far-off blotch which is Swansea. A pencil-line of Gower coastline ends in the Bristol Channel, the whole land panorama rising to the faint outlines of the Brecon Beacons. Looking due west now, your gaze moves across the linking line of sea over the white exclamation mark of the lighthouse on Flat Holm Island, before the perspective suddenly shortens to swoop over the green nose of Brean Down's west knoll where the Iron Age field banks make square mounds in the turf. Then the distant land reappears – the tiny red huddle of Minehead under Exmoor's shadow, another long curve of coastline moving nearer past the grey boxes of the nuclear power station at Hinkley Point to the silver tongue of the River Parrett where it meets the sea below Burnham. After all this coastline and brown estuary, streaked into white lines by the wind, it's a shock to see green fields below you as you look eastward at the rump of Mendip, end-on to you and running away as it climbs inland.'[20]

Landward of Brean Down the River Axe opens into the southern port of Weston Bay, and as we cross it we leave Somerset for the county of Avon, established when boundaries were re-drawn in 1974.

Weston-super-Mare

From Weston-super-Mare there are fine views out to Steep Holm and Flat Holm, islands of Mendip Limestone: Steep Holm is owned by a Trust set up in memory of the writer, Kenneth Allsop. Ships pass on their way to and from Avonmouth.

Weston-super-Mare has long been popular with Welsh tourists. A poem by Idris Davies, called 'Tonypandy', told of an excursion:

> *Do they remind you, David, you son of Tonypandy,*
> *Of summer afternoons on holiday beaches,*
> *And cheap excursions to Weston-super-Mare,*
> *With the steamer chuff-chuff-chuffing across the Channel*
> *And the Flatholm in the distance, and the sunshine*
> *Radiant over the Somerset cliffs and gardens,*
> *And your Martha, with her mouth wide open,*
> *Leaning against you on the crowded deck,*
> *And the Sunday School parties all around you*
> *Sweating with singing the sad, sad hymns ?*
> *And O it was sweet in the evening, Dai,*
> *After the bathing and the dancing and the pastries and the ice-cream,*
> *And the gardens of roses behind the coloured town,*
> *And the nut-brown ale in the pub by the pier,*
> *Ay, it was sweet upon the evening waters*
> *To watch the sun go down in scarlet*
> *Behind the far promontory, and gaze upon*
> *The velvet undulations of the sea,*

And sweet it was to dream, Dai bach,
With Martha warm and fragrant, close against you,
Martha from Treorchy nestled in your arms,
Sweet it was to coo of love and summer
To the rhythm and the moaning of the darkening sea,
And the pleasure-boat chuff-chuff-chuffing homewards
Towards the lights of Cardiff in the bluish distance,
And the waiting quays and the quayside station,
With your Day Excursion tickets sticky in your hands.[21]

In 1872 the Reverend Francis Kilvert was enjoying nude swimming here: '4th September. Bathing in the morning before breakfast from a machine. Many people were openly stripping on sands a little further on and running down into the sea, and I would have done the same but I had brought down no towels of my own.

'5th September. I was out early before breakfast this morning bathing from the sands. There was a delicious feeling of freedom in stripping in the open air and running down naked to the sea, where the waves were curling white with foam and the red morning sunshine glowing upon the naked limbs of the bathers.'[22]

Bel Mooney was here after 'the beginning of autumn term, so the beach was empty, and the donkeys looked disconsolate – although in fact they probably drooped their heads with relief. The few figures on the beach were turned, by a trick of the autumn sunlight, into images in a Lowry painting. Footsteps sounded hollow on the wooden boards of the Grand Pier – which seemed almost totally given over to the old, who sat under elegant spiderweb ironwork reading tabloid newspapers or rode the little train to the end. Some women were knitting in the warm sun. Nobody spoke much. And in the Terrace Café the musak was an upbeat yet still mournful verison of *The Way We Were.*'[5]

Paul Theroux stopped here on his journey: 'The beach was long and mostly empty and very grey, and it was flatter than the water. Parked on the sand, as in a cartoon of desert mirages, were a red Punch and Judy booth, and two yellow huts, one labelled 'Tea-Stall' and the other 'Shellfish Bar'. A flapping pennant said 'Donkey Rides – 20 pence'. The few people on the beach lay heavily bundled-up on the sand, like war wounded on a beach-head. Their faces were tight with discomfort. A fat old lady with wild hair, wearing a winter coat but barefoot, stood and howled 'Arthur!' The donkeys stamped and shuddered in a little group, looking thoroughly baffled. And here on the promenade hunched-over ladies with big handbags tipped their stoutness into the wind and breathed loudly through their teeth. Across the street at the Winter Gardens people were buying tickets for tonight's show, 'Cavalcade of Song'.

'I was so unaccustomed to a place like Weston-super-Mare that with a little concentration I saw it in a surrealistic way. What were all these different things doing there? They had accumulated over the years, slowly, piling up like the tide-wrack, and because it had happened so slowly, no one questioned it or found it strange. And this was also why I could spend days in the seaside resorts, fascinated by the way the natural coast had been deranged and cluttered. It did not matter much whether a town was pretty or ugly – although ugly ones were often the most telling.'[23]

Clevedon

Coleridge lived here at Old Church Road in 1795-96, and wrote about it in his poem 'Reflections on Having Left a Place of Retirement' (1795):

> *Low was our pretty Cot: our tallest Rose*
> *Peep'd at the chamber-window. We could hear*
> *At silent noon, and eve, and early morn,*
> *The sea's faint murmur....*
> *But the time, when first*
> *From that low Dell, steep up the stony Mount*
> *I climb'd with perilous toil and reach'd the top,*
> *Oh! what a goodly scene! Here the bleak mount,*
> *The bare bleak mountain speckled thin with sheep;*
> *Grey clouds, that shadowing spot the sunny fields;*
> *And river, now with bushy rocks o'er-brow'd,*
> *Now winding bright and full, with naked banks;*
> *And seats, and lawns, the Abbey and the wood,*
> *And cots, and hamlets, and faint city-spire;*
> *The Channel there, the Islands and white sails,*
> *Dim coasts, and cloud-like hills, and shoreless Ocean -*
> *It seem'd like Omnipresence!*[3]

He also lay on the slopes of Wain's Hill and looked seaward:

> *....the world so hush'd!*
> *The stilly murmur of the distant Sea*
> *Tells us of Silence.*
> *....... on the midway slope*
> *Of yonder hill I stretch my limbs at noon,*
> *Whilst thro' my half-clos'd eyelids, I behold*
> *the sunbeams dance, like diamonds, on the main,*
> *And tranquil muse upon tranquillity.*[3]

Berta Lawrence said that Coleridge 'called it "the valley of seclusion" and that is exactly what it was in 1795. Today it is difficult to imagine that this description ever fitted Clevedon. A seemingly endless line of bungalows has extended under the hanging woods and the hidden prehistoric Cadbury Camp. The twentieth century has added Edwardian villas, modern houses, bungalows, shops, garages, and a murderous flow of traffic that passes noisly through Coleridge's valley of seclusion. Even by 1840 the population numbered little more than 1,100, and, Coleridge's little grey fishing village could not have held more than a quarter of that number.

'It sheltered beneath the long, rocky height called Dial Hill, at its western extremity. It consisted of a handful of thatched and tiled stone cottages – a few of these survive – built at some distance from the parish church of St. Andrew that dominates Clevedon Pill and whose tower, squat as it is, was a familiar mark to sailors out in the bay.

'Sometimes he walked along the shore where black seaweed strewed the dark mud beyond the shingle at low tide. When he walked in the direction of Portishead he saw men gathering samphire below craggy yellow cliffs, one of which he described in his notebook as hanging over to 'glass' a rugged forehead in the calm sea.

'If we walk the long steadily climbing cliff path between the shoulder of Wain's Hill and the sea – the sea lies on the right far below the steep fall of the yellow cliffs that in places are clouded with blue scabious in summertime – we walk where Coleridge certainly walked and see the landscape and seascape of which details are condensed in the Clevedon poems.'[17]

Clevedon Court, a fourteenth century manor house, became 'Castlewood' in Thackeray's *Henry Esmond*, but he transferred the story to Hampshire. He also wrote part of *Vanity Fair* while staying there. It was the home of Tennyson's friend, Arthur Hallam, and his poem 'In Memoriam' commemorated his friendship with Arthur, who died in Vienna at the age of 22 and who is buried in St. Andrew's Church:

The Danube to the Severn gave
The darkened heart that beat no more;
They laid him by the pleasant shore,
And in the hearing of the wave.

There twice a day the Severn fills,
The salt sea-water passes by,
And hushes half the babbling Wye,
And makes a silence on the hills.[24]

Tennyson may also have been writing about Clevedon and Hallam in

Break, break, break,
  On thy cold grey stones, O sea!
And I would that my tongue could utter
The thoughts that arise in me.

And the stately ships go on
  To their haven under the hill;
But O for the touch of a vanish'd hand,
  And the sound of a voice that is still![24]

John Hadden remarked: 'Today it is still the romantic appeal of dramatic, though small-scale scenery, fine views, winding walks, little parks, many trees, fine villas, elegant Regency houses of the earlier development along the shore, and the alternating of rocks and pebbles along the coast, which constitute Clevedon's main attraction.'[25]

Portishead

Portishead has a pleasant Esplanade and gardens but a muddy and marshy foreshore. Michael Havinden found that: 'The old village of Portishead was more than a mile inland, lying in the eastern lee of Portishead Down, but connected to the sea by Portishead Pill, a tidal estuary now converted into a modern dock entered by a lock. This enables ships to supply fuel to the immense electric power station which has been built there, whose towers dominate the scenery for miles around. This industrial development has rather spoiled the Victorian resort which had grown up between the old village and the sea.'[26]

Grahame Farr recalled that 'It was very peaceful as I stood on the lawn of the Royal [Hotel, Portishead] and so quiet that I could hear the tide rushing down past the Firefly Buoy, a few hundred yards from the shore beneath. The great black cone was heeling over at an impressive angle which ably demonstrated the strength of the current. Beyond the semi-derelict wooden pier were the mud flats between the meadows of Saint George's Wharf and the ancient anchorage of King Road. The flats stretched ahead into the haze and beyond could be made out the massive grain silos, tall cranes and lighthouse-tipped piers of Avonmouth docks.'[19]

Avonmouth

Avonmouth is famous for its huge tides, among the largest in the world, with a range of more than 50 feet at springs. Upstream is the Avon Gorge and the city of Bristol. The coastline runs on towards the Severn Bridge and the narrowing estuary, with Gwent and the mouth of the River Wye over on the northern shore. Avonmouth and the flatlands beside the Severn are dominated by vast chemical works, fuel depots and warehouses.

Ethel Thomas, a native of Avonmouth, explained that 'the name was a very modern innovation, and was given to the present industrial parish little more than one hundred years ago, at the coming of the new port. Down through the ages, the land surrounding the mouth of the Avon has been referred to merely as "River's Mouth" or, as marked on a map of 1567, "The Salt Marsh"'

'In 1865 Avonmouth Hotel was built, in conjunction with the Bristol Park and Pier Railway, on the banks of the River Severn. It was estimated that 100,000 passengers annually would be attracted to an outing to the Avonmouth Hotel and pleasure gardens, and certainly tea and shrimps at Avonmouth became a popular objective in a half-holiday programme, while the Hotel gardens and the fêtes held in them at Easter and Whitsuntide attracted thousands of pleasure-seekers from Bristol. This brave attempt to make Avonmouth a popular seaside resort was ill-fated, which resulted in heavy losses to the original projectors. The odds were too great. Not destined to be a summer resort, and with land a loss to agriculture, Avonmouth's real destiny was yet to come.'[27]

It was through the part of Avonmouth that bananas were first introduced to this country.

Severn Beach

Severn Beach has a sea wall and a caravan and camping site. It is a somewhat unlikely place for a seaside holiday, as Michael H.C. Baker, a writer of railway books, observed 'The station consists of a windswept, almost empty platform, the terminus of a suburban service from Bristol Temple Meads set beside a large expanse of mud. In short, it has to be said that it is the least prepossessing seaside resort I have ever come across. However, back in the 1930s, when choice and money was in vastly shorter supply and the line continued on past Severn Beach Station and curved inland to join the Severn Tunnel main line at Parkway, it was deemed sufficiently attractive for the LMS to run seaside specials to it from Redditch, Birmingham, Great Malvern and Gloucester. One trusts that the excursionists got their money's worth; but one doubts it.'[28]

From Severn Beach one can see under construction the second Severn Bridge which will span the estuary between nearby Redwick and Caldicot on the Gwent shore, a distance of 5 kilometres. It is on a similar alignment to the Great Western Railway tunnel, built between 1873 and 1886 by Sir John Hawkshaw and designed by Charles Richardson.

Aust and the Ferries

The Romans depended on ferries to cross the Severn to get to the great camp at Caerleon beside the River Usk. The Tintern Abbey Charter, between 1138 and 1148, mentioned a ferry service between Beachley and Aust, the Old Passage, used by the monks, their servants and cattle. On his tour of England and Wales Daniel Defoe came to 'an ugly, dangerous, and very inconvenient ferry over the Severn, to the mouth of the Wye.......the badness of the weather, and the sorry boats, deterred us from crossing there. When we came to Aust, the sea was so broad, the foam of the Bore of the tide so formidable, the wind also made the water so rough, and which was worse, the boats to carry over both man and horse appeared so very mean, that in short none of us cared to venture: so we came back, and resolved to keep on the road to Gloucester.'[11]

In 1838 Thomas Telford viewed the Old Passage at Aust as 'one of the most forbidding places at which an important ferry was ever established – a succession of violent cataracts formed in a rocky channel exposed to the rush of a tide which has scarcely equal on any other coast.'[29] He proposed a suspension bridge from Aust to Beachley, but this idea was well ahead of its time.

Aust is now a quiet, leafy village where one can walk along beside the estuary, past the ruins of the ferry pier to stand beneath the great span of the Severn Bridge, running out from Aust Cliff.

In 1791 Edward D. Clarke and his party arrived here: 'We came to the New Passage House upon the banks of the Severn. There are no small boats kept at this place; but when passengers arrive too late for the larger vessels, they light a bundle of straw, the smoke of which gives notice to the people on the opposite shore that some persons are wanting to cross. We took the opportunity of dining while this ceremony was going forward, and beheld from our window a charming prospect of the Severn, bordered with the rich pastures of Wales, whose meadows, rising from the banks of the river, present a distant but inviting specimen of the country.

'Our boat soon made its appearance, manned with four stout rowers, who conducted us three miles across this beautiful piece of water, although as yellow as the Avon at Bristol, nevertheless like that river presents such beautiful scenery on each side of it, that unmindful of its colour we glide over its muddy waters with delight. The passage over the Severn is, from the great rapidity of that river, rendered often unpleasant and sometimes dangerous. The number of sand banks, and sharp black rocks, which are dispersed in different places, make it necessary to have a good pilot upon those occasions.'[30]

The Severn Bore

The Severn Bore is a wave that moves upriver during spring tides. Fred Rowbotham wrote that 'it could be said to have its beginnings where the incoming tide from the Atlantic first feels the constriction and rising bed of the Bristol Channel. It develops in the sand-locked channels of the Severn's lower estuary, and is fully grown when it has run upstream into the relatively narrow inland river.

'I have watched the bore's growth from the air, noted the first tangible swell and followed its changing character through adolescence and maturity to final extinction at Gloucester. Looking down on the vast banks of mud and sand which at low water half fill the broad estuary opposite Avonmouth, the first indication of the incoming tide is the advance over the lowest sands of a sheet of water fronted by the thinnest of white lines – a little wave barely two inches high. The sands are so flat that the rapidly rising tide spreads quickly, pushing its little wave along faster than you could get away from it on foot if taken unawares. As yet there is no visible swell on the water in the deep channels, but as the vanguard of the tide moves further upstream it acquires just a trace of a roll, or rather a succession of three or four rolls – long, smooth, very shallow unbroken waves.'[31]

William Wickenden, a Gloucestershire farmer's son wrote a verse about the Bore in the 18th century:

> *And see, hoarse Boreas shakes the craggy shore,*
> *And circling eddies mark the whitening bore,*
> *And wave impelled by wave, tremendous sound,*
> *And like a deluge whelms the hissing ground.*[32]

Camden described the 'rage and boisterousness of waters, which I know not whether I may call a gulph or whirlpool, casting up the sands from the bottom, and rowling them in heaps, it floweth with a great torrent. The watermen us'd to it, when they see this Hygre coming do turn the vessel, and cutting through the midst of it avoid its violence.'[33]

Defoe also watched the Bore 'rolling forward like a mighty wave: so that the stern of a vessel shall in a sudden be lifted up six or seven feet upon the water.'[11]

J.H.B. Peel sailed up-river: 'Astern I see a twilight of sky and waves. Somewhere ahead, in the gloom, green fields wait, and quiet lanes, and a river leading to its source among mountains. The Ordnance Survey map bears the words *Mouth of the Severn*, which it emphasizes by marking a lightship and several shallows...Middle Ground, Welsh Hook, Usk Patch. The Admiralty chart is even more vivid, for it utters fathoms and other maritime mysteries. Yet not even the Hydrographer of the Royal Navy can precisely separate the river from the estuary, the estuary from the sea. One fact, however, is indisputable; the estuary tonight looks very much as it did when a Severn schoolmaster, T.E. Brown, described it a century ago: "The sulky old gray brute..."[34]

The Severn Bridge
Nearly a century after Thomas Telford first suggested the idea, a conference held in Chepstow advocated bridge construction, but it was not until 1927 that the scheme was adopted. In 1961 the foundations were laid. It took five years to complete, and was opened by HM Queen Elizabeth II on 8th September 1966. It is here, in the shadow of the great bridge that crosses to Wales, that our literary traverse of the south-west coast of England comes to an end.

ACKNOWLEDGEMENTS

Kenneth Allsop: from *In the Country*, 1972. Hamish Hamilton. Reprinted by permission of the Peters Fraser & Dunlop Group Ltd.

John Amis: from *Amiscellany, My Life, My Music*, 1985. Reprinted by permission of Faber & Faber Ltd.

W J Arkell; from *The Geology of the Country Around Weymouth, Swanage, Corfe and Lulworth*, 1947. Reprinted by permission of the Controller of HMSO.

Paul Ashbee: from *Ancient Scilly*, 1974. Reprinted by permission of David & Charles.

Stephen Austin: from *From the Footplate: Atlantic Coast Express*, 1989. Reprinted by permission of Ian Allan Publishing Ltd.

Frank Baines: from *Look Towards the Sea*, 1958. Published by Eyre & Spottiswoode. Reprinted by permission of David Higham Associates.

Michael H.C. Baker: from *Railways to the Coast*, 1990. Published by and reprinted by permission of Patrick Stephens Ltd, Sparkford, Somerset.

Jack Battrick: from *Brownsea Islander*, 1978. Reprinted by permission of Gail Lawson and the Poole Historical Trust.

Derrick Beckett: from *Brunel's Britain*, 1980. Reprinted by permission of David & Charles.

Quentin Bell: *Virginia Woolf: A Biography*, 1972. Reprinted by permission of Random House UK Ltd.

Hilaire Belloc: from *The Cruise of the* Nona, 1925. Reprinted by permission of the Peters Fraser & Dunlop Group Ltd.

Claude Berry: *Portrait of Cornwall*, 1963. Reprinted by permission of Robert Hale Ltd.

John Betjeman: 'The Town Clerk's Views', 'Cornish Cliffs' and 'St. Enodoc Church' from Collected Poems, 1948 and *John Betjeman's Cornwall*, 1984. Reprinted by permission of John Murray (Publishers) Ltd.

Lord Birkenhead: from *Rudyard Kipling*, 1978. Reprinted by permission of Weidenfeld & Nicolson.

Nicholas Blake: from *The Beast Must Die*, 1938. Reprinted by permission of the Peters Fraser & Dunlop Group Ltd.

Lilian Bond: from *Tyneham – a Lost Heritage*, 1956. Reprinted by permission of The Dovecote Press Ltd.

Harriet Bridle: from *Woody Bay*, 1991. Reprinted by permission of the author.

S.H. Burton: from *Exmoor*, 1969. Reprinted by permission of Robert Hale Ltd.

Nigel Calder: from *The English Channel*, 1986. Reprinted by permission of the author.

Victor Canning: from *The Mask of Memory*, 1974. © Victor Canning. Reproduced by permission of Curtis Brown Ltd., on behalf of Mrs Adria Canning.

Sir Francis Chichester: from *Gipsy Moth Circles the World*, 1967. Reprinted by permission of Hodder & Stoughton Ltd./New English Library Ltd.

Agatha Christie: from *An Autobiography* © Agatha Christie Ltd., 1977. *Evil Under the Sun*, © Agatha Christie Mallowan 1941. Reprinted by permission of Hughes Massie Ltd.

V.C. Clinton-Baddelley: from *No Case for the Police*, 1970. Reprinted by permission of Victor Gollancz Ltd.

Vaughan Cornish: from *The Scenery of Sidmouth, Its Natural Beauty & Historic Interest*, 1940. Reprinted by permission of Cambridge University Press.

Noel Coward: from *Present Indicative*, 1937. © 1937 by the Estate of Noel Coward by permission of Michael Imison Playwrights Ltd., 28 Almeida Street, London.

Idris Davies: 'Tonypandy' from *Collected Poems*, 1945. Reprinted by permission of Gomer Press.

Ann Davison: from *Last Voyage*, 1953. Heinemann. Reprinted by permission of A.M. Heath.

Walter de la Mare: 'Sunk Lyonesse', 1969. *The Complete Poems*. Reprinted by permission of The Literary Trustees of Walter de la Mare, and the Society of Authors as their representative.

Eric R. Delderfield: from *The Lynmouth Flood Disaster*, 1953. Reprinted by permission of the author.

Daphne du Maurier: Reproduced with permission of Curtis Brown Ltd., London on behalf of the Chichester Partnership. *Rebecca* © 1938 by Daphne du Maurier Browning. *Frenchman's Creek* © 1941 by Daphne du Maurier Browning. *Jamaica Inn* © 1936 by Daphne du Maurier Browning.

The House on the Strand, 1969, and *Vanishing Cornwall*, 1967, reprinted by permission of Victor Gollancz.

Aaron Elkins: from *Murder in the Queen's Armes*, 1990. Reprinted by permission of Harper Collins Publishers.

Danial Farson: from *A Window on the Sea*, 1977. Michael Joseph. Reprinted by permission of A.M. Heath.

E.M. Forster: from *Howards End*, 1910. Reprinted by permission of The Society of Authors, with acknowledgements to The Provost and Scholars of King's College, Cambridge.

John Fowles: from *The French Lieutenant's Woman*, 1969. Jonathan Cape. Reprinted by permission of Sheil Land Associates Ltd. *A History of Lyme Regis*, 1982. Reprinted by permission of the Dovecote Press Ltd. *Islands*, 1978. Reprinted by permission of Random House UK Ltd.

Bryn Frank: from *Everyman's England*, 1984. Reprinted by permission of J.M. Dent & Sons Ltd.

Maxwell Fraser: from *Companion Into Somerset*, 1947. Methuen, London. Reprinted by permission of Reed Book Services Ltd.

Christopher Fry: from *Thor, With Angels*, 1949. Oxford University Press. Reprinted by permission of Oxford University Press.

David Garnett: from *The Sailor's Return*, 1929. Chatto & Windus. Reprinted by permission of A.P. Watt Ltd., on behalf of the Literary Executors of the Estate of David Garnett.

Winston Graham: from *Poldark's Cornwall*, 1983. The Bodley Head and Webb & Bower. Reprinted by permission of A.M. Heath.

Geoffrey Grigson: from *History of Him*, published by Martin Secker & Warburg. Reprinted by permission of Reed Book Services Ltd. From *Country Writings*, reprinted by permission of David Higham Associates.

John Grimson: from *The Channel Coasts of England*, 1978. Reprinted by permission of Robert Hale Ltd.

John Hadden: from *Portrait of Avon*, 1981. Reprinted by permission of Robert Hale Ltd.

Charles Hadfield: from *Atmospheric Railways*, 1967. David & Charles. Reprinted by permission of the author.

Christopher Hassall: from *Rupert Brooke: A Biography*, 1964. Reprinted by permission of Faber & Faber Ltd.

Michael Havinden: from *The Somerset Landscape*, 1981. Reprinted by permission of Hodder & Stoughton Ltd.

Richard Holmes: *Coleridge: Early Visions*, 1989. Reprinted by permsiion of Hodder & Stoughton Ltd.

W.G. Hoskins: from *The Making of the English Landscape*, 1955. © 1955 by W.G. Hoskins. Reprinted by permission of Hodder & Stoughton Ltd./New English Library Ltd.

Barry Humphries: from *More Please*, 1992. Viking, London. Reprinted by permission of Penguin Books Ltd.

Paul Hyland: from *Purbeck – The Ingrained Island*, 1978. Reprinted by permission by The Dovecote Press Ltd.

Brian Jackman: from *Dorset Coast Path*, 1979. Reprinted by permission of The Controller of HMSO.

Mary Lakeman: from *Early Tide – A Mevagissey Childhood*, 1978. Reprinted by permission of Harper Collins Publishers.

Lois Lamplugh: *Barnstaple – Town on the Taw*, 1983. Reprinted by permission of Phillimore & Co. Ltd.

Berta Lawrence: from *Coleridge and Wordsworth in Somerset*, 1970. Reprinted by permission of David & Charles.

John Le Carré: from *A Perfect Spy*, 1986. Reprinted by permission of Hodder & Stoughton Ltd./ New English Library Ltd.

Brian Le Messurier: from *South Devon Coast Path*, 1980. Reprinted by permission of The Controller of HMSO.

Rachel Lloyd: from *Dorset Elizabethans*, 1967. Reprinted by permission of T. Hamilton-Fletcher.

Kenneth McConkey: *British Impressionism*, 1989. Reprinted by permission of Phaidon Press Ltd.

Compton Mackenzie: *My Life and Times: Octave Four*, 1965. Published by Chatto & Windus. Reprinted by permission of The Society of Authors as the literary representative of the Estate of Sir Compton Mackenzie.

Ruth Manning-Sanders: from *The West of England*, 1949. Reprinted by permission of B.T. Batsford Ltd.

John Masefield: from *Christmas 1903*, 1923: Heinemann. Reprinted by permssion of The Society of Authors as the literary representative of the Estate of John Masefield.

Barbara Milne: from *The House at Ashley Combe*, 1992. Reprinted by permission of the author.

Bel Mooney: from *Somerset*, 1989. Reprinted by permission of Weidenfeld & Nicolson.

Christopher Morris: from *The Illustrated Journeys of Celia Fiennes c. 1682- c. 1712*, 1982. Reprinted by permission of Dianne Coles Agency.

Laurence O'Toole: from *The Roseland between River and Sea*, 1978. Reprinted by permission of Lodenek Press, Truro.

Derek Parker: from *The West Country and the Sea*, 1980. Published by Longmans. Reprinted by permission of David Higham Associates.

J.H.B. Peel: from *Portrait of the Severn*, 1968. Reprinted by permission of Robert Hale Ltd.

John Cowper Powys: from *Autobiography*, 1934. MacDonald, London and *Weymouth Sands*, 1934. Simon & Schuster, New York. Reprinted by permission of Laurence Pollinger Ltd., on behalf of the estate of the late John Cowper Powys.

Gerald & Sylvia Priestland: from *West of Hayle River*, 1980. Wildwood House, London. Reprinted by permission of Mrs Priestland.

J.B. Priestley: from *The Balconniny and Other Essays*, 1929. Methuen. Reprinted by permission of the Peters Fraser & Dunlop Group Ltd.

Sir Arthur Quiller-Couch: from *Poems*, 1929. Reprinted by permission of G.F. Symondson.

Jonathan Raban: from *Foreign Land*, 1985 and *Coasting*, 1986. Reprinted by permission of Harper Collins Publishers.

Arthur Ransome: from *Missee Lee*, 1941. Reprinted by permission of Random House UK Ltd.

Henry Handel Richardson: from *The Fortunes of Richard Mahony*, 1930. William Heinemann Ltd. Reprinted by permission of Reed Book Services Ltd.

Fred Rowbotham: from *The Severn Bore*, 1970. Reprinted by permission of David & Charles.

A.L. Rowse: from *A Cornish Childhood*, 1942 and *A Cornishman at Oxford*, 1965, reprinted by permission of the author. *From A Cornishman Abroad*, 1976, reprinted by permission of Random House UK Ltd.

Bertrand Russell: from *The Scientific Outlook*, 1931. Reprinted by permission of Routledge.

John Seymour: from *The Companion Guide to the Coast of South West England*, 1974. Reprinted by permission of Harper Collins Publishers.

Ken Small: from *The Forgotten Dead*, 1988. Reprinted by permission of Bloomsbury Publishing Ltd, 1988.

Christopher Somerville: from *Britain Beside the Sea* published by Grafton Books 1988, © Christopher Somerville 1989 and *Coastal Walks in England and Wales* published by Grafton Books 1988, © Christopher Somerville 1988. Reprinted by permission of Richard Scott Simon Ltd.

Howard Spring: from *There is no Armour*, 1948. Published by Collins. Reprinted by permission of David Higham Associates.

Derek Tangye: from *A Gull on the Roof*: Michael Joseph, 1961. © Derek Tangye 1961. Reproduced by permission of Michael Joseph Ltd.

Paul Theroux: from *The Kingdom by the Sea*, 1983. Reprinted by permission of Hamish Hamilton Ltd.

Dylan Thomas: from *The Collected Letters*, 1985. Published by Macmillan. Reprinted by permission of David Higham Associates.

Leslie Thomas: from *The Hidden Places of Britain*, 1981. Reprinted by permission of the author.

E.V. Thompson: from *Ben Retallick*, 1980. Published by Macmillan. Reprinted by permission of the author.

H.M. Tomlinson: from *Gifts of Fortune*, 1926. Heinemann. Reprinted by permission of Susan Gibson for the Estate of H.M. Tomlinson.

Leo Tregenza: from *Harbour Village*, 1977. Published by William Kimber & Co.Ltd., an imprint of Harper Collins Publishers Ltd. Reprinted by permission of Harper Collins Publishers Ltd.

Anne Treneer: from *School House in the Wind*, 1944. Reprinted by permission of Random House (UK) Ltd.

James Turner: from *The Stone Peninsula*, 1975. Published by William Kimber & Co.Ltd., an imprint of Harper Collins Publishers Ltd. Reprinted by permission of Harper Collins Publishers.

Denys Val Baker: from *The Waterwheel Turns*, 1982, and *Britain's Art Colony by the Sea*, 1959. Reprinted by permission of Martin Val Baker.

J.H. Wade: from *Rambles in Devon*, 1930. Methuen, London. Reprinted by permission of Reed Book Services Ltd.

Mark Wallington: from *500 Mile Walkies*, 1986. Reprinted by permission of Random House UK Ltd.

Rex Warner: 'Chough' from *Poems*, 1937. Boriswood, London. Reprinted by permission of Random House UK Ltd.

Henry Williamson: from *Tarka the Otter*, 1927. The Bodley Head and 'Stumberleap': from *The Old Stag and Other Hunting Stories*, 1926. Macdonald. Reprinted by permission of A.M. Heath.

John Willing: from *A History Little Known*, 1984. Reprinted by permission of the author.

Virginia Woolf: from *Moments of Being*, 1939. Reprinted by permission of Random House UK Ltd.

There are instances where we have been unable to trace or contact the copyright holder before our printing deadline. We apologise for this. If notified the publisher will be pleased to rectify any errors or omissions at the earliest opportunity.

REFERENCES

Chapter 1 - Dorset

1 Sheila D. Herringshaw, 1981: *A Portrait of Highcliffe*. (Privately printed).
2 William Stewart Rose, 1837: *Rhymes*. (Privately printed).
3 C.J. Cornish, 1895: *Wild England of To-day*. Nelson.
4 John Grimson, 1978: *The Channel Coasts of England*. Robert Hale.
5 Robert Louis Stevenson, 1920: *Underwoods*. Chatto & Windus.
6 Paul Verlaine, 1877: *Bournemouth*. [Quoted from Geoffrey Grigson, 1980: *Poems and Places*. Faber & Faber.]
7 John Wells [Quoted from Richard Ingrams, 1949: *England - An Anthology*. Collins.]
8 John Betjeman, 1948: *Collected Poems*. John Murray.
9 Thomas Hardy, 1876: *The Hand of Ethelberta*. Smith, Elder & Co., London. [Quoted from the 1973 Greenwood edition, Macmillan, London].
10 Thomas Hardy, 1891: *Tess of the D'Urbervilles*. Osgood M'Ilvaine & Co., London. [Quoted from the 1975 New Wessex Edition, Macmillan, London].
11 Malcolm Muggeridge: 'Bournemouth.' [Quoted from in Yvonne Cloud (ed.) 1934 *Beside the Seaside*. Stanley Nott, London.
12 Frederick Treves, 1906: *Highways and Byways in Dorset*. [Quoted from 1981 edition Macmillan, London].
13 Kenneth Allsop, 1972: *In the Country*. Hamish Hamilton, London.
14 Daniel Defoe, 1724-26: *A Tour Through the Whole Island of Great Britain*. [Quoted from Pat Rogers (ed.), 1971 Penguin edition, Penguin, Middlesex.]
15 Eric Shanes, 1981: *Turner's Rivers, Harbours and Coasts*. Bookclub Associates [in conjunction with Chatto & Windus, London].
16 Christopher Morris (ed.), 1982: *The Illustrated Journeys of Celia Fiennes c.1682-c.1712*. Webb & Bower, London.
17 Jack Battrick, 1978: *Brownsea Islander*. (As told by Gail Lawson). Poole Historical Trust.
18 Donald Maxwell, 1927: *Unknown Dorset*. John Lane, The Bodley Head Ltd., London.
19 Paul Hyland, 1978: *Purbeck – The Ingrained Island*. The Dovecote Press Ltd., Dorset.
20 Paul Theroux, 1983: *The Kingdom by the Sea*. Hamilton, London.
21 Hilaire Belloc, 1935: *The Cruise of the Nona*. [Quoted from the 1983 edition, Hutchinson, London].
22 E.M. Forster, 1910: *Howard's End*. Edward Arnold, London.
23 James Gibson (ed.), 1979: *The Valorium Edition of the Complete Poems of Thomas Hardy*. Macmillan, London.
24 Christopher Somerville, 1989: *Britain Beside the Sea*. Grafton Books, London.
25 W.J. Arkell, 1947: *The Geology of the Country around Weymouth, Swanage, Corfe & Lulworth*. Memoir of the Geological Survey of Great Britain. HMSO, London.
26 J. Meade Falkner, 1898: *Moonfleet*. Arnold, London.
27 Lilian Bond, 1956: *Tyneham – a Lost Heritage*. The Dovecote Press, Dorset (1984 edition).
28 F.J. Harvey Darton, 1922: *The Marches of Wessex*. Newnes, London.
29 John Keats, Sonnet. [Quoted from H.W. Garrod (ed.) 1982: *Keats Poetical Works*. Oxford University Press].
30 Christopher Hassall, 1964: *Rupert Brooke: A Biography*. Faber & Faber, London.
31 Thomas Hardy, 1871: *Desperate Remedies*. Tinsley, London [Quoted from the 1966 Greenwood edition. Macmillan, London].
32 Thomas Hardy, 1874: *Far From the Madding Crowd*. Smith, Elder & Co., London. [Quoted from 1975 New Wessex edition, Macmillan, London].
33 Llewelyn Powys, 1935: *Dorset Essays*. The Bodley Head, London.
34 Llewelyn Powys, 1926: *Skin for Skin*. The Bodley Head, London [1948 edition].
35 David Garnett, 1929: *The Sailor's Return*. Chatto & Windus, London.
36 Thomas Hardy, 1880: *The Trumpet Major*. Smith, Elder & Co., London [Quoted from the 1975 New Wessex edition, Macmillan, London].

37 J. Hemlow et al. (eds.), 1972-84: *The journals and letters of Fanny Burney (Madame d'Arblay).* 12 volumes. Clarendon Press, Oxford.

38 William Holloway, 1798: 'Weymouth' Poem.

39 Thomas Hardy, 1878: *The Return of the Native.* Smith, Elder & Co., London. [Quoted from 1975 New Wessex edition, Macmillan London].

40 Thomas Hardy, 1908: *The Dynasts.* Macmillan, London [Quoted from the New Wessex edition, 1978, Macmillan, London].

41 John Cowper Powys, 1934: *Autobiography.* MacDonald, London.

42 John Cowper Powys, 1934: *Weymouth Sands.* Simon & Schuster, New York.

43 Charlotte M. Mason, 1881: *The Forty Shires.* Hatchards, London.

44 Victor Hugo, 1869: *The Laughing Man.* Thomas Nelson & Sons London.

45 Thomas Hardy, 1896: *The Well-Beloved.* Osgood, McIlvaine & Co., London [Quoted for the 1975 New Wessex edition, Macmillan, London].

46 Ethel Mannin, 1972: *England my Adventure.* Hutchinson, London.

47 Thomas Hardy, 1873: *A Pair of Blue Eyes.* Tinsley, London. [Quoted from the 1975 New Wessex edition, Macmillan, London].

48 Ann Davison, 1953: *Last Voyage.* Heinemann, London.

49 H.M. Tomlinson, 1926: *Gifts of Fortune – with some hints for those about to travel.* Heinemann, London.

50 Jonathan Raban, 1985: *Foreign Land.* Collins Harvill, London.

51 The Story of the attempt to drain The Fleet is recounted in the *Dorset County Magazine* for 1971: vol. 17, pages 8-10, and vol. 21, page 25.

52 Ward Lock, 1931: *A Pictorial and Descriptive Guide to Swanage and South Dorset.* 8th Edition. Ward Lock, London.

53 J.B. Priestley, 1929: 'Out of it' in *The Balconinny and Other Essays.* Methuen, London.

54 Thomas Hardy, 1888: 'Fellow-Townsmen.' In *Wessex Tales*, vol.1. Macmillan, London. [Quoted from the 1975 New Wessex edition. Macmillan, London.

55 Bennet Copplestone (F. Harcourt Kitchin), 1922: *The Treasure of Golden Cap.* John Murray, London.

56 Rachel Lloyd, 1967: *Dorset Elizabethans At Home and Abroad.* John Murray, London.

57 Jane Austen, 1818: *Persuasion.* John Murray, London [Quoted from the 1980 edition. Oxford University Press].

58 Aaron Elkins, 1990: *Murder in the Queen's Armes.* Collins, London.

59 Francis Bickley, 1911: *Where Dorset Meets Devon.* Constable & Co.Ltd., London.

60 John Fowles, 1969: *The French Lieutenant's Woman.* Jonathan Cape, London.

61 Brian Jackman, 1979: *Dorset Coast Path.* H.M.S.O, London.

62 E.M. Ward, 1922: *English Coastal Evolution.* Methuen, London.

63 John Fowles, 1982: *A History of Lyme Regis.* Dovecote Press, Wimborne.

64 Brian Wilks, 1978: *Jane Austen.* Hamlyn, London.

65 Hallam Tennyson, 1897: *Alfred Lord Tennyson: A Memoir by his Son.* Macmillan, London.

66 F.T. Palgrave, 1874: *A Lyme Garland.* Lyme Regis.

67 Henry Handel Richardson, 1930: *The Fortunes of Richard Mahony.* Heinemann, London. [Quoted from the Australian Classics edition (1983), Angus and Robertson, Melbourne].

68 Beatrix Potter, 1930: *The Tale of Little Pig Robinson.* Frederick Warne, London.

69 Nicholas Blake (Cecil Day-Lewis) 1938 *The Beast Must Die.* Collins, London.

Chapter 2 - South Devon

1 John Fowles, 1969: *The French Lieutenant's Woman.* Jonathan Cape, London.

2 Hallam Tennyson, 1897: *Alfred Lord Tennyson: A Memoir by his Son.* Macmillan, London.

3 Jane Austen, 1818: *Persuasion.* John Murray, London. [Quoted from the 1980 edition. Oxford University Press].

4 Sheila Bird, 1985; *Lyme Regis, Uplyme and Charmouth Companion.* N.J. Clarke Publcations, Lyme Regis.

5 William Buckland, 1840: *On the Landslip near Axmouth.* Ashmolean Society, Oxford.

6 John Grimson, 1978: *The Channel Coasts of England.* Robert Hale, London.

7 G.P.R. Pulman, 1875: *The Story of the Axe*. [Quoted from the 1969 facsimile edition, Kingsmead, Bath].

8 Reverend J.B. Smith, 1835: 'Seaton Beach': A Poem. Longmans & Co., London.

9 William Plommer (ed.), 1944: *Selections from the Diary of the Reverend Francis Kilvert*. Jonathan Cape, London.

10 Jack Rattenbury, 1837: *Memoirs of a Smuggler*. [Quoted from the 1964 edition, Graham, Newcastle-upon-Tyne].

11 J.L.W. Page, 1895: *The Coasts of Devon & Lundy Island*. Horace Cox, London.

12 Brian Le Messurier, 1980: *South Devon Coast Path*. HMSO, London.

13 W.H. Hudson, 1923: *Afoot in England*. Dent, London

14 John Seymour, 1974: *The Companion Guide to the Coast of South West England*. Collins, London

15 Edmund Butcher, 1805: *An Excursion from Sidmouth to Chester in the Summer of 1803*. H.D. Symonds, London.

16 Anonymous, 1810: *Guide to All the watering and Sea-Bathing Places*. [Quoted from Maggie Lane, 1986: *Jane Austen's England*. Robert Hale, London].

17 Peter Orlando, 1881: *A History of the Town, Parish and Manor of Sidmouth*. Hutchinson. [Quoted from Unpublished Manuscript, Devon County Council Library].

18 W.M. Thackeray, 1850: *Pendennis*. Smith, Elder, London. [Quoted from the 1910 Everyman edition, Dent, London].

19 Bryn Frank, 1984: *Everyman's England*. Dent, London.

20 Stephen Reynolds, 1908: *A Poor Man's House*. Macmillan, London [Quoted from the 1980 London Magazine edition].

21 Vaughan Cornish, 1940: *The Scenery of Sidmouth, Its Natural Beauty & Historic Interest*. Cambridge University Press.

22 Rising Bray, 1949: *I Give you Sidmouth*. The Market Press, Sidmouth.

23 V.C. Clinton-Baddeley, 1970: *No Case for the Police*. Victor Gollancz Ltd., London.

24 Quoted from J.J. Cartwright (ed.), 1888-9: *The travels through England of Dr Richard Pococke*. Camden Society, London.

25 J.H. Wade, 1930: *Rambles in Devon*. Methuen & Co., London.

26 Mary E. Insull, 1965: *Lympstone Heritage*. Caldicotts Ltd., Gainsborough.

27 W.G. Hoskins, 1954: *Devon*. Collins, London.

28 John Willing, 1984: *A History Little Known*. The Strand, Topsham.

29 W.G. Hoskins, 1955: *The Making of the English Landscape*. Hodder & Stoughton, London.

30 Charles Hadfield, 1967: *Atmospheric Railways*. David & Charles, Newton Abbot.

31 Sidney Heath, 1910: *The South Devon & Dorset Coast*. T. Fisher Unwin, London.

32 Annie R. Ellis (ed.), 1907: *The Early Diary of Frances Burney*. Bell & Sons, London.

33 Humphry House & Graham Storey (ed.), 1959: *The Journals and Papers of Gerard Manley Hopkins*. Oxford University Press.

34 Rudyard Kipling, 1937: *Something of Myself*. Doubleday, Doran & Co., New York. [Quoted from the 1981 edition, Macmillan, London].

35 Lord Birkenhead, 1978: *Rudyard Kipling*. Weidenfeld and Nicolson, London.

36 Edmund Gosse, 1928: *Father and Son: a study of two temperaments*. Heinemann, London.

37 Betty Miller, 1954: *Elizabeth Barrett to Miss Mitford*. John Murray, London.

38 *Murray's Handbook for Devon and Cornwall*, 1859.

39 Quoted from C. Carrington, 1955: *Rudyard Kipling*. Macmillan, London.

40 Quoted from *The Complete Works of Alfred Lord Tennyson*, 1894. Macmillan, London.

41 Rupert Brooke, 1908: 'Seaside'. In *Collected Poems* [Quoted from Christopher Hassall, 1964: *Rupert Brooke: A Biography*. Faber and Faber, London].

42 Tickner Edwardes, 1910: *Lift-luck on Southern Roads*. Methuen, London. [Quoted from the 1931 edition, Methuen, London].

43 Agatha Christie, 1977: *An Autobiography*. Collins, London,

44 Charles Kingsley, 1890: *Glaucus*. Macmillan, London.

45 Darrell Bates, 1976: *The Companion Guide to Devon & Cornwall*. Collins, London.

46 John Le Carré, 1986: *A Perfect Spy*. Hodder & Stoughton, London.

47 Thomas Macaulay, 1848: *The History of England*, vol. 2. [Quoted from the 1906 Everyman edition, Dent, London].

48 Geoffrey Chaucer, 1387-1400: *The Canterbury Tales*. [Quoted from *The Complete Works*. Ed. by Walter W. Skeat. OUP]

49 Daniel Defoe, 1724-26: *A Tour through the Whole Island of Great Britain*. [Quoted from Pat Rogers (ed.), 1971 Penguin edition. Penguin, Middlesex].

50 Arthur H. Norway, 1897: *Highways and Byways in Devon & Cornwall*. [Quoted from 1923 Macmillan edition, London].

51 Jonathan Raban, 1986: *Coasting*. Collins Harvill, London.

52 Ken Small, 1988: *The Forgotten Dead*. Bloomsbury, London.

53 Mark Wallington, 1986: *500 Mile Walkies*. Arrow Books, London.

54 Raymond Cattell, 1937: *Under Sail through Red Devon*. Alexander Maclehose & Co., London.

55 Hilaire Belloc, 1925: *The Cruise of the Nona*. Century Press, London.

56 John Masefield 'Christmas 1903', 1923.: *The Collected Poems* (1932 edition). Heineman.

57 Eric Shane, 1981: *Turner's Rivers, Harbours and Coasts*. Book Club Associates and Chatto & Windus, London.

58 Agatha Christie, 1941: *Evil Under the Sun*. Collins, London.

59 Thomas Hardy, 1873: *A Pair of Blue Eyes*. Tinsley Brothers, London [Quoted from the 1975 Wessex edition, Macmillan, London].

60 Nigel Calder, 1986: *The English Channel*. Chatto & Windus, London.

61 Nicholas Monsarrat, 1978: *The Master Mariner*. Cassell, London.

62 Shirley Harrison, 1986: *The Channel*. Collins, London.

63 Francis Chichester, 1967: *Gipsy Moth Circles the World*. Hodder & Stoughton, London.

64 Sir Arthur Quiller-Couch, 1929: *Poems*. Oxford University Press.

65 Ernest Radford, 1906: *A Collection of Poems*. [Quoted from Jack Simmons, 1971: *A Devon Anthology*. Anthony Mott, London].

66 James Gibson (ed.), 1979: *The Valorium edition of the Complete Poems of Thomas Hardy*. Macmillan, London.

67 Geoffrey Grigson, 'Hardy's Plymouth' from *History of Him*. Martin Secker & Warburg

68 R.A.J. Walling, 1950: *The Story of Plymouth*. Westaway Books Ltd., London.

69 Derrick Beckett, 1980: *Brunel's Britain*. David & Charles, Newton Abbot.

Chapter 3 - South Cornwall

1 Philip E.B. Porter, 1905: *Around and About Saltash*. Dingle & Co., Saltash.

2 Lady Ernestine Edgcumbe, 1897: 'Mount Edgcumbe.' *Pall Mall Magazine*, reprinted in the *Cornish Magazine*, 2 (1899): 28-42.

3 Nigel Calder, 1986: *The English Channel*. Chatto & Windus, London.

4 Wilkie Collins, 1851: *Rambles Beyond Railways*. Richard Bentley, London [Quoted from the 1948 edition, Westaway Books, London].

5 Geoffrey Grigson, 1984: *Country Writings*. Century Publishing, London.

6 Evelyn E. Atkins, 1976: *We Bought an Island*. George Harrap, London.

7 Darrell Bates, 1976: *The Companion Guide to Devon & Cornwall*. Collins, London.

8 Jonathan Couch, 1871: *The History of Polperro*. W. Lake, Truro.

9 Paul Theroux, 1983: *The Kingdom by the Sea*. Hamish Hamilton, London.

10 Arthur H. Norway, 1897: *Highways and Byways in Devon and Cornwall*. [Quoted from the 1923 edition Macmillan, London].

11 S.C. Roberts (ed.), 1944: *Memories and Opinions: an unfinished autobiography by 'Q'*. [Sir Arthur Quiller-Couch].

12 A. Quiller-Couch, 1899: 'The Harbour of Fowey', in *A Fowey Garland*. [Quoted from F. Brittain, 1948: *Q Anthology*, Dent, London].

13 A. Quiller-Couch, 1893: 'Prologue', in *The Delectable Duchy*. Dent, London.

14 A. Quiller-Couch, 1888: *The Astonishing History of Troy Town*. Everyman Library, Dent, London.

15 Kenneth Grahame, 1908: *The Wind in the Willows*. [Quoted from the paperback edition, 1961. Methuen, London].

16 Peter Green, 1982: *Beyond the Wild Wood: the world of Kenneth Grahame*. Webb & Bower, Exeter.

17 Daphne Du Maurier, 1938: *Rebecca*. Victor Gollancz, London.

18 Daphne Du Maurier, 1969: *The House on the Strand*. Gollancz, London.

19 Ruth Manning-Sanders, 1949: *The West of England*. Batsford, London.

20 Noel Coward, 1937: 'Present Indicative.' Heinemann, London.

21 A.L. Rowse, 1942: *A Cornish Childhood.* Jonathan Cape, London.

22 A.L. Rowse, 1965: *A Cornishman at Oxford.* Jonathan Cape, London.

23 A.L. Rowse, 1976: *A Cornishman Abroad.* Jonathan Cape, London.

24 E.V. Thompson: *Ben Retallick*

25 Mary Lakeman, 1978: *Early Tide - A Mevagissey Childhood.* William Kimber, London.

26 John Amis, 1985: *Amiscellany. My Life, My Music.* Faber & Faber, London.

27 Colin Wilson, 1981: *Discovering Cornwall.* [Quoted from J.C. Trewin (ed.) *The West Country Book.* Webb & Bower, Exeter].

28 Anne Treneer, 1944: *School House in the Wind.* Jonathan Cape, London.

29 Laurence O'Toole, 1978: *The Roseland between River and Sea.* Lodenek Press, Padstow.

30 Graham J. McEwan, 1986: *Mystery Animals of Britain and Ireland.* Robert Hale, London.

31 Winston Graham, 1983: *Poldark's Cornwall.* The Bodley Head and Webb & Bower, Exeter.

32 Arthur Ransome, 1941: *Missee Lee.* Jonathan Cape, London.

33 W.P. Hodgkinson, *The Under Road.* [Quoted from *A Cornish Chorus.* Muriel Hawkey (ed.) 1948. Westaway Books, London].

34 Susan E. Gay, 1903: *Old Falmouth.* Headley Brothers, London.

35 Howard Spring, 1948: *There is no Armour.* Collins, London.

36 Ida Procter, 1982: *Visitors to Cornwall.* Dyllansow Truran, Cornish Publications, Redruth.

37 Daphne Du Maurier, 1941: *Frenchman's Creek.* Gollancz, London.

38 Charles Kinglsey, 1866: *Hereward the Wake.* Macmillan, London.

39 A.E. Copping, 1907: *Gotty and the Guv'nor.* [Quoted from 1979 edition, Mallard Reprints, Lavenham, Suffolk].

40 Frank Baines, 1958: *Look towards the Sea.* Eyre & Spottiswood, London.

41 Sheila Bird, 1989: *Cornish Curiosities.* Dovecote Press, Wimborne.

42 C.C. Rogers (Lady Vyvyan), 1926: *Echoes in Cornwall.* John Lane, London.

43 Daphne du Maurier, 1967: *Vanishing Cornwall.* Gollancz, London.

44 J.C. Trewin (ed.), 1981: *The West Country Book.* Webb & Bower, Exeter.

45 Charlotte Mason, 1881: *The Forty Shires.* Hatchards, London.

46 H.D. Rawnsley, 1887: 'The Gull Rock.' *Sonnets Round the Coast.* Swan, Sonnenschen, Lowry & Co. London.

47 C.A. Johns, 1848: *A Week at the Lizard.* SPCK. London.

48 Compton Mackenzie, 1965: *My Life and Times: Octave Four.* Chatto & Windus, London.

49 S. Baring-Gould, 1899: *A Book of the West: Cornwall.* Methuen, London [Quoted from the 1981 Wildwood House edition, London].

50 Alfred Lord Tennyson, 1859-1885: 'Idylls of The King.' [Quoted from The New American Library edition, New York].

51 A.G. Folliott Stokes, 1909: *From Land's End to the Lizard.* Greening & Co., London.

52 W.G. Maton, 1796: *Observations on the Western Counties of England.* [Quoted from R. Pearse Chope (ed.), 1918: *Some early tours in Devon and Cornwall*, Commin, Exeter].

53 Roger Jones, 1985: *West Country Tour: Diary of an excursion through Somerset, Devon and Cornwall in 1797 by John Skinner.* Ex Libris Press, Bradford-on-Avon, Wiltshire.

54 Alphonse Esquiros, 1865: *Cornwall and its Coasts.* Chapman and Hall, London.

55 Joseph Farington, 1810: *The Farington Diary.* Hutchinson, London.

56 John Davidson, 1894: *Ballads & Songs.* John Lane, London.

57 James Turner, 1975: *The Stone Peninsula.* William Kimber, London.

58 Edmund Spenser, 1595: *Colin Clouts Come Home Againe.* William Ponsonbie, London. [Quoted from J.C. Smith and E. de Selincourt (eds.), 1912: *Spenser: poetical works.* Oxford University Press].

59 Thomas Hardy, 1885: 'A Mere Interlude.' Reprinted 1913, in *A Changed Man and Other Tales.* Macmillan, London.

60 Leslie Thomas, 1981: *The Hidden Places of Britain.* Arlington Books, London.

61 Kenneth McConkey, 1989: *British Impressionism.* Guild Publishing, London by agreement with Phaidon Press.

62 Charles Hemming, 1988: *British painters of the Coast and Sea.* Gollancz, London.

63 Mrs Lionel Birch, 1906: *Stanhope A. Forbes, A.R.A., and Elizabeth Stanhope Forbes, A.R.W.*
64 Dylan Thomas, 1985: *The Collected Letters.* (Ed. by Paul Ferris) J.M. Dent, London.
65 Jean Goodman, 1988: *What a Go! – The Life of Alfred Munnings.* Collins, London.
66 Leo Tregenza, 1977: *Harbour Village.* William Kimber, London.
67 J.T. Blight, 1861: *A Week at the Land's End.* Longman, Green, Longman and Roberts, London.
68 S.P.B. Mais, 1932: *The Cornish Riviera.* Great Western Railway Company, London.
69 W.H. Davies, 1942: *Collected Poems.* Jonathan Cape, London. (1955 edition).
70 Derek Tangye, 1961: *A Gull on the Roof.* Michael Joseph, London.
71 Derek Parker, 1980: *The West Country and the Sea.* Longmans, London.
72 Rex Warner, 1937: *Poems.* Boriswood, London.
73 Sheila Bird, 1992: *Tales of Old Cornwall.* Countryside Books, Newbury.
74 Walter White, 1855: *A Londoner's Walk to the Land's End.* Chapman and Hall, London.
75 W.H. Hudson, 1908: *The Land's End.* Hutchinson, London.
76 Humphry Davy, c. 1858: *On Land's End.* [Quoted from *A Cornish Chorus*, Muriel Hawkey (ed.) 1968 Westaway Books, London.

Chapter 4 - Isles of Scilly

1 Walter de la Mare, 1969: *The Complete Poems.* Faber, London.
2 Ruth Manning-Sanders, 1949: *The West of England.* Batsford, London.
3 William Borlase, 1754: *Antiquities Historical & Monumental of the County of Cornwall.* E.P. Publishing Ltd., Yorkshire.
4 Wilkie Collins, 1851: *Rambles Beyond Railways.* Westway Books Ltd., London (1948 edition).
5 John Fowles and F. Fodwin, 1978: *Islands.* Jonathan Cape, London.
6 Alphonse Esquiros, 1865: *Cornwall & Its Coasts.* Chapman & Hall, London.
7 Sir Arthur Quiller-Couch, 1907: *Major Vigoureux.* J.M. Dent, London (1949 edition).

8 Walter Besant, 1900 *Armorel of Lyonesse, A Romance of Today.* Chatto & Windus, London.
9 Wendy Aldridge, 1956: *Hobnails & Sea-Boots – Flower-Farming in the Isles of Scilly.* George G. Harrap, London.
10 Kevin Crossley-Holland, 1972: *Pieces of Land – Journeys to Eight Islands.* Victor Gollancz, London.
11 Paul Ashbee, 1974: *Ancient Scilly.* David & Charles, Newton Abbot, Devon.
12 Mary Wilson, (No date): *A Journey to Scilly.* (No Publisher).

Chapter 5 - North Cornwall

1 Wilkie Collins, 1851: *Rambles Beyond Railways.* Westway Books Ltd., (1948 Edition) London.
2 R.M. Ballantyne, 1869: *Deep Down A Tale of the Cornish Miners.* James Nisbet, London.
3 W.H. Hudson, 1908: *The Land's End.* Hutchinson, London.
4 Bertrand Russell, 1931: *The Scientific Outlook.* Allen & Unwin, London.
5 Gerald & Sylvia Priestland, 1980: *West of Hayle River.* Wildwood House, London.
6 Edwin Way Teale, 1970: *Springtime in Britain – A Journey Through the Land.* Cassell & Co., London.
7 John Seymour, 1974: *The Companion Guide to the Coast of South-West England.* Collins, London.
8 D.H. Lawrence, 1923: *Kangaroo.* Heinemann, London.
9 Barry Humphries, 1992: *More Please.* Viking, London.
10 Denys Val Baker, 1982: *The Waterwheel Turns.* W.M. Kimber, London.
11 Hilary Taylor, 1978: *James McNeill Whistler.* New Orchard Edition, London.
12 Denys Val Baker, 1959: *Britain's Art Colony by the Sea.* George Ronald, London.
13 Alphonse Esquiros, 1865: *Cornwall and its Coast.* Chapman & Hall, London.
14 Arthur H. Norway, 1897: *Highways and Byways in Devon and Cornwall.* Macmillan, London.
15 Virginia Woolf, 1939/40: *Moments of Being.* (Unpublished autobiography & writings). Ed. by Jeanne Schulkind. 1976 University Press, Sussex.

16 Quentin Bell, 1972: *Virginia Woolf: A Biography*. Hogarth Press, London.
17 Virginia Woolf, 1927: *To the Lighthouse*. Hogarth Press, London.
18 Frank Morley, 1980: *Literary Britain*. Hutchinson, London.
19 James Payn, 1916: *A Cornish Harbour: A Story of old Newquay*. Chatto & Windus, London.
20 G.T. Roberts, c.1970: *Surfing: what it's all about*. Harvey Barton, Bristol.
21 H.T. Moore (ed.), 1970: *D.H. Lawrence: The Collected Letters*, Vol. 1. Heinemann, London.
22 Claude Berry, 1963: *Portrait of Cornwall*. Robert Hale, London.
23 Stephen Austin, 1989: *Atlantic Coast Express*. Ian Allan Ltd., London.
24 E.P. Leigh-Bennett, 1932: *Devon and Cornish Days*. Southern Railway Company, London.
25 S.P.B. Mais, 1937, *The Atlantic Coast Express*. McCorquodale, London.
26 James Turner, 1975: *The Stone Peninsula*. William Kimber, London.
27 John Betjeman, 1958: *Collected Poems*. John Murray, London [Quoted from the 3rd edition, 1970].
28 John Betjeman, 1984: *Betjeman's Cornwall*. John Murray, London.
29 John Merrill, 1979: *Turn Right at Land's End*. Oxford Illustrated Press.
30 Daphne Du Maurier, 1936: *Jamaica Inn*. Gollancz, London.
31 Alfred Lord Tennyson, 1859: 'Idylls of the King' (The Coming of Arthur). [Quoted from WHO edition], 1894. *The Complete Works of Alfred Lord Tennyson*, Macmillan, London].
32 Algernon Charles Swinburne, 1927: *Collected Poetical Works*, Heinemann, London.
33 Christopher Fry, 1949: *Thor, With Angels*. Oxford UP.
34 Daphne du Maurier, 1967: *Vanishing Cornwall*. Gollancz, London.
35 Algernon Charles Swinburne, 1959: *The Swinburne Letters*, Vol.1 (ed. by Cecil Y. Lang) Yale University Press.
36 S.H. Burton, 1955: *The Coasts of Cornwall*. Werner, Laurie, London.
37 Emma Hardy, 1911: *Some Recollections*. (ed. by Evelyn Hardy & Robert Gittings) 1961 OUP, London.
38 Thomas Hardy, 1873: *A Pair of Blue Eyes*. Tinsley, London [Quoted from the 1975 New Wessex edition, Macmillan, London].
39 Thomas Hardy, 1870: James Gibson (ed.) 1979 *The Valorium Edition of the Complete Poems of Thomas Hardy*. Macmillan London.
40 S.P.B. Mais, 1928: *The Cornish Riviera*. Great Western Railway Co., London.
41 C. Fox Smith, 1937: *The Ketch Ceres*. Bude, Cornwall.
42 Bryan Dudley Stamp, 1972: *Ebbingford Manor*. Bude, Cornwall.
43 S. Baring-Gould, 1899: *The Vicar of Morwenstow*. Methuen, London.
44 Rev. Robert Stephen Hawker, 1825: *The Song of the Western Men*. (From *Cornish Ballads & Other Poems*: Robert Stephen Hawker – selected and edited by Piers Brendon). 1975 Elephant Press.
45 Charles Kingsley, 1855: *Westward Ho!* Thomas Nelson, London.

Chapter 6 - North Devon

1 J.L.W. Page, 1895: *The Coasts of Devon and Lundy Island*. Horace Cox, London.
2 R. Pearse Chope, 1925: *Hercules Promontory*. Reprinted for the Devonian Year Book.
3 S.H. Burton, 1953: *The North Devon Coast*. Werner Laurie, London.
4 W.G. Hoskins, 1955: *The Making of the English Landscape*. Hodder & Stoughton, London.
5 Charles Dickens, 1860: Christmas Stories from *Household Words* and *All the Year Round*. Hazell, Watson & Viney, London.
6 Daniel Farson, 1977: *A Window on the Sea*. Michael Joseph, London.
7 Charles Kingsley, 1855: *Westward Ho!* Thomas Nelson & Sons, London.
8 Rudyard Kipling, 1899: *Stalky & Co*. Macmillan, London.
9 Maj-Gen. L.C. Dunsterville, 1928: *Stalky's Reminiscences*. Jonathan Cape, London.
10 G.C. Beresford, 1936: *Schooldays with Kipling*. Victor Gollancz, London.
11 Clive Gunnell, 1981: *Somerset & North Devon Coast Path*. HMSO, London.
12 Henry Williamson, 1927: *Tarka the Otter*. The Bodley Head, London.
13 Christopher Somerville, 1989: *Britain Beside the Sea*. Grafton Books, London.
14 Ernest H. Rann, 1927: *The Homeland of English Authors*. Methuen, London.

15 Daniel Defoe, 1724-26: *A Tour Through the Whole Island of Great Britain*, 1912. Dent, London.

16 Lady Rosalind Northcote, 1908: *Devon, its Moorlands, Streams and Coasts*. Chatto & Windus, London.

17 Lois Lamplugh, 1983: *Barnstaple – Town on the Taw*. Phillimore, Chichester.

18 R.D. Blackmore, 1869: *Lorna Doone*. Heron Books, London.

19 Victor Canning, 1974: *The Mask of Memory*. Heinemann, London.

20 Richard T. Bass, 1992: *Spirits of the Sand - History of the US Army Assault Training Centre*, Woolacombe. Lee, Devon.

21 E.P. Leigh-Bennett, 1937: *Devon and Cornish Days*. Waterlow & Sons, London.

22 Philip and Emily Gosse, 1853: *Sea-side Pleasures*. Society for Promoting Christian Knowledge, London.

23 Charles Kinglsey, 1873: *Prose Idylls New and Old*. Macmillan, London.

24 Michael Drayton, 1622: *Polyolbion*

25 Kevin Crossley-Holland, 1972: *Pieces of Land – Journeys to Eight Islands*. Victor Gollancz, London.

26 Henry Jame, 1905: *English Hours*. Heinemann, London.

27 R.N. Worth, 1895: *A History of Devonshire*. Elliot Stock, London.

28 Daniel Benham, 1849: *Diaries of Daniel Benham*. In Ilfracombe Museum.

29 Robert Southey, 1851: *Common Place Book*. (Ed. by John Wood Warter). Longman, Brown, Green & Longmans, London.

30 E.A. Newell Arber, 1911: *The Coast Scenery of North Devon*. Kingsmead Reprints, Bath.

31 S.H. Burton, 1969: *Exmoor*. Robert Hale, London.

32 Henry Williamson, 1926: *Stumberleap from The Old Stag and other Hunting Stories*. [Taken from 1970 Macdonald, London, edition]

33 R.N. Worth, 1883: *Tourist's Guide to North Devon and the Exmoor District*. Edward Stanford.

34 Harriet Bridle, 1991: *Woody Bay*. Merlin Books, Devon.

35 Samuel Taylor Coleridge, 1798: 'The Wanderings of Cain.' From *The Complete Poetical Works* (ed. E.H. Coleridge) Oxford Standard Authors, 1912.

36 Paul Theroux, 1983: *The Kingdom by the Sea*. Hamish Hamilton, London.

37 Arthur L. Salmon, 1908: *West Country Verses*. Wm. Blackwood & Sons.

38 Eric R. Delderfield, 1953: *The Lynmouth Flood Disaster*. E.R.D. Publications Ltd., Exmouth, Devon.

Chapter 7 - Somerset and the Severn Estuary

1 Barbara Milne, 1992: *The House at Ashley Combe*. Privately printed.

2 Richard Holmes, 1989: *Coleridge – Early Visions*. Hodder & Stoughton, London.

3 Samuel Taylor Coleridge, 1797: *Complete Poetical Works* (ed. E.H. Coleridge). (Oxford Standard Authors), 1912.

4. G.J. Whyte-Melville, c.1900: *Katerfelto*. Ward Lock.

5 Bel Mooney, 1989: *Somerset*. Weidenfeld & Nicolson, London.

6 John Collinson, 1791: *The History and Antiquities of the County of Somerset*. R. Cruttwell. Bath.

7 Robert Southey, 1799: *Poems*. Oxford University Press, 1909 Edition.

8 Richard Warner, 1800: *A Walk Through some of the Western Counties of England*. London, R. Cruttwell. Bath.

9 Henry James, 1905: *English Hours*. Heinemann, London.

10 Ralph Whitlock, 1975: *Somerset*. Batsford, London.

11 Daniel Defoe, 1724-26: *A Tour Through the whole Island of Great Britain*, 1912: Dent, London.

12 Robert Southey, 1851: *Common Place Book*. (Ed.) John Wood Warter. Longman, Brown, Green & Longmans, London.

13 Gerard of Trent, 1633

14 Maxwell Fraser, 1947: *Companion Into Somerset*. Methuen, London.

15 Dorothy Wordsworth, 1798: *Journals of Dorothy Wordsworth*. OUP 1987 edition.

16 William Wordsworth, 1805: *The Prelude*.

17 Bertha Lawrence, 1970: *Coleridge and Wordsworth in Somerset*. David & Charles, Newton Abbot.

18 William Gresswell, 1903: *The Land of Quantock*. Barnicott & Pearce, Taunton.

19 Grahame Farr, 1954: *Somerset Harbours*. Christopher Johnson, London.

20 Christopher Somerville, 1988: *Coastal Walks in England and Wales*. Grafton Books, London.

21 Idris Davies, 1945: *Collected Poems*. Ed. by Islwyn Jenkins. Gomerian Press, Llandysul.
22 William Plomer (ed), 1944: *Selections from the Diary of the Reverend Francis Kilvert*. Jonathan Cape, London.
23 Paul Theroux, 1983: *The Kingdom by the Sea*. Hamish Hamilton, London.
24 Alfred Lord Tennyson, 1850: 'In Memoriam.' [Quoted from the *Complete Works of Alfred Lord Tennyson* 1894. Macmillan, London].
25 John Hadden, 1981: *Portrait of Avon*. Robert Hale, London.
26 Michael Havinden, 1981: *The Somerset Landscape*. Hodder & Stoughton, London.
27 Ethel Thomas, 1979: *Avonmouth Story*. D. Bailey & D. Archer.
28 Michael H.C. Baker, 1990: *Railways to the Coast*. Patrick Stephens Ltd., Northants.
29 Thomas Telford, 1838: *Life of Thomas Telford*. (Ed. John Rickman). James & Luke G. Hansard, London.
30 Edward D. Clarke, 1793: *A Tour Through the South of England, Wales and part of Ireland made during the summer of 1791.* R. Edwards, London.
31 Fred Rowbotham, 1970: *The Severn Bore*. David & Charles, Devon.
32 William Wickenden, c1700.
33 William Camden, 1586: *Britannia*.
34 J.H.B. Peel, 1968: *Portrait of the Severn*. Robert Hale, London.

INDEX

The Cornish World of **DENYS VAL BAKER**
by Tim Scott
This is the remarkable story of Denys Val Baker – writer, editor, seafarer and family man – from childhood years in North Wales, through war-time in London to his fateful discovery of Cornwall, where he and his ever-growing family moved through a succession of rather eccentric old houses, and where it was always a case of 'too little earned money chasing too much owed money.'

In West Cornwall Denys Val Baker was a writer among tists, and his amiable nature and generous spirit won him a wide circle of friends among the art colony of St. Ives and throughout Cornwall. Included here is the story of Denys's creation, the *Cornish Review*, his county arts magazine, 'Born originally in 1949, prematurely retired in 1952, resurrected in 1966 and finally buried in 1974.'

During the 1960s an unexpected inheritance enabled a life-long ambition to be fulfilled with the purchase of a sixty-foot motor fishing vessel named *Sanu*, in which the whole family found adventure – and misadventure – at sea. It was these voyages which provided so much material for the series of autobiographical books for which Val Baker is perhaps best known.

In *The Cornish World of Denys Val Baker*, Tim Scott chronicles the life of a prolific writer who is fondly remembered by the many who knew him, especially in Cornwall, and the thousands more who enjoy his books – and perhaps envied the lifestyle – of one who was a rebel to the end.
128 pages; Illustrated throughout; Bibliography; Price £4.95

EX LIBRIS PRESS books are available through local bookshops or may be obtained direct from the publisher, post-free, on receipt of net price, at 1 The Shambles, Bradford on Avon, Wiltshire, BA15 1JS.

Please ask for our free illustrated catalogue of around 50 titles.